# The Traitor

# The Traitor

ANDRÉ GORZ

**Foreword by Jean-Paul Sartre**

Translated by Richard Howard
and revised by the Author

**VERSO**
London · New York

First published by Editions du Seuil, Paris, 1958
First published in English by Simon & Schuster, New York, 1959
This edition published by Verso 1989

**Verso**
UK: 6 Meard Street, London W1V 3HR
USA: 29 West 35th Street, New York, NY 10001-2291

Verso is the imprint of New Left Books

**British Library Cataloguing in Publication Data**
Gorz, André
    The traitor.
    1. Existential sociology. Biographies
    I. Title II. Traître. *English*
    301'.092'4

    ISBN 0-86091-228-0
    ISBN 0-86091-941-2 pbk
    ISBN 978-0-86091-941-4


**US Library of Congress Cataloging-in-Publication Data**
Gorz, André
        [Traître. English]
        The traitor / André Gorz : foreword by Jean-Paul Sartre :
    translated by Richard Howard and revised by the author.
        p.   cm.
        Translation of: Le traître.
        Reprint. Originally published: New York : Simon and Schuster.
    1959.
        ISBN 0-86091-228-0 : —-ISBN 0-86091-941-2 (pbk.)
        1. Existentialism.    2. Gorz, André.    3. World War, 1939-1945
    —Personal narratives, Jewish.        I. Title
    B819.G6513  1989
    142'.78—dc19

Typeset by Leaper & Gard Limited, Bristol, England
Printed in Great Britain by Bookcraft (Bath) Ltd

*A Toi dite Kay*

# CONTENTS

Here the Traitor reveals his original situation, which is (virtual) treachery. In so doing, he 'betrays' us, since this situation is our own as well. But it is by announcing our position that we betray, to the degree that we claim to be altogether on one side or the other. As for him, he does not betray, since he unremittingly makes explicit, represents his ambiguity: his double relation and his double exclusion.

— FRANÇOIS JEANSON,
*Sartre par lui-même*

# FOREWORD
## *Of Rats and Men*

'They corrected his strabismus with glasses, his lisp with a metal loop, his stammer by mechanical exercises, and he spoke perfectly, but with a voice so low and so fast that his mother was forever complaining, "What are you saying? Talk louder! What are you mumbling about now?" and they nicknamed him Mumbler . . .'

This muffled, monotonous, courteous voice is the one you are about to hear, and you will recognize it among all others from now on. To whom does it belong? To no one. As if language had begun speaking all by itself. Occasionally the word 'I' is mentioned and we expect to catch a glimpse of the speaker of this speech, the subject who selects the terms. Pure illusion; the subject of the verb is merely an abstract word, the sentence has followed its familiar course, has taken a personal inflection for the sake of convenience. As a matter of fact, someone *is* here – 'a thin fellow with hollow cheeks and eyes, receding forehead and chin, a long neck poking forward above a slightly hunched back, with the gait of a heron and parsimonious gestures, as if he were trying to contain his being within himself.' But he has nothing to say. He is an 'object', every proposition reorganizes him, designates him. If it weren't for this mute creature, the voice would be quite uninhabited; he lives in it, extends his verbal body through the words; the voice tells us that 'he' is apprehensive, that 'he'

1

has finished a philosophical work, that 'he' is preparing to show it to someone named Morel.

'What do we care about this anonymous whispering?' you will ask. 'What we want is books constructed by real authors. Literature is like a high-wire act – our only pleasure is being able to appreciate the artist's work; we attach no more importance to the shudders that run through an abandoned language than to the wind in the reeds.' Then put down this book. In its last pages, as a matter of fact, a certain Gorz, emerging from the slime, affirms his retrospective rights over the language that has engendered him. He has not wanted to create a work of art, he says. You will readily believe him. From the first moment you hear this forsaken voice, you will notice its continual uncertainty, the flaccidity of all natural things; it is a kind of arid guest, unconscious of itself and always on the verge of being choked by its own words. Yet art is a motionless image of movement; when you begin reading a novel, even confessions, everything has long since been consummated, 'before' and 'after' are nothing but operative signs, the dawn of love and its death agony exist simultaneously, each spread out upon the other, in the eternal indistinction of the moment; to read is to make a time transfusion; the hero lives on our life, his ignorance of the future and the dangers that surround him are our own; it is with our patience as readers that he creates for himself a parasitic duration whose course we break off and resume as we please. As for style, that great, vainglorious flourish – style is death. Its illusory speed sweeps us back into the author's past. The latter may groan all he likes, may torture himself under our very eyes; he feels nothing, he is telling himself. By the time he picks up his pen the die has long since been cast, his friend has betrayed him, his mistress has left him, and he is determined to hate them or to hate the human race. He writes to communicate his hatred, and style is a hammer to crush our resistance, a sword to slice our rationalizations to ribbons. Everything is ellipsis, syncope, flea-jumps and false collusion; rhetoric becomes terror; rage and insolence, humiliation and pride control the attack and the turn of a phrase. The great writer – this madman, this maenad – hurls himself upon language, conquers it, enslaves it, mistreats it, *faute de mieux*; alone at his desk, he is an autocrat. If he slashes his paper with a streak of lightning that will dazzle twenty generations, it is because he looks to this verbal ukase for the symbol of respectability, of the humble powers his contemporaries persist in refusing him. A dead man's vengeance, for scorn has long since killed him; these thunderclaps conceal a defunct child who puts himself ahead of everything else; the child Racine, the child Pascal, the child Saint-Simon – these are our classics. We enjoy strolling among the tombs of literature, that calm cemetery, spelling out the epitaphs and momentarily resuscitating eternal words. It is reassuring that such phrases *have lived*; their meaning is fixed forever, they will not take advantage of the brief survival we deign to accord them and start up inopportunely, sweeping us on toward some unknown future. As for the novelists who are not yet so fortunate as to be in their coffins, they play dead. They will fish words out of their stock ponds, kill them, gut them, season, cook and serve them up – *au bleu, meunière,* or *grillés*.

*The Traitor* will be set both within and beyond the scope of a literary enterprise. This Gorz is not dead; he is even impertinent enough, at the beginning, not to be born yet. Therefore, no rhetoric. Who would there be to persuade us? And of what? Nor is there any question of tapping our duration to feed a fictional hero or direct our dreams by words. There is only this voice – this voice searching and ignorant of what it is searching for, desiring and ignorant of what it desires, this voice speaking in the void, in the darkness, perhaps to give a meaning by words to the words which have just escaped it, or perhaps to disguise its fear.

For it is afraid; we can no longer doubt the fact. It said, '*He* is afraid, *he* is apprehensive because he has finished his book.' But the voice claimed impassivity; it was merely a sonorous medium where various objective meanings collected, it discussed the passions of the thin chap with hollow eyes without suffering them. But we are not fooled. At first imprisoned in this alien body, in the individual referred to, the passions have spread outside their envelope, can no longer be localized; anguish colours the voice in every register, creates the inert urgency of this mumble; these groping, scrupulous, modest words have caught the fever. This is the voice of care speaking. This time we have understood, the individual referred to is the individual speaking; but the two do not manage to create a single person. There exists at least one man on earth who eats, drinks, works, sleeps, who looks just like us, in short, and yet is condemned by some obscure spell to remain Other in his own eyes.

Has his inner life been pounded and pulverized to the point of leaving only a swarm of words in a decomposed body? Or is his consciousness, still intact, so deeply buried that it no longer recognizes him at such a distance? No one knows yet, for this divided creature is no one. There is the dummy with hollow eyes, this pure object which has no control over itself, and there is this tiny tumult of words that dies away in the empty darkness and does not hear itself. As a matter of fact, to whom is this voice speaking? To us? Certainly not. To talk to men, you must already be a man. This voice does not care about being listened to; it is the fissure that deepens itself by trying to fill the gap; it is the stitches of language that have begun to unravel. Without references, roused by a nameless anxiety, the words work on. If they are determined to designate this human carcass, it is because they are obscurely trying to assimilate it, to dissolve it into themselves. The voice is born of a danger. It must destroy itself or gain the right to speak in the first person.

That is why this soliloquy is so disconcerting – we overhear it. You will smile at my naïveté, you will say, 'After all, Gorz *published* his book.' Yes, when there was a Gorz to make the decision; but he has added nothing, altered nothing of this beginning that seemed to be going nowhere and was intended for no one. I remember being told, whenever I chattered too much as a child, 'Keep still, you sound like a trickle of warm water.' A trickle of warm water is about to be turned on inside you now. It will consist of these long inchworm sentences interrupted by parentheses, swollen with the retrospective particulars they have engendered, expunged by scruples and regrets, suddenly inverted by backward glances. Where is order? Where is ceremony? Where is mere politeness? In vain you will try to

cling to these first declarations; they are constantly being transformed by the action of those that follow. What you read on page
30, you learn on page 80 *he* did not really believe – *he* merely
supposed he believed it; on page 150 you learn *he* did *not* suppose
he believed it, and on page 170 you find out *he* had not even
written it – *he* had written a certain sentence imagining he was
writing another one; and on page 200 you discover that imagined
and written significations are strictly interchangeable and are
both false besides. But you must not assume you are witness to a
confession deceptive at the start and gradually inventing its own
sincerity. Here there is no confessor in either sense, no confes-
sional, and nothing to confess; when the voice began – I know, I
can bear witness – it had nothing to say, its truth did not exist. It
spoke words by chance because it had to begin somewhere; such
words are transparent, they refer only to themselves and conceal
no strategy of exposition in the defenseless stammer. Nothing is
more sincere, nothing less artificial than this enterprise. It begins
in anguish, in penury, here, under your eyes, by these very
words; it loses its way and we miscarry with it. *It is true* that it
loses itself and will find itself. *It is true* that it breaks free and
grows rich.

Accustomed to the mind's calisthenics, we imagine, from the
first words, that we have grasped the movement of this thought,
the intention that presides over the construction of a paragraph;
these sudden anticipations, these implied conjectures, these
guesses and forebodings ordinarily permit us to understand the
way of the world and the actions of men. We easily outstrip the
developments still to come and wait for this language-in-action,
comfortably installed at the finish line. But in the present
instance such a procedure is of no use. We discover an intention,
and in so doing were not mistaken, only the intention changes in
its course. No one is there to maintain it; 'the master is in the
Styx',* or, rather, 'in Limbo', and there are only these trinkets of

---

*From a sonnet of Stéphane Mallarmé: 'Car le Maître est allé puiser des
pleurs au Styx'. [A.G.]

sonorous inanity* which change as they incarnate themselves, and each of which, by its mere presence, modifies all the rest. Leaning against the goalpost, we see the verbal stream flowing toward us, and then, suddenly, it contracts, wavers, slips down another slope and leaves us in the lurch. The indefinite recurrence of our disappointments makes a prattling disorder out of what will later seem an order-in-the-making.

For this slow, unpredictable progress *is* an order, a truth in the process of becoming; this is a whole human life shifting from the abstract to the concrete, from poverty to plenitude, from the universal to the individual, from anonymous objectivity to subjectivity. There are reasons for our surprise. Books are corpses, yet here is one which, scarcely in our hands, becomes a living creature. We must open it, of course, turn the pages and awaken the signs, but the mere movement of reading will provoke an unforeseeable occurrence of which neither the moments nor the end are given in advance; you imagine you are lending it your own duration, and it is the book that imposes its duration upon *you*; you will discover the laws of this dangerous language at the very moment it is engendering them, but you will know at the same time that they will be unceasingly changing and that the whole system transforms them to the very degree it is based upon them.

This hoarse, muffled voice, this breaking voice will live in your ears. Its slowness is a kind of speed, for it guides us towards a real future, the only future that is not a masquerade of memories, toward a place no one knows, which does not exist, and which, nevertheless, will be. It strips away its appearances; neither warm nor soft nor fluid, it reveals the inflexible order of enrichment; each sentence gathers within itself all that have preceded it, each is the living medium in which all the rest breathe, endure and transform themselves; in fact, there is only one sentence, rolling over all kinds of terrain, sustained by all kinds of soil, always heavier, fuller, denser, swelling to the bursting point, to the point

---

*'Aboli bibelot d'inanité sonore' [A.G.].

of becoming a man. From moment to moment the sentence runs a real risk: it might explode, might come to a pitiful halt and fall back on itself, a great inert mass clotted in the desert of the present; we sense this risk inside ourselves as we read on, anxiously. Of course, the book seems to be finished; after this page come others, but what does that prove? Everything can end up in nothingness or, worse still, in quicksand. What reassures us, however, is that behind the hesitations of life and language we glimpse a kind of arid passion, cold and sharp, a steel wire stretched between the lacerations of the past and the uncertainty of the future – an inhuman passion, unconscious of itself, an anxiety casting about for its cause, the maniac silence at the heart of language. It drills through the readers' time and draws after it this whole cavalcade of words; we will trust it.

If the work of art cries to all comers the name of its artist, the Late Great who has settled everything, then *The Traitor* is not a work of art; it is an event, a sudden precipitation, a disorder of words assuming an order. You hold in your hands this surprising object – a work in the process of creating its author. Of the latter we know nothing save this one negative characteristic: he will not be, he cannot be that sacred monster known as the Writer; if, at the end of his struggle, he finds himself, it will be as Anyman, a man like the rest, for the voice is in search of a man, not a monster. Therefore do not expect the gesture which is style; here everything is action. But if you prize a certain flavour in our great authors' words, a particular harmony in their sentences, a physiognomy of the feelings and of thought, then read *The Traitor*. At first you will lose everything, but everything will be restored to you; it is its renunciation, its passionate search, the break in its tone that make this voice inimitable; in this writing without subject, the radical impossibility of style ultimately becomes a transcendence of all known styles, or, if you prefer, the style of death gives way to a style of life.*

---

*I do not claim to establish Gorz's superiority, but his originality. Like everyone else, I love death as much as life, for both comprise our fate.

The undertaking is scarcely one that will please. We like whoever likes us; if you want to be read, you have to know how to give yourself, how to pluck your words cunningly to make them resound, how to let your voice grow husky with feeling. But *he*, the object, the 'third person', how could he like us? How could this voice like us? We are confronting a man cut in two, trying to join his stumps together. This occupation leaves him no leisure; perhaps tomorrow there will be time for such trifling. To which you will doubtless reply that your time is short too, and that the problems of joint surgery do not interest you. But how do you know? I happen to read science fiction, invariably with pleasure, for this genre offers an exact measure of our fear of ourselves. One piece particularly delights me: men from Earth land on Venus; no sooner have they stepped out of their rocket than these future colonists happily start hunting for the natives of this planet, their future subjects, who do not show themselves at first. You can imagine the arrogance of the king of nature, the intoxication of his victory, his new freedom. Everything soon collapses before the intolerable evidence: the conquerors are in a cage, their every movement foreseen; every path they decide to take has already been determined for them – by someone. Invisible as they lean over the glass cage, the Venusians submit these captive higher mammals to various intelligence tests. Such, it seems to me, is our common condition. With this difference: that we are our own Venusians and our own guinea pigs. Open *The Traitor* and you are a colonist, you observe with a shrug of the shoulders a curious creature, perhaps a native running terrified across the soil of Venus, but it will not take you two minutes to realize that the native is a rat and that this rat is none other than yourself. The book was a trap, and we have fallen into it; now we are scampering down the corridors of this oversized labyrinth under the experimenter's eyes – that is, under our own. The experiment is taking place; we are trying to find out if there is a single action in this rigged world of which we can say, *I* have done it. Do we recognize our undertakings? Do they not become 'Other' in becoming real? And do not 'Others ' pursue them in our place, Others who are dearer to us than ourselves and who feed upon our blood? Scarcely has this stranger in my heart of hearts determined my behaviour for me than I hear the uproar of the crowd that inhabits me; a sudden agitation seizes all these people I do not know, they condemn my initiative and protest that it concerns only me! *Je suis un autre*, says the Traitor. I consider this to be quite modest. In his place, instead of saying, 'I am an Other', I would say, 'I am Others', and I would refer to myself in the third person plural. Each of my acts, registered upon the passivity of being, becomes a turnstile whose imperious inertia defines me as *its man*, in other words, its slave, the Other I must be in order to provide the first impulsion and incessantly renew it. My slightest action, my sincerest commitment suggest inanimate faces; I must slip into this merry-go-round and revolve like a circus horse in order to make it turn with me. *He*, the author writing this Preface, is an Other, at this very moment someone I don't like. I like the book and I said I would write a preface for it because you always have to pay for the right to like what you like; but once I picked up my pen a tiny invisible carrousel started up just above the paper. This was the foreword-as-a-literary-genre, which requires its specialist – an Olympian old man, a silver-haired Academician. I wasn't an Academician? It didn't matter; *he* would become one for the occasion. How dared I present someone else's book if I wasn't on my own deathbed? *He* would get inside the character's skin, make himself great-elderly-diaphanous-and-astounded; *he* has written the foregoing with a long pale hand which my own stubby fingers were manipulating, *he* thrusts his tentacles into me, sucks up my words and my ideas to produce his slightly superannuated graces. If I try to wrench myself from his grasp, to write naturally, it is worse still; I no longer know what is natural, *he* filters it out and transforms it into *bonhomie*. He will hold onto the pen until the end of this exercise and then he will disappear. But whatever I start on next – pamphlet, lampoon, autobiography – other vampires lie in wait for me, future intermediaries between my consciousness and my written page.

At least I can hope that the intruder will go away, but it is just as likely he will stay on, that I am the victim and the accomplice of his permanent installation. One day Mirandola felt called upon to bring out under the pseudonym Jouvence one of those vehement, vital books which exhort the reader to courage and which for this reason are considered courageous. The work was successful; men who had been down and out glimpsed between the lines an austere and sacred countenance which restored their hopes. In short, Mirandola's book, once it cooled off, created Jouvence, its true author. Today, Jouvence is recognized for his public utility, his virtues are taught in our primary schools, he constitutes a part of our national patrimony and often represents France abroad; he lives on Mirandola, and Mirandola dies of him. The other day at some opening night or other, Mirandola and Jouvence were given only a side seat in the balcony; Mirandola is modest, almost timid, yet he took it upon himself to protest loudly, trembling with rage. 'I wouldn't have said anything if it had been just I,' he exclaimed as he stalked out, 'but I couldn't let them do it to Jouvence!'

Is it his fault? Is it yours? After all, we don't ask for these undesirable guests; it is *the Others* who impose them upon us. The Others or their instruments, those petrified fingers continually pointing at us – the little black bag and the patient making the doctor out of a fat scatterbrained man, creating an angelic dictator, an enlightened despot who pursues our welfare against ourselves while we look forward to his orders, his remonstrances, his adorable severity. Sometimes we would like to muzzle the vampires and to show ourselves as we are; no one is listening, it is They who are expected. Faced with disappointment or general indifference, we ruefully decide, 'If that's the way everyone wants it . . .' and then we unleash the monsters; it always turns out badly. Soon after the war I made the acquaintance of a foreign painter who came over from London; we used to chat in a café. He was a Traitor too, or thought he was. He liked himself so little that other people detested him; it was his name that they liked. I thought he was quite charming. Authoritarian and weak, mistrustful and naïve, drunk with pride and shame, mischievous and kindhearted, fascinated and inconvenienced by his celebrity, he was still quite stupefied at having behind him a considerable body of work which he nevertheless despised. This Don Quixote could respect himself only by winning on another battlefield the war he knew in advance he would never even manage to declare. It all came to an end, in fact, two years later in a burst of laughter. Unstable, unhappy, romantic, he depended on the time of day, on the light in the sky, on a note of music, on women, and especially on men, on all men. All together we might have saved him; lacking this unanimity he vacillated between arrogance and a defenceless kindness. Sometimes, to forget his Treason, that old, badly cared-for blennorrhagia, he let himself be entirely devoured by the celebrated creature he represented for others, and then there remained of him nothing more than a shiny bug; and sometimes fear, warmheartedness and good faith changed him into himself, an ordinary man who painted pictures. On this particular day, a little old man at another table was staring at us. I knew this little old man too; it was one of his compatriots, an *émigré* like himself, but one who had had no luck. Finally, unable to resist any longer, the little old man came over to introduce himself to my friend, who, off his guard, naïvely returned his smile. Glory and genius vanished together; there remained only two exiles who recognized each other without knowing each other, neither of whom was happy, and who talked together like friends.

It was the unluckier of the two who reignited the halo around his interlocutor's head; there had been a misunderstanding, he had not been speaking to the man but to the Painter. You mustn't ask too much of artists; provoked by a respect that was all too manifest, by a few servile inflections, the Great Man appeared; he was perfect – understanding, modest, so inspiredly simple that he drove his compatriot away. The latter hastily gathered up the papers that littered his table and left the café with a bitter, disappointed look, unaware that he had been the artisan of his own misfortune. The painter and I sat there together, and after an uneasy silence the great man murmured something I shall not forget: 'Another failure!' And that meant: *He* had decided he would forget his name, his fame, his voluminous presence; *he* would be merely an exile sitting across the

table from a companion in exile. But since it was the Incomparable Artist that was expected of him, *he* resigned himself to it, *he*
lent his body and his voice to this Other who was not even his
private parasite, who at that very moment was infecting over a
thousand people from Peking to Valparaiso by way of Moscow
and Paris, and he heard it speak out of his own mouth, with that
dreadful sweetness meaning 'Oh, no, it's nothing, *I'm* nothing,
I've done nothing more than you, I've been lucky, that's all.' And
he realized that he had once again missed his chance, and that
his chance would turn up again every day, every moment, and
that every day, every moment, he would miss it.

The test is not over; we are still scampering through the labyrinth. The voice is still speaking. These tourists, these hitchhikers
who inhabit us by the month or the day are not concerned by
this investigation. We will not be asked to account for the
furnished rooms, the halls of mirrors we rent out to our transient
guests; everyone will be released after identifications have been
checked, save for one mysterious and seldom seen visitor, a
usurper who claims to be a prisoner and who is actually nothing
more than our oldest lodger. This individual is precisely the
person whom the voice persists in calling 'he'. Besides, listen to
the voice now, it's not quite the same any more. At the start, it
confined itself to a commentary on our occupant's actions; later,
it revealed that this person was under observation, it described
the tests he was made to undergo, and it gave the results. Now,
louder, more insistent, sometimes brutal, it interrogates; the
Venusians have turned into secret police and the rats into
suspects. Of course, at first we are led to believe we are merely
witnesses of a preliminary investigation. No one seems to bother
about us. It is someone named Gorz who is on the stand; his
name has just been pronounced, he is unremittingly questioned,
his alibis are exploded, they are trying to force him to contradict
himself. What was he doing in Vienna on a certain winter day in
1936? And before that, in his earliest childhood? And later on,
during the Anschluss, he admits he frequented young Nazis,
admired them. Why? Then he claims to have broken off with
them. Did he really? Of his own free will? Can he honestly say, '*I*

broke off?' Wasn't he forced by circumstances? By his 'objective nature'? And where did he get this objective nature from? From whom? From what? Silent, embarrassed, we attend this interrogation and do our best to feel indiscreet. What luck if we could remind ourselves, I was not in Vienna under Chancellor Dollfuss; this business has nothing to do with me. But no, we are stuck, and we know it. At the very moment we explain to the guards that our presence in the torture chamber is due to a misunderstanding, we have already long since started on our own confessions. Executioners and victims, as always, it is we, the police, who begin questioning the Traitor. But as soon as he denounces his first inhabitant, that misshapen dwarf who might be dead or in hiding or whose sly face has just now pressed against the window to mock us, we remember suddenly the little weakling that inhabited us so long, and we try to reconstitute the suspect circumstances of his disappearance: in 1920 I existed, and *he* still existed, so who had so cruelly mutilated him? I remember I didn't like him much, and then I didn't see him any more; there was a murder, I think. But which of us killed the other? The voice is still talking; it has found words for the seam, the scar, the chasm that separates us; the first guilty parties have left their fingerprints on a knife; it won't take us long to identify them.

In fact, the world still seems to be inhabited by savages stupid enough to see reincarnated ancestors in their newborn children. Weapons and jewellery belonging to the dead man are waved under the infant's nose; if he makes a movement, there is a great shout – Grandfather has come back to life. This 'old man' will suckle, dirty his straw and bear the ancestral name; survivors of his ancient generation will enjoy seeing their comrade of hunts and battles wave his tiny limbs and bawl; as soon as he can speak they will inculcate recollections of the deceased. A severe training will 'restore' his former character, they will remind him that 'he' was wrathful, cruel or magnanimous, and he will be convinced of it despite all experience to the contrary. What barbarism! Take a living child, sew him up in a dead man's skin, and he will stifle in such senile childhood with no occupation save to reproduce the

avuncular gestures, with no hope save to poison future child-
hoods after his own death. No wonder, after that, if he speaks of
himself with the greatest precautions, half under his breath, often
in the third person; this miserable creature is well aware that he
is his own grandfather.

These backwards aborigines can be found in the Fiji Islands,
Tahiti, in New Guinea, in Vienna, in Paris, in Rome — wherever
there are men. They are called parents. Long before our birth, even
before we are conceived, parents have decided who we will be. They
have called us 'he' years before we could say 'I'. We existed at first as
absolute objects. By means of our family, society assigns us a situation, a being, a set of roles; the contradictions of history and class
struggle determine in advance the character and the destiny of
generations to come.

Algeria 1935: the parents are exploited, oppressed, reduced
to poverty in the name of a racism which refuses them their
status as men, Arabic is taught as a dead language, there are so
few French schools that the great majority of Algerians are illiter-
ate; rejected by France, without rights, without culture, without
a past, they find relief and assistance only in religion or the
negative pride of a dawning nationalism. Are not their sons, the
*fellagha* of 1957, predetermined? And who has predetermined
them thus, if not the French *colons*? Who has forced upon them,
since Bugeaud, this destiny of wrath, despair and blood? Who
has built these infernal machines which must one day explode
and destroy the colonial system? Everywhere, the role is there,
waiting for its man. For this one it is the role of a Jew; for that
one, the role of a property owner. But these occupations are still
too abstract. They are made specific *en famille*; we have all been
forced to reincarnate at least one deceased person, generally a
child who is the victim of his next of kin, killed at an early age,
and whose wretched ghost survives in the form of an adult – our
own father or mother. Zombies. Scarcely out of the womb, each
child of man is taken for another; he is pushed and pulled to
make him play his part like children the *comprachicos* stuffed into
porcelain jars to keep them from growing. At least the latter were
not the sons of their executioners; sometimes they were bought,

often kidnapped. But who is not a kidnapped child, more or less – stolen from the world, stolen from his neighbour, stolen from himself? The custom has been perpetuated; it is from kidnapped children that kidnappers are made. We knew all this, we have always known it. A solitary voice constantly told us so, but we preferred to pass it over in silence, it was speaking in the desert, in our desert. *He* was doing this or that in our place, and we were *his* straw man; out of cowardice, out of complacency, we declared, 'I did it', and everyone pretended to believe us on condition that we did the same for them. Thus for thousands of years humanity, ashamed of yielding to fear, to blackmail, covers up for the profitable racket that has been feeding on it. Fortunately, someone has just given away the show, a 'traitor', someone like the American dockworkers who, disgusted by their own cowardice, inform against the gangsters exploiting them and are later found in the Hudson. A traitor, a man with as many cracks and crevices as ourselves, but a man who could no longer stand the double-dealing. He has broken the silence, refused to cover up for the intruder who was impersonating him, refused to say, 'I did it'. Suddenly the Others – the Zaras, the loas, the dark angels, the sons of Cain, all our parasites – are shown naked. Naked but not dead. We are torn between scandal and terror; from one minute to the next we expect the mobsters' reprisal, an informer's execution. In fact, we have gained nothing; we find our own cracks, we discover our occupants, that is all. But we are undeceived. We thought that this little gnawing noise came into us through our ears, but no – it is in our hearts that it was born; this time we have recognized the universal mumble of enslaved consciousness, the human voice – and we are not likely to forget it.

Which, of course, does not keep the Traitor from belonging to a very particular species; he has his own way of being anyone at all. Neither the Extravagant Doctors nor the Braggart Heroes have chosen him as their domicile. If he refers to himself in the third person, it is not out of excess but by default. The temperate actions committed in his name he regards as *his* only if he manages to find motives for them; he has conducted hundreds of

investigations, always in vain; from which one might conclude
that he cares about nothing. *He* travels without wanting to travel;
*he* meets people, makes visits, invites guests without enjoying
company; on other occasions, *he* goes to earth, shuts himself up
without any desire to be alone. Is he blasé? Not at all. To rid
yourself of this world's goods, you have to have cared for them
once. And we certainly cannot reproach him for 'having come
back from somewhere, anywhere, without ever having been
there.' For there is nothing of the *revenant* about him; he has never
left, this is his real misfortune. Why? Because he didn't want to
enough. His heart, moreover, shows no trace of that arrogant
insatiability which has served as our alibi for three literary generations. The infinite, the eternal Elsewhere, the Dream – he
couldn't care less, thank God. Some men I know feel justified in
despising the world by comparing it with some perfect prototype.
But the Traitor despises no one, nothing. Then is it Drieu La
Rochelle's famous 'empty suitcase'? No. The valise trick was
good for the years between the wars – you opened it, you asked
the spectator to see for himself that there was nothing in it
besides a pair of pajamas and a toothbrush. Today we know that
the valise had a false bottom, that it was used to carry arms and
drugs; the *jeunesse dorée* skillfully concealed in it anything that
could be used to destroy the race and precipitate the succession
of the Inhuman. But the Traitor has no interest in blowing up
the world; the Inhuman is already his fate, since he does not
share the objectives of men. In a word, I classify him with the
Indifferents. This subgroup is of recent origin, its representative
members are no more than thirty; no one knows yet what they
will become. All we know now is that we lose all means of understanding them if we insist on saddling them with an aristocratic
nonchalance. What distinguishes them, in fact, is their eagerness.
Gorz has a job, cultivates his body and his mind, has taken a
wife. If you met him carrying his elegant leather briefcase at the
Palais de Justice or the Bourse, you would take him for someone
like yourself. He is punctual at his office, scrupulous to the point
of being niggling; no one is more affable; in his daily relationships he betrays only a faint shadow of reserve which his

colleagues smilingly explain as timidity; but ask him to do you a favour and he drops everything to execute it as fast as he can. Superficial observers will judge him to be insignificant. As a matter of fact, he speaks infrequently, he looks like everyone else; this effacement and this skillful mimicry will assure his popularity. But when you look at him more closely, this imposter is exposed by his very zealousness. Most people, convinced of their status as men from father to son, and since Adam, treat their human nature with some negligence; they have rights to it so ancient and so little contested that they calmly follow their personal inclinations, certain that they can take a piss, if they want to, or kill a man, quite humanly. But the Indifferent does not recognize his own right to his inclinations; he has to force himself to take a drink or get into a fight, drink without thirst, take revenge without anger for an affront he has not suffered, all in order to do as the rest do. His first impulse is not to have one – that is what he must conceal, constantly deny; this curious product of our societies, terrified of falling to the level of the angels or that of conditioned rats, forces himself to imitate the Adamites in every detail; he disappears. In the excellent little book in which he describes his war experiences, Paulhan calls himself 'the diligent warrior'. The Indifferent, on the other hand, rouses suspicion for the simple reason that he is a diligent *man*.

Too diligent to be honest. If he is so anxious to pass for a man like myself, it must mean that he isn't one. Could the human community contain *false* men? Men who cannot be distinguished from the real ones? Then how could you know if the real ones exist at all? Who is to check their qualifications? I have occasionally heard that man was his own future, on other occasions that he was his past – never his present. We are all false men; the Traitor has given away the game again; by his passion to make himself human, he reminds us that our race does not exist. The author of this book is a rat, as we might have suspected. And what is more, a rat possessed. By another rat? By the rat-in-itself? Certainly not. This Other a lonely voice continually refers to, this pure object, this receding perspective, this absence – is Man, our tyrant. We are all exposed, rats a prey to Man. Now the Indifferent's folly is immediately recognizable, it is our own. We all pursue a ghost down the corridors of an experimental labyrinth; Gorz is at the head of the line. If he catches that ghost and eats him, if he assimilates into his own substance that parasite he has fed so long on his anxieties and exhaustions, then our race is possible; somewhere, between the rats and the angels, it is in the process of being born; we will get out of the labyrinth.

Once again, the sense of this book has been transformed. It is not a question of knowing oneself but of changing life; we are not being spoken to, but whether we like it or not it is of us that the fundamental question is asked: By what activity can an 'accidental individual', as Marx calls him, realize the human person in himself and for everyone else?

This book is organized like a feedback machine: the present ceaselessly metamorphosizes the past from which it issues. In the early pages, the voice seemed to gather up words accidentally, no matter where, to escape its anguish and to have something behind it, no matter what – anything but silence. And that was true; at that moment, that was true. But the question of man has been asked. A new light is now shed on the beginning of the enterprise, a metamorphosis: before the voice, Gorz already existed, was already suffering from his indifference, was protecting himself against it with the means at hand. Suddenly he changes his tactics and reverses his relation to himself. This rupture constitutes in itself an absolute event, but it would be wrong to construe it as an interior adventure whose chief merit would be to have produced a book; in fact, it is in the book that the event occurs, it is through the book and by the book that this rupture develops and becomes conscious of itself. *The Traitor* does not claim to *tell us* a convert's story; it *is* the conversion itself.

Gorz is thirty-two; for thirty-two years, whatever he does, it invariably seems to him that he might have done the opposite and that the result would have been the same; that is, null – or, worse still, insignificant. For thirty-two years, his existence has escaped him, he has no proof of it beyond an insurmountable boredom: *I'm bored, therefore I am.* But he has struggled, has searched, has thought he found the way to carry it off, deciding, 'Because I belong nowhere, to no group, to no enterprise, because I am exiled from all such groups and enterprises, there is only one alternative: either to be a marginal note of society and history, the supernumerary of the human race ... reduced to the boredom of living, to the acute awareness of the contingency of everything around me, or to raise myself in conscience to the absolute – that is, to regard everything, philosophically, as a moment of the spiritual adventure and then ... to recover, starting from such speculative interests, a taste for the concrete. ... I can achieve ... the real only by starting with the Idea.' In other words, since he is so constituted as to be unaware of possessing any particular desire, he will put his indifference to good use. Because he cannot – or will not, nothing is certain yet – be a certain Gorz, he will make himself into the Universal Man; he will determine his behaviour by concepts and give himself this rule: Always act so that the circumstances and the moment serve as a pretext for your actions to realize in and beyond yourself the generality of the human race. This is why he undertook, at twenty, to write a philosophical work; when you are immunized from birth against the violences of fear, concupiscence or anger, you must either do nothing at all or base everything on reason, even the act of opening an umbrella if it is raining.

Everything is clear now. We are no longer surprised that he has 'betrayed'; he is one of those people who have their heads full of words, who analyse everything, who always want to know the why and the how; a critical and destructive spirit – in short, a damn intellectual. I wouldn't dream of denying it – that's even why I like him; I'm one myself. Not long ago a literary paper asked the prince of counterfeit what he hated most of all; he didn't hesitate a moment: 'Intellectuals'. I happen to be the friend of this forger. He is a true poet and a good man; but I wonder what was the matter with him that day. Everyone knows his hunted looks, his arias about time, death and destiny, anthology pieces from a perpetual and suppliant vindication, these congestions of words in his throat, his charming hands that are words too, turning palms outward to implore pardon, this harassed, exhausted intellect, but still running, leaping nimbly from one idea to the next without realizing that it is merely turning the treadmill in its cage, these skyrocket improvisations whose scaffolding can be found in the texts of the day before and which, as they fade and go out, offer glimpses of the incurable sadness of that frozen stare. This man seeks a tribunal for himself only in order to corrupt it; if he meets you, you will be judge and jury, he will not let you off from a single detail of his behaviour and will let you go only if you have acquitted him. But don't fool yourself, he knows it all, he knows he was condemned at the century's start to the sentence he wants to head off, he knows he is a convict and has been working out that sentence for over fifty years; for he is condemned to plead even in old age the cause which his adolescence has judged without appeal. What would you call this Devil's Advocate if not an intellectual? I know others, of course, who would oppose such chatter with the great silences of the earth or of the peasants. But if you open them up, what a hubbub! Their heads are humming with words that describe other people's silence. Gorz is the first, I think, to have formulated the problem concretely; and I am grateful to him for that. It matters little whether you speak about language or about silence, about the poet's confused intentions or about reason's clear and distinct ideas; what matters is that these speakers must speak, are compelled to speak. In the cause of the heart's shadows, our forger has offered more reasoning than Kant to establish the rights of Reason. He was compelled to; discourse, concepts, argumentation – this is our fate. Why? Because the intelligence is neither a gift nor a fault, it is a drama – or, if you prefer, a temporary solution which generally becomes a life sentence. Someone once told our Traitor, 'You stink of intelligence the way some people stink from under their arms.' And its true; intelligence stinks. But not more than stupidity; there are odours for every taste. Stupidity smells of animals; intelligence, of men. To begin with, this is because there are certain lacerated, condemned, exiled individuals who try to surmount their conflicts and their solitude by pursuing the fleeting image of unanimity; it is that image we see reflected in their eyes, that image their timid smiles offer us. Apropos of anything and everything, the appeal is there, permanently etched on their faces; the voice insists, whatever it says, on universal agreement; but humanity, weighed down by its particularities, by its close-packed interests, by its passions, detests anyone who would dissolve its differences and its hates in the formal harmony of assent.

And then, intelligence is scrupulous: it wants to start everything over at the beginning, even what everyone thinks he already knows how to do. It takes apart walking or breathing and puts them back together again, it learns how to wash an ear, how to blow a nose, according to principles. That is what makes intellectuals walk like wounded men learning how to use their artificial limbs. But you must understand them – they are reinventing everything to compensate for the great rummage sale that has liquidated their every impulse, every obstinacy; they need it to replace the signals that have not been inscribed on their flesh, the habits they have not been given, the paths they have not been shown – in short, to live. I remember seeing a puppy after the partial ablation of its cerebellum. It moved across the room and only rarely bumped into furniture, but it had become thoughtful; the animal carefully established its itinerary, deliberated before avoiding an obstacle and took a long time to accomplish the movements previously made without paying any attention at all. In the language of the period, the animal's cortex had assumed the functions of the lower centres; what we had was an intellectual dog. I don't know if the creature was very useful or very harmful to his fellows, but we can suppose it had lost what another exile, Genet, has so aptly called 'the sweet natal confusion'; ultimately, the creature must either crack up or reinvent the dog. And the rest of us, rats without half our brains, are so constituted that we have to crack up or invent man. Moreover, we are well aware that he will be invented without us, by work and by conflict, that our models grow obsolete from one day to the next, that not even a knucklebone will figure in the finished product; but the creation would be performed in the dark, blindly, by tinkering, by puttering and patching, if we, the lobotomized, were not here constantly repeating that you must work according to principles, that it is not a matter of darning but of cutting, that our race, finally, will be the concrete universal or not be at all.

Gorz's intelligence is immediately and strikingly apparent. It is one of the sharpest, the most agile that I know; he must have great need of this tool to have sharpened it so well. But when he undertakes his philosophical treatise, he still does not escape the contradiction proper to intellectuals. He wants to act only in terms of the human condition; yet, once performed, the action buries itself in the particular; what remains is the fortuitous realization of one possibility out of a thousand. Why particularly that one? The worst is that it compromises him; he cannot even breathe without adding a new brushstroke to a portrait-without-a-model which is none other than his own. He would have to become every possible Gorz at once for these futile equivalents to cancel each other out, in order to be, finally, *only* man by becoming *all* man. But no – 'We are born several and we die only one', says Valéry's Socrates. Gorz cannot keep from living or from shrinking with use. His universal intelligence exceeds his personal adventure and is disgusted at the appearance of the physiognomy of the Gorz who will die only one; his intelligence refuses this one, does not even want to recognize him. It would accept him gladly as anyone at all; now he is not even that; a series of accidents has given him a definite individuality that distinguishes itself from the rest by a number of inanities.

We all know this listless, sugary anguish – we, that is, we intellectuals. We think we are universal because we play with concepts, and then, suddenly, we see our shadow at our feet; we are *here*, we are doing *this* and nothing else. Once, in Brooklyn, I thought I was going crazy. It was my own fault – I was strolling, and you don't stroll in the United States. Therefore I was crossing sidewalks, passing apartment buildings, staring at people on the street. And from one street to the next, apartment buildings, people and sidewalks were all the same or, at least, seemed all the same to me. I turned right, left, turned back, continued straight ahead, always to find the same brick buildings, the same white steps in front of the same doors, the same children playing the same games. At first I liked this – I had discovered the city of absolute equivalents; universal and anonymous, I had no more reason to walk on *this* sidewalk than on the same one ten blocks ahead; recommenced a thousand times, the wave of stone carried me on, made me share in its inert renewal. What gradually exhausted me was to be advancing constantly *to get nowhere*; I walked faster, I was almost running, and I was still in the same place. Suddenly I was conscious of an infinite refusal; all these standardized products, all these stubs of streets running side by side, resembled each other further in that they were equally empty of me – except for one, in fact, which was in no way different from the rest, in which I had no more reason to be than in the neighbouring blocks and which, for an unknown reason, or even with no reason at all, tolerated my presence. Suddenly my movements, my life, my own weight seemed illegitimate to me. My person was not real, since I had no particular reason to be at this point on the forty-second parallel rather than at any other; still, I was an individual being, irreducible since my position by latitude and longitude rigorously defined me. Neither everyone nor someone, nor quite something – a determination of space, a guilty and contagious dream that haunted, in spots, the overheated asphalt, a fault in being, a defect. An obstinately moving body, my presence in the mechanical universe of repetition became a crude accident as stupid as my birth. Ubiquity would have saved me; one must be legion, prowl a hundred thousand sidewalks at once – that alone would have allowed me to be any stroller in any Brooklyn street. Since I could not abandon myself, or multiply myself, I dashed into the subway, returned to Manhattan and, back in my hotel, recovered my usual ordinary *raisons d'être*, scarcely convincing, but human.

There is no subway for young Gorz, no hotel and no *raison d'être*. He is outside even in his room, hence illegitimate everywhere; and hoaxed into the bargain: he thinks he can escape his insignificant person by parading the disgust it inspires in him; now, it is first of all this disgust that singles him out; the peculiarity of intellectuals is precisely their vain desire for universality.

But he has just finished his treatise, he steps back to get a
better look at it, and the entire hoax vanishes; the notion of the
universal contracts, condenses, assumes a contour, a physiognomy – it resembles him; he is at the origin of a supernumerary
object – this bundle of typed pages – and at the same time he is
imprisoned within it. For a long time now other people have
claimed to recognize him by his most ordinary gesture, his way
of eating, sitting down, opening a telegram – 'Oh yes, that's you
all right, that's just like you, I'd know you anywhere by that,
what you just did is pure Gorz, the spit and image.' God knows it
made him angry enough, but has he not just performed a
voluminous gesture that has closed over him? The others will be
all too pleased, they will lean over the transparent walls of his
prison and they will recognize him. 'That way of writing, *mon
vieux*, that way of correcting yourself, of entering into your
subject little by little, of testing the water with your toe before
jumping in – why, that's you, that's you all right, and those
ideas, they're pure Gorz, only Gorz could have such ideas!' Like
a devil in a bottle, whether he opens cans, other people's
concepts or his own umbrella, he has only one and the same
gesture, only one way to enter the views of a seventeenth-century
philosopher and a girl friend's apartment. One by one he takes
up the sentences of his book. Gestures! Gestures! Gestures! Gorz
is here, under his eyes, stretching out his long neck, pinching his
thin lips. '*Tel qu'en lui-même enfin . . .*'* In short, he has tried to
live, and he has failed. Now he knows he was condemned to fail
and that he was secretly determined to besides.

It is at this very moment that we first hear the voice – a tiny,
almost unintelligible mumble born of anguish and recrimin-
ation, ruminating this surprising and foreseen defeat. The voice
merely establishes a fact: That's him, that's him all right, the
spitting image. Which is enough for everything to collapse. It was
other people who claimed to know this parasite that fattened on

---

*'As into himself at last [eternity transforms him]', from the first line of
Mallarmé's sonnet on Poe [Tr.].

his acts, while the Indifferent's universal gaze passed through him like light through a windowpane. Suddenly he is there, opaque, encumbering. 'Confess – you saw him, you spoke to him, we know you did; your alibi is totally unconvincing, we know the time and place of your meetings. You're finished!' The voice changes to a confession: 'All right, yes, I know him better than anyone else, I've always known him, I'll tell you everything I know about him!'

Was I not right just now when I said we should always speak of ourselves in the plural? There are two people living on this unfortunate creature: there is the Universal Man, an elusive, well-armed tyrant, and then there is the other one, the failure. *One* becomes a *certain* Gorz by trying to be merely man; and, to tell the truth, one wants to become *all man* because one refuses to be a certain Gorz. But then, who refuses to be Gorz if not Gorz himself? This refusal explains and defines him. If one accepted being in other words, accepted having been the greedy boy with the long neck who wants to preserve his futile universality; if one unremittingly spoke of him, if one detailed all his private obsessions, if, instead of passing through him, the intellectual gaze brought him to light, would not this 'original' disappear with the stubborn negation that comprised his originality? Of course, it is not Millennial Man who would come to take his place, but another private individual whose fundamental obsessions would merely risk being more positive. What is there to be gained? Is the game worth the candle? As a matter of fact, it is too late to reckon profit and loss; the voice is speaking, the enterprise has begun. The Traitor has chosen as his goal his own particularity.

It is not a question of knowing that particular nature, not even of changing it, but first of all of changing *oneself* by wanting to know it. The Indifferent has no such foolish project as to describe himself; he wants to modify the fundamental relation that unites him to Gorz. When he turns back toward the child and the adolescent he has been, when he questions his witness, his investigation is already an action. He calls a halt to his headlong flight, forces himself to look at himself without disgust, transfers to himself his taste for generalities and, lacking All Man, he claims first to become for himself All Gorz.

This is not easy; having neglected himself so long, he is lost inside himself, like Crusoe on his desert island. How rediscover the lost paths? Creepers and briars cover everything. He can still glimpse certain memories, but what is a memory? What is the truth of this inert miniature? And its importance – what is its importance? Is it the past that explodes in the present like a bomb? Is it the present making itself up to look like the past? Or both together? To answer these questions we must know: Who is this Gorz I am? Who made me so that I am Gorz, so that I refuse so fiercely to be Gorz? But how decide? Where are the tools? Of course, there is no lack of offers; there are well-tried methods which hurriedly propose themselves and even make little test demonstrations to prove their effectiveness. 'Your class,' says one, 'is decaying. Without principles and without hope, it expends all its strength maintaining itself and has not enough heart, or, if you prefer, enough naïveté, to undertake anything new. Your indifference betrays the anxious uncertainty of your class; exist-ence seems without a purpose to you because bourgeois life no longer has a meaning. As for your philosophical malaise, how else account for its origin? The bourgeoisie no longer has any confidence in its old idealism and tries to conceal it with new tinsel; you have taken these bright rags into your hands, you have seen the threadbare warp, and you have been disgusted, unable to satisfy yourself with these outworn notions, unable to find a new rationale.' He listens, he approves, he is not altogether convinced; he has no difficulty admitting he is a young bourgeois. Without needs, quite abstract, a 'pure consumer of water, air, bread and other people's work, reduced to ... the acute awareness of the contingency of everything around me.' But he knows many other bourgeois his age who do not in the least resemble him. Of course, he could, without abandoning the method, recover the historical and social circumstances which might explain his peculiarities. He tells us himself that he is Austrian, half Jewish, that he had to leave Austria during the Anschluss and that he lived in Switzerland for several years. He is convinced that these factors are not without an influence on his present attitude. But just what influence is here at work? And how is it wielded? And in a more general manner, is there anything more surprising, more obscure than the action of people, of events or of objects on a man's development? Around him everyone is in agreement: we are conditioned; he finds no one to doubt the existence of this conditioning and to question its nature; these are things handed down from father to son; their quarrels begin when they try to classify the conditions and to determine their importance. But all these people are inheritors; these presuppositions, these supposed evidences comprise an ancient legacy which each generation palms off on the one following, and of which no one has ever made an inventory. The Indifferent, on the other hand, has inherited none of their convictions; the Exile from all groups must also be exiled from all ideologies. When he comes to consider that he is 'the son of a Jew' and at the same time that he has an 'acute awareness of the contingency of everything', he admires the isolation, the opacity, the lofty irreducibility of these two facts at such variance with each other. Considering them quite naïvely, it is as if they were two miniatures of medieval cities girdled with ramparts and moats; each was painted long ago and framed, and they were hung at the same level on the wall; between them there is no visible connection for they do not exist in the same world. Yet he is not unaware that people come and go in this private museum of theirs, that they pass from a Circumcision to a Flagellation without even looking for the painters' names, saying: 'That is because of this; I am the unfortunate product of my race, of my father's Jewishness, of my friends' anti-Semitism', as if the real link between these mysterious images of himself were quite simply the wall on which the pictures had been hung; but when he thinks of the peaceful assurance of these heirs, he falls into a trance of wondering.

This is when the other method seems more likely, this strange dogma based on absolute scepticism. Does he remember his early years, the aversion that his mother felt, that she was able to inspire in him, for the Jew she had married, the intolerable tension of the family group, the severe training he was made to

undergo as soon as he could speak? Then let him ask whether he
was not the victim of a tyrannical, castrational mother, and if it is
not from this obscure period, from this oppression submitted to
in bewilderment, that he must date the appearance of the
'complexes' that today divide him from the world. '*He*', finally –
would *he* not be the Honorary Aryan, a character an outraged
wife wants to impose upon her son because she ceaselessly
reproaches a certain Jew for being the only husband she could
find? The docility of a moulded child survives in the adult as
apathy.

To which he replies that his education has in fact given him
certain complexes. His mother wanted to make him this Other
whom he has in part become; during his first years, he suffered,
as now, from an anxious and overzealous indifference. But he
cannot understand how these famous complexes perpetuate
themselves. He was apathetic at eight, he is apathetic today. Is it
the same apathy? Has it been preserved by an inert perseverance
of being? But he will not believe so easily in human passivity; all
his experience rejects this notion, despite its convenience, and
the metaphysic that supports it as well. Will he admit, on the
other hand, that he has coddled his complexes, that he feeds and
fattens them now, that the adolescent and the adult have
developed, emphasized, enriched the child's first characteristics
by a kind of continuous creation? Then he would be responsible
for everything; it is he, from day to day, who makes himself
indifferent.

He cannot reach a conclusion so quickly. None of these interpretations is completely satisfactory, none is altogether clear in
his eyes; a traitor once again, like the child in the fairy tale who
sees the emperor naked, he takes inventory of our philosophical
heritage, finds the coffers empty, and says so ingenuously
enough. Why, moreover, should he be interrogated by the other
people's methods, why should he hand himself over to the
psychoanalytic or Marxist third degree? It depends on him, in
fact, to put these investigation procedures to the test in the questions he asks himself about himself. This Oedipus interrogates
his own past, the validity of his memory, the rights of experience

and the limits of reason, and the legitimacy, finally, of the prophetic gifts claimed by our Tiresiases. But he turns his back on the universal. He invents the method by reflecting on his own case, it will substantiate itself by his success; in order to bring himself to light as an individual totality, he must confine himself in the experience of his individuality, which he will invent for himself by inventing his own interrogation and the means of answering it. The Traitor erases everything and begins himself all over again. That is what gives us, today, the opportunity to read a *radical* book.

For a long time we have been listening to 'his master's voice'. Now it is Gorz speaking. The monologue's end catches up with its beginning, envelops it, absorbs it; the meaning of the work appears in broad daylight. First of all there was a question, asked in the darkness by no one: Under what conditions could the man named Gorz say 'I'? But, immediately afterward, a creature still indistinct emerged from the shadows. It is not merely a question of determining these conditions, the book becomes Gorz's living effort to satisfy them. *He* knows, now, that *he* will have done nothing if he does not wring the necks of the vampires that dress, wash and feed him in order to feed upon him. The first action of my hands, depending only on itself and the obstacles to be overcome, turning back on itself to develop and check itself – that is the action which will say my first 'I'; this imperceptible pressure of an action upon itself, that will be I. And who keeps him from acting? He knows that too: it is the too prompt desire to be too quickly universal. He reminds himself now that his future action will necessarily borrow *his* eyes, *his* mouth, *his* arms, that it will have *his* expression; and, above all, that it will be more rigorously defined every day by the ephemeral agitation it will communicate to the objects around him. Taken outwardly, that's all a man is – an anxiety working over matter in the limits of a rigorously defined area. Singular old enterprises impose their singularity on a new enterprise which refers to all the rest in order to singularize them still more: 'I' is this perpetual coming and going. Whatever it does, it will be itself; but one must accept

oneself in order to act. Who keeps him from doing that? What is
the reason for his futile desire for universality? He discovers an
accumulation of failures piled up in his heart: his childhood; he
attempts to sweep it away, but that is not enough. He can no
longer conceal from himself the fact that he is constantly
reinventing his bastardy, the weight of his old miseries, his old
weaknesses; because he is not everything, it is he, today, who
flings himself into a proud passivity so that everyone will know he
receives his determinations from the exterior and without
consenting to them; it is he who annihilates himself of his own
free will or, at least, who absents himself, letting the habits other
people have made him acquire assure his place in the world,
assume the natural and social functions of his body; it is he who
has voluntarily decided, like Saint John of the Cross but without
mysticism, to do nothing at all in order to be free to 'be nothing
at all'. Then is he free? Of course; he never doubted it. They
have made him, marked him, poured him into the mould – and
he is free? Yes; predestination and free will create in him one and
the same thing. How can this be? He will try to say, to tell
himself; but his purpose remains practical: it is, for him, a
question of inventing the dialectical movement that can sum up
the changing relations of past, present and future, of objective
and subjective, of being and existence, of mechanism and freedom, in order to be able to affirm himself and at the same time
perpetually dissolve himself until at last he can generate in his
heart the authentic impulse that ravages him as it leaves his
hands and reaches external completion in that holocaust of
objects called an 'action'.

Such is his task. He has just understood it, he puts what he has
understood on paper; and, at that moment, he realizes that his
most intimate desire leaves his heart through his hands; that he
is already launched on an enterprise; that yesterday's words and
today's and those of the month past gather together, organize to
show him his new face; that he is dissecting himself by words so
that he can someday create himself by actions; that this destruction creates him, that it determines him irreversibly, that it transforms him little by little into that incomparable and ordinary

creature each of us is for himself while our vampires are asleep; that he has, finally, 'jumped in', condemned, whatever he does, to have no other springboard ever again but himself. This is the moment. *Hic Rhodus, hic salta*; the enterprise turns back on itself, provides a thousand fluctuations of consciousness, the thousand rings of reflection, brushes against itself, smells itself, sees itself. The enterprise is the voice. The voice recognizes itself. In it, action discovers itself and says 'I'. I am making this book, I seek myself, I write. Somewhere a hollow-eyed chap sighs, intimidated, 'How pompous to use the first person!' and then dissolves. Gorz appears. I am Gorz, it was my voice that was speaking, I am writing, I exist, I have submitted to myself and I create myself, I have won the first round.

Is it worth crying victory? Who is Gorz, after all? Someone 'of no social importance', a failure of the universal who has flung out these abstract speculations to fascinate himself with his own insignificant person. Where is the gain? Where is the progress? This is a question Gorz will not answer, I imagine; but we can answer for him. For we have followed step by step this fantastic Cuvier who finds a bone, reconstructs the whole animal from the meagre remains, and realizes, at the end, that the creature he has put together is none other than himself. The method was valid only for him, he has said so a hundred times; he can experience it only in his own case. But we have followed him, we have understood the meaning of his actions along with him, we have watched his experiments, seen the muscles reborn around the knucklebone, the organism reconstitute itself step by step, author and book create each other by means of each other. Since what we understand belongs to us, Gorz's method is ours; when he tries to interpret his life by Marxist dialectic or by psychoanalysis without ever quite succeeding, his failure involves us, we will be able to make the test, and we know the result in advance. And when he asks his own object, that is, himself, to create his method for him, we grasp at once the significance of this singular attempt. For we are like him in this, that each of us, too, is a unique someone. Then what is this object that makes itself into a subject by invoking a method? Gorz, or you and I? You are not

indifferent, you will have other questions to ask about yourself;
by inventing himself, Gorz has not relieved you of your duty, the
duty of inventing yourself. But he has proved that the general-
izing invention is possible and necessary. Closing this book, each
reader confronts his own undergrowth, the poisonous trees of his
private jungle; it is up to him to hack out his own paths, to clear
his own ground, to drive off the vampires, to burst the old iron
corsets, the exhausted actions into which resignation, fear and
self-distrust have laced him. Will we recover the universal by
putting our chips on the individual? No, that would be too easy.
We are no longer altogether animals, without quite being men;
we have not yet taken advantage of that dreadful catastrophe
which has fallen on some representatives of the animal kingdom
– thought. In short, we shall be mammals stricken by disaster for
a long time still; this is an age of fury, fetish and sudden terrors,
universality is only a dream of death at the heart of separation
and fear. But for several decades now our world has been changing. At the very depths of its hatred, reciprocity reveals itself;
even those who enjoy emphasizing their differences must be
willing to ignore a fundamental identity. This new disturbance,
this modest but stubborn attempt to communicate across the
incommunicable, is not the stale and always somewhat stupid
desire for an inert and already realized universal; this is what I
should prefer to call 'the movement of universalization'. Nothing
is possible yet; no agreement is foreseen among the experimental
creatures; our universals separate us; they provide the permanent occasion of private massacres. But if one of us, stirred by
anxiety, turns back on his singularity *to go beyond it*; if he tries to
recognize his solitude in order to escape it, to launch the first
bridges, whatever the cost – in a strange, empirical language like
the speech invented by the aphasiac – between the islands of our
archipelagos; if he replaces our intransigent loves – which are
disguised hatreds – by applied preferences; if he tries, in circumstances that are always individual and dated, to ally himself with
others whom he scarcely approves of and who do not approve of
him, to make the reign of Injustice a little less unjust, then he will
force those others to reinvent this same stubborn effort, to ally

themselves by the recognition of their diversities. This is what Gorz has attempted; this Traitor has broken the tables of the universal, but in order to find the movement of life, that slow universalization which realizes itself by the affirmation and the transcendence of the particular. The immediate consequence: At the very moment when at last he can say, *I* am doing this, *I* am responsible for it, he realizes that he is speaking to *us*. For today there are only two ways of speaking about oneself: the third person singular and the first person plural. We must know how to say 'we' in order to say 'I' – that is beyond question. But the opposite is also true. If some tyranny, in order to establish the 'we' first, deprives individuals of the subjective image, all 'interiority' disappears and all reciprocal relations with it. 'They' will have won forever, and 'we' never stop running through their experimental labyrinths, crazed rodents at the mercy of vampires.

Gorz's book concerns us all. If he stammers at first, if he doesn't know where he's going, if he transforms himself incessantly and if we feel his fever and his chills in our own hands, if he contaminates us without seeing us and if, finally, he speaks directly, intimately, to each reader, it is because he is altogether alive with the movement that animates us, the movement of our times. Radical and modest, vague and rigorous, banal and inimitable, this is the first book after the defeat; the vampires have made a memorable carnage, they have extinguished hope; we must catch our breath, play dead a while, and then get up, leave the charnel house, begin everything all over again, invent a new hope, try to live. The centuries' great slaughters have made Gorz into a corpse; he revives by writing an Invitation to Life.

— JEAN-PAUL SARTRE

# *We*

*Hic Rhodus, hic salta.*

He stared at the silhouettes appearing behind the window curtains across the Place de Rennes. The die was cast; he had to take the jump. For ten years he had clung to his manuscript. He had set out to solve the world's problems. With no certainty save that certainties can be acquired and remain subject to dismissal, he had thought he could begin living the day he answered this question: When, how, for whom can life have a meaning?

The silhouettes wavered behind the curtain. The light went out. He glanced at the shadows of the doorway. That was where they would come out, and the manuscript would stay on the shelf, a corpse. Would they even read it? Not tonight. Tomorrow maybe. He wanted to be angry with them, but could not.

*Hic Rhodus, hic salta.* He had promised himself to write these words in his journal the day he finished writing this book. He had clung to it for ten years; it had become his justification. He had discovered that when a man is incapable of living, or when life has no meaning for him, he always invents this way out for himself: to write about the nonmeaning of life, to look for an explanation, an escape, to demonstrate that all roads are blocked save one – this demonstration itself, and the remedy it provides against the experience it contradicts. Writing had become a passion; he had purged himself of all problems; he had resolved

35

them in the abstract. And when, after nine years, he had felt he was near the end, the beginning of the end, he had realized that the essential thing was eluding him. The essential thing: himself. He felt empty and bone-dry. He wondered if he would even suffer if his book (ten years!) were refused. 'The Essay' had slowly died as he drew near the end, had fallen outside himself; it had given him something to think about for ten years, but these ruminations had not reached him. He was the same as he had been before, with this exception: he had learned to think about life. He had not learned to endure himself. He had escaped himself by posing his problems in the abstract, and he found himself intact. Now everything had to be begun all over again; he must take a look at himself rather than at 'man in general'. He must stop believing a problem can ever be 'solved'. He must reach this certainty: A philosophy cannot dispense with life – the question persists and you have to put up with yourself indefinitely.

Then it had begun to seem laughable. This book had not come from *him*. It was a lie. It was not looking for his way, it was looking for The Way. And all it had given him was his feeling, today, of mounting anguish. I have not tried to resolve problems, but to get rid of them. Using a technique not my own, I have tried to make everything abide by the laws of this technique. I have wadded reality together and tied it up with Morel's string. I have asked myself the questions he left open (What is pure reflection? Morality? Authenticity? Value?), but I have refused to live them. I have lined up various cogitations, supposing that by repeating what he had suggested I would discover the Truth. I have done nothing except imitate without understanding.

That is why he finds himself empty today, the earth giving way under his feet. No need to wait for Morel's verdict. He knows it will be negative. Ten minutes' conversation with Morel and he came back to all the questions of ten years before, questions he hadn't known how to pose, with this one into the bargain: What made me think I was competent to begin this anyway?

Betrayed. The question shimmers before him like a trap. Atheist he might be, but the question betrayed his profound religiosity. He had a God. God, for him, was called Morel, and all he had done for ten years was to pray to Morel as you pray to God: spiritual exercises in order to enter into communion with Morel; exegeses of texts in order to receive the absolute Truth from Morel's mouth (Morel's pen). Competent to begin! To begin what? As for my questions, who else would be competent to begin? But that was just it, they were Morel's questions, not mine; his. I didn't care about 'me' – I didn't like 'me'. I liked Morel, because it was easier; you got rid of yourself to become – by immolating yourself on the altar of – Morel. Like Kay. Kay doesn't love herself, so she loves me; I am the anti-Kay in whom Kay lovingly abolishes herself. And I, I'm nothing unless I abolish myself worshipping Morel. I'm a fake. I've often wanted to scream at Kay. 'You're in love with a fake', to tell her I don't exist, that I'm the empty vessel waiting for the Lord's wine. I loaded her up with all of Morel's books, and if she hadn't said she liked them, I think I would have dropped her. (And when she happens to disagree with Morel, he becomes exasperated and refuses to argue; he explains why Morel thinks as he does and is furious that this explanation is not enough.) She expects a personal contribution from me, but I have nothing to give her.

I want to see Morel and tell him, 'Don't waste your time, I'm worthless; it's all a cheat; just intellectual games, words.' And then he'd send me away. 'Unworthy son,' he would say, 'I condemn you to eat dry sand forever.' I'll say, 'Yes, yes', sobbing, and I'll feel the floor swaying, as it did when the school principal told me, 'Dirty Jew, we're doing you a favour keeping you on', and when the priest said, 'Can't your father go to mass?'

Let them condemn me. He had been asking for it a long time now. He who is damned is saved, for the damned are never alone. There is always a God pointing his finger at them, they are saved from themselves. Respectful, obedient, impotent, their entire infernal existence is a submission: there is God and the Law above them; they are relieved of themselves, in security.

The worst, and the best too, that could happen to him is that he might lose his respect for Morel; then there would be nothing left. If Morel could make a fool of himself, then he would have to find his own truth by himself. But Morel will pump me. He won't say: 'This is good and that's bad.' He'll want to know how I got there, and then I'll show him my nothingness: intellectual speculation, logical delirium, eclecticism; as he said of X, 'He takes a little here and a little there, but he lacks unity, a sense of synthesis.' I'm going to disappoint Morel terribly; he liked me because he thought I was trying to find ... But I haven't tried; this interminable labour was nothing but a sterile evasion.

He turns back, he rereads his words, he recognizes himself. Take any event, pursue your sense of it as far as you can go, and it will be like pulling one thread in a tangled skein – the entire skein comes with it. He was all there: his arrogant humility, his weakness for 'lucidity', his taste for self-destruction. And, as always, everything he said had a ring of truth in it: he was object-ively right, his philosophical intentions *were* an escape; but the discovery of this truth manifests a still deeper truth: the taste for self-destruction. So he can ask himself, 'Is it this depraved taste that allows me to see clearly, or does it falsify my sense of the event, or does the event, by a quasi-miraculous coincidence, justify this depraved taste?'

He is dealing with philosophy's most disturbing question; it will take him hundreds of pages to elucidate it, and this is now his aim, an aim he still doesn't dare claim as his present task, for he doesn't know how or even if he'll achieve it. All he knows is that the event seems to justify his taste, his profound choice, to such a degree that there is always reason to wonder, Is it the event which has provoked the choice, or the choice that has provoked the event? Given his condition, was another choice possible? And given his choice, another condition? What is the proportion of (historical, social, individual) fatality, and what is the proportion of freedom? An impossible question; neither can be fixed. They must be taken together, in their experienced unity. But where begin?

Not by trying to explain the event by psychoanalysis; not by trying to explain the person by the event. Fatal as it may be objectively, the event is always the image of the person to whom it happens as well; whatever happens to me, it is I who happen to myself. The proof: he always recognizes himself in what happens to him – not, of course, in the raw event, inconceivable in itself, but in the meaning which this event, immediately integrated into his situation, assumes for him, in the familiar, anticipated countenance it turns toward him, though in reality it has not been anticipated. This is the 'mystery of life'. It's not so mysterious after all; in every event he recognizes himself, recognizes his destiny (tells himself, 'I could have guessed that, it's no surprise, you've got what you deserve'), recognizes a will he has actually never produced, because, from the fact that this event happens to me, it becomes me, an occasion for me to perpetuate my being, to recover myself as I am, with a 'miraculous' air of the *déjà vu* about it, although it may be altogether unique. So with this business of Morel: Morel has still not said anything to me; I'm doing the talking. I'm the one who heaps abuse upon myself in advance (a preventive accusation – he anticipates abuse in order not to be crushed when and if Morel heaps abuse upon him; pride), because I cannot believe in what I have done; because he has always doubted his success, because it seemed impossible he should succeed in such an undertaking, because he has begun it with every expectation of failure – the big one, the final catastrophe, as when you work ten years on something, stake your life on it, aim at the highest, so when the failure does occur, everything will collapse, nothing will remain. Nothing save the impossibility, now complete, of being anything at all. That is what I call 'a successful failure': one that cures you of the little fiascos you incur all your life without wanting them, one that will at least be entirely attributable to me and will raise me above everything; it is the annulment of my life, my nonwork. My hell. It will cast him back into that nullity which is his condition in fact and which can only be transcended philosophically. Because I belong nowhere, to no group, no enterprise, because I am exiled from all groups and enterprises, there is only one alternative: either to be marginal in regard to society and history, the supernumerary of the human race, the pure consumer of air, water, bread and other people's work, reduced to the boredom of living, to the acute awareness of the contingency of everything around me, or to raise myself in conscience to the absolute – that is, to establish everything philosophically as a moment of the spiritual adventure and then, having gone so far, to recover, starting from this speculative interest, the taste for the concrete.

This is the first rational thing he has said in six pages; the rest is sterile lucidity. Which leads to another question. What he has called his desire for failure, his evasion, his logical delirium, boils down to this: Given my condition, I can achieve the concrete only by starting from the abstract, the real by starting from the Idea; given my condition, it is impossible for me to believe in anything I do, to believe in my own reality, in any form of success. Living in this condition of nullity, I cannot imagine emerging from it. And I shall not start emerging from it until I learn from other people – and for me 'other people' means Morel first of all – that I really have done something, that I'm not a blank in being, but an existing man. If I achieve this recognition of my reality, my history will begin; but I can no more imagine this history than the Chinese can imagine the accomplishment of their tenth five-year plan. I have not worked in order to fail; I have worked in order to emerge from failure without knowing how I would manage afterward, and therefore quite ready, in case of a new failure, to fall back into my situation of nullity which I have not yet really transcended.

Here the ground is firm, at last he has the sense of having put things properly. But even to get this far, he had to start from the sentiment of nullity, doubt, impotence, failure, the taste for self-destruction – from the personal choice, from his complexes. If he does not start by acknowledging how he feels, he will not discover the condition motivating his way of being; if he does not start by an interest in the world's affective colouring, he will not discover the 'destiny' he is living. The objective, materialist explanation cannot come first; how can he become conscious of his condition in fact, if not through the felt experience he necessarily has of it? How can he even conceive of changing his condition if he doesn't first bring it into perspective by reflection, doesn't first acknowledge the absolute subjective misery which this condition occasions?

No further. There is something ignobly satisfying in the explanation of himself by his condition (the vulgar Marxist explanation): Of course you're like that, because (because the world, society, your history are like that) you're a victim of circumstances. This is false and leads back to the same problem as before, the problem of the 'miraculous coincidence': It is not my condition of objective nullity that has determined my desire for subjective nullity, it is the inverse. There was an encounter, an encounter between his immemorial taste for annihilation (. . . as a child of four or five, he still knew nothing of his 'condition', he didn't know who his father was, that every group would reject him; at four or five he was already hiding under couches, tables, the piano, disappearing behind curtains or into closets; he would huddle into dark corners and make believe he was a tiny animal, fallen out of someone's hand or pocket, whom no one wanted, and then he would cry to himself quietly, comfortably, full of self-pity, and after he had mourned his exile he would harden himself by knocking his head against the wall until he saw stars, and then, to punish himself, to destroy himself further, he would do the things that were hardest of all: pull out his hair and eat it, lick the soles of his shoes after walking over dogs' shit, or not drink water for three days . . .) and an objective condition of nullity, an encounter between infantile complexes and adolescent and adult problems which the child could in no way anticipate. Everything happened as if the meek, ascetic little boy had unconsciously prepared himself for a destiny which would justify him.

And this was the retrospective illusion, the hoax *par excellence*, the 'miraculous coincidence' – miraculous, as a matter of fact, if he admits that his condition was imposed upon him ready-made, that he fell into it by accident as into a snare prepared only by God or by chance. But isn't it true that this condition is not attributable to him, that he fell into it? True, yes, that he one day discovered Father was a Jew. (One day – he was seven or eight – they were walking home from school past a fence where someone has pasted up a lot of fly bills with human heads, faces with big, fleshy, arched noses, drooling mouths, and *paiessl*

curling down the cheeks, and Felix said, 'That's your father.'
'My father doesn't look like that', he said. Felix laughed and
said, 'Oh yes he does, because he's a Jew!' And Borck burst out
laughing and said that *his* father was a baron. He inquired at
home and his mother told him that his grandfather on *her* side
was a count and that a count was more than a baron because his
crown had seven prongs and the baron had only five. But Borck
said that didn't matter, it was your father who mattered, and a
Jew couldn't be a noble. 'My father was a captain during the
war. What was yours? Jews are never officers. They don't know
how to fight.' And although his mother showed him a photograph
of his father in uniform with a long sabre, she had to admit his
father hadn't been an officer and hadn't been in the fighting
either. He had been a clerk and his sabre was a general-staff
clerk's sabre.) True too that his mother took him to Switzerland
on the eve of the war; true that, half-Jew in anti-Semitic Austria,
then Austrian half-Jew in the Pan-German Reich, then Austrian
half-Jew with a German passport in a Switzerland favouring the
Reich, he was neither Jew nor Aryan, nor Austrian, nor German,
nor Swiss – nothing, in short, except the nothing that he was. But
true too that before knowing that he was this nothing, he already
regarded himself as nothing, was nothing for himself. At five, his
four-year-old little neighbour gave him a smack and he ran away
in a state of shock. 'I won't play with him any more', he told his
mother. 'He hit me.' 'And you didn't hit back, silly?' his mother
said. At six, Strauss, a Jewish boy, caught up with him on the
way home from school and tripped him up on the freshly tarred
street, and he was afraid of Strauss, he did not fight back but kept
out of his way for the next few days, but Strauss caught him
again and rolled him in the tar. And his mother complained to
the teacher and asked him to walk her son home. Protected by
the teacher at the age of six, when he still didn't know anything.

His conclusion, then: He himself was responsible for the
'miraculous coincidence' of his infantile complexes and his
objective condition of nullity. This condition of nullity, although
objective, was his own work. And because it was his own work it
fitted him like a glove. Not that he had invented this condition

altogether, of course; but he recognized himself in it, established himself in it, subjectively an accomplice because subjectively prepared for it. Others, in his place, would have considered such a condition temporary, provisional. Not he; to him it seemed immutable, he abandoned the idea of being at home somewhere, disavowed his family, his Church, the Reich, Austria, the Jews, his mother tongue, everything, and decided that he would be the one thing which he was least of all – he would be French. To read, write, think in French (to think in French in a German school, in 1940, after the fall of France, was a splendid self-destructive *ascesis*, a transparent choice of nullity) and to despise everything around him that wasn't French. An objective condition of nullity, yes, but maintained, willed, rendered still more null by virtue of a choice anterior to it, a choice that had not been occasioned by that condition.

I said he must start with this choice! A Hegelian–Marxist notion that the human condition is man's own work; not because he has created it *ex nihilo*, but because it is his only insofar as he has already assumed it, chosen to live it, recognized himself in the meaning he gives it. For man adapts himself to his condition only insofar as the fact of living it has founded a choice which gives it value, a choice occasioned or awakened by 'complexes' which cause him to feel comfortable in that condition, resigned to it, or proud of it. Had I not given a value to that condition, I would already be trying, here and now, to transform it, no longer its accomplice, no longer able to explain myself by it.

To start from the personal choice, what would be the use of wanting to change your condition if you didn't know what had made you choose it in the first place, establish yourself within it, if you didn't revoke this choice, a revocation which is your only reassurance that you're not going to reproduce the same condition all over again? To start from the personal choice – that is, to understand how you have arrived at your condition, how you have chosen yourself starting from there, how you have let yourself be infected by it, half victim, half accomplice, how it has been possible that you have agreed to live it.

His head has emptied itself out. He feels he is at the foot of a huge, slippery mountain. He has to climb it from all sides at once. He doesn't know where to begin. To understand yourself as the choice of your condition – of course, but since this choice itself is conditioned . . . He wants to know how it has been possible for him to adapt himself to his own condition. He says two apparently contradictory things (he adds 'apparently' for caution's sake, hoping that the contradiction will prove to be dialectical, but actually he doesn't see how he will escape it). He has accepted or, better still, he has created his objective condition of nullity by virtue of a choice of nullity that reaches far back into his childhood; that is the subjective explanation. He juxtaposes to it an objective explanation: his infantile choice of nullity was encouraged to develop because he was placed in an objective condition in which he recognized himself, an accomplice. Very pretty; the difficulty has been forced to retreat, and the indigestible residue is the question, What has occasioned this infantile choice? Or, since it is this choice which explains his complacency toward his empirical condition, the way he has adapted himself to it, must he then yield himself up to a complete psychoanalysis, delving back into the infantile clamminess in order to revoke his original choice and thus be enabled to transform his condition? Does not this priority he has accorded to the psychoanalytic viewpoint condemn him to perform first and foremost a subjective conversion, a catharsis? And how would he have the means to perform this conversion, since the condition he has made for himself, which is his choice sedimented in being, conditions him in return, consigns him to the nullity which he claims he wants to transcend?

He is not yet through with the theory; he must clarify matters. He sums up: (1) There is no concrete hope of transforming his condition if he does not at the same time revoke his choice of this condition. (2) His choice of this condition is conditioned by it, therefore there is no concrete hope of modifying it if he does not modify his condition at the same time. (3) His choice of this empirical condition is conditioned not only by the condition but by one anterior to it, the infantile condition. Three possible conclusions:

(a) This is a vicious circle, since the subjective conversion supposes the transformation of the objective condition, and since inversely the transformation of the objective condition supposes the subjective conversion if it is to be effective. (b) The subjective conversion must (see 3) start with a psychoanalysis of the infantile choice, the infantile condition being the original basis of the total choice; but how can this psychoanalysis be effective, since there can be no question of transforming the infantile condition, moreover buried in oblivion? (c) (Here he has got hold of something, he begins to see a way, and it is only out of complacency that he continues accumulating difficulties.) The subjective conversion and the transformation of the objective condition must go hand in hand, react dialectically against each other, the former causing his factual condition to appear in a new light, showing new ways out by an initial transforming action, consolidating the conversion and furnishing it, for at this point it is merely an abstract self-doubting, virtually disincarnated intention, with a content, a body it cannot derive from itself, the beginnings of a new condition, conditioning new possibilities.

A momentary temptation: to say that psychoanalysis of the infantile choice is therefore superfluous, that the way out (the way to salvation) is in action, that action, once initiated, will develop dialectically and, upon contact with concrete reality, will cause the unanticipated means of conversion, the new man, to appear. This is false. For how initiate the subjective conversion which will cause the objective condition to appear in a new light? By what means? How transform the instruments employed by the total choice to develop itself, on which it leans as on a total attitude, consolidated by habit, if you do not know them? And how know them if not by a scrupulous investigation of my history (and of history itself, from a Hegelian–Marxist viewpoint; for we cannot conceive our world, our condition, explicitly, since our concepts are a part of the world which we comprise and have no point of view upon the worldly and intellectual means they are putting to work; the only point of view we can acquire upon these means is historical – the study of their genesis, of their objective meaning, both imperceptible to the subject who 'lives' the sociocultural heritage as closely as he lives his own body), which will reveal the themes, obsessions, dominant motifs of my life, the progressive elaboration, in contact with people and changing realities, of that arsenal of habits in which each being-for-itself is enclosed, just as a pudding conforms to a mould it has already left.

Again, he wonders if he has not produced contradictory declarations, and at the very moment he picks up his pen to write that he is wondering this (the first time he has permitted himself this luxury of writing down the questions, instead of writing only the result of his cogitations about them), he sees the issue appear again before him: the savoury nebula in which thought dawns, fast taking form; this is a moment he likes to prolong, feeling, tonight, that his thoughts will be scarce (not so much scarce, perhaps, for a crowd of ill-assorted ideas rushes forward, but difficult to bring to birth). So on the one hand he declares he must start from the 'personal choice', meaning by this the subjective – he must become aware of the original intention that goes hand in hand with the situation-in-fact it has elaborated, in order to modify it. On the other hand, he has just realized that this modification of the fundamental intention (the subjective conversion) has no means of functioning if it is not based on his becoming objectively aware of the instruments of which his original intention constitutes the existence, and which are its flesh. Why not say right away that the subjective conversion must begin by an objective investigation? What does this mean?

It means so many things that he must be careful not to let the idea vanish before he has managed to put it into words. First of all it means that the first intention of subjective conversion is a formal and empty intention (a pious hope, an abstract wish for 'something to change', unaware of its content and its real possibilities), for not only does this first intention not have the means to come into being, it is even unaware what content it must apply its means to once they are created. In other words, the subjective conversion from which he says he must start is at first nothing but the abstract *intention* of subjective conversion, a resolution to become aware of his original choice through the instruments of unveiling (skills, habits, obsessions, 'natural' behaviour) in which that choice is incarnated. And to become conscious of these instruments, he must be able to stop using them, stop living them so closely that he has no point of view upon them. To know them instead of clinging to them, of existing them, he must use different instruments of unveiling: a method affectively neutral, 'scientific, objective', as Marx and Freud both put it. A fruitful notion of incarnation, which will perhaps allow him to thread his way between Marxism and psychoanalysis. ('You cannot juxtapose these two techniques,' Morel said, 'You must adopt a perspective which will create their unity.' And Morel said that such unity was 'the person', was lived before being thought. But how establish this unity in thought without exploding?) The personal choice is not a 'subjective' intention deliberately creating the means of its own realization; it is an incarnated intention, enclosed within the mould of his body. In one sense, the personal choice is 'interiority' though it will not grasp itself as such save by a turning back upon itself, when in hesitation and anxiety it discovers its own nothingness; in another sense, it is deployed altogether externally, existing in things as their signification for me, their quality, their potentialities. The personal choice is inscribed in being like a certain face, a certain truth, a version of the world indistinguishable from its reality. Forever developing yet endowed with the permanence of things, this world tends to persevere in its being, thereby lending a solid consistency, a quasi inertia to the choice sedimented within it.

His idea, then, is that there is an objective bent to the personal choice; that the situation of a person and his choice are one and the same, for his situation is the incarnation of his choice, the sum of the instruments he is in order to produce and develop himself. The meaning of the choice is there, outside, existing in things (but also inside – in my body's taste, my past, my being-for-others). His idea, now, is that all things (the world) are operated and that insofar as all things are the objective unity and dialectic of operating choice, they are not only meaningful and human, but also the sedimentations of choices operated by others, sedimentations which require our comprehension (and not our scientific knowledge) and request us to reproduce in ourselves the choices which have produced them.

He reminds himself that this is all somewhere between Hegel, Marx and Merleau-Ponty, and that he is still nowhere near out of it; he is afraid of once more losing himself in abstract speculations which, so far as he is concerned, lead to nothing, to everything save himself. But that remains to be seen. He is also astonished by that intellectual toy, Marx's concept of 'work' – essence of the apparent world – though where Marx says 'production' or operation, he would say 'choice producing and incarnating itself'. And he glimpses a vague possibility of making this concept into a bridge to phenomenology by arranging matters as follows: starting from the world as it presents itself to us and, by entirely re-creating it in the imagination, seeing how it has been possible – that is, what is its human signification, what is the project, the operative choice that has 'operated' and produced this world. And this is precisely Marx's procedure too: not relying on 'appearances' but, starting from the labour-value, finding the 'essence' beneath appearances, that is, the project which has produced – and has alienated itself in – capital. The idea, then, that the world has a meaning, is a knot of tangled significations; that, upon appearing in this world, the individual is at once enlisted in an anonymous project which is inherent in the facts and whose instruments are immediately furnished to it, to the exclusion of other immediate instruments. Enlisted: provoked to play a role, to choose between the roles the institutional world offers him from the outset and on the basis of which – transcending or repeating them – he will make himself into a person.

Good; still to be discovered is the point of view from which he can interpret the anonymous project which a given interworld proposes to the individual – a world which is an 'order' already here and addressing itself to him, but which in truth is merely produced and reproduced over and over again by the operative choices which determine themselves for and start from it. Here the methods begin to diverge radically.

Then is the anonymous project (which every individual willy-nilly assumes by becoming its conscious defender, its involuntary accomplice, its victim or its critic) a project of this human order? Precisely not; that order is the alienation of the very work which produces it. No one recognizes himself in such an order. If we have produced it, we have not desired it but somehow produced it into the bargain, as the unforeseen result of an intention aiming at something else (much less than an order: a little comfort, security, pleasure, privacy). But from the fact that this order has been produced it has repercussions upon the anonymous social and cultural project of the group, making of this project – insofar as the group is not willing to surrender its purpose and its avowed ideology – 'its solemn complement, its general rationale of consolation and justification, its idealist point of honour', and actually obliging that project to complicate itself, to produce the intentions of actions other than the actions initially intended. Actions not produced by express intention arouse intentions after the fact, the objective has repercussions upon the subjective, the men who have produced an involuntary order are led to will that order. It is a fruitful idea of Marx's, then, that the reality of this order is the work which produces it despite itself and alienating itself in that order; further, that this order is imputable to the dominant class, that the latter therefore has to answer for it, but that this class itself is transcended and alienated by the consequences of its avowed intentions, produced by its product. The essential question remains: What is the anonymous project of an institutional order really the project of? What is its meaning?

### To begin with, Marx

For Marx, there is the project's factual meaning, which in the present situation (the bourgeois world) is an absurdity for the bourgeois who conceal it from themselves; they are doing something other than what they think they are doing and, in so doing, are digging their own graves. But there is also the project's potential meaning, which for Marx, a moralist and a Hegelian, is that

man's fundamental project must be the project of man, a project
to create man, so that the producer of the world can recognize
himself in his product (Marx even dreamed that man can
coincide with his product, but here he was mistaken). This
potential meaning of the project is unfortunately only the ideal
and unrealized meaning of the project, which latter alienates
itself, and it is this alienation that man must become conscious of
in order to work at transcending it by changing the world.

Thus Marx assumes an idealist point of view with regard to
reality – he judges and interprets it with an initial requirement
that alienation be suppressed and that man's relation to man be
an unmediated human relation, the production of a human
world, a human man. For Marx, man is what he makes, and it is
essential that he make what he is – that is, that he make man,
that he be able to recognize himself in what he makes. The
categorical imperative of Marxist morality is: Make what you are
– in order to be what you make. And what man is, for Marx, is
freedom at work. His projected disalienation is the possibility
required for freedom to will itself through what it does, instead of
doing things in which it is engulfed. The fundamental requirement of Marxist morality is that the human reality be totally
penetrated with freedom to the point of being total freedom, that
it may realize itself and become its own goal on every level at
once; the total man is the happy synthesis in action of the biological and the human, of the individual and the social, at the
heart of the personal unity, the person created within the social
project and the social project created within the person. The
person totally realizes himself and accedes to the universal means
and reality of the recognition of all by each and of each by all.
Perfect; as a matter of fact this is the requirement of moral freedom: a world which would be the means and the occasion of
total accomplishment as an individual person and as a citizen,
and vice versa. Is this possible? It doesn't matter; here is an
absolute goal, the requirement of man-as-value. Starting here, it
is possible to expose every alienation responsible for the fact that
today as yesterday we are not what we produce and do not
produce 'ourselves', but only things which enslave us. The

fundamental reason for our alienation is the present social and economic order, for in this world of ours, enmeshed in its praxis, we cannot, even with the best will in the world, desire in the name of freedom what we actually do, whatever our intention, simply because we have assumed, by merely choosing to live, the present social condition, the incarnation of a praxis in regard to which abstention is not possible. Man is impossible in this world of ours, therefore it is this world which must be changed; imperatively; it is the final and determinant reason for man's impossibility. Whatever my subjective conversions and psychotherapies may be, they will never be a solution, for the cause of all misfortunes is my real condition, and what I can best achieve is the consciousness of its contradictions and the resolution to change it.

He is quite content with these conclusions and quite in agreement with them; he wonders what he can add, now that he discovers himself a Marxist. Never, he feels, has he thought more lucidly, or been in possession of stronger evidence, and were he not condemned to write in order to feel he existed, he would announce that there was nothing more to say and would continue his meditations as a member of the Communist Party.

Now he tells himself, 'Luckily I mentioned the CP.' Because the CP has always been a strong temptation, an impossible temptation which has nothing (or not much) to do with the reasons he has just revealed for the first time. The CP will always (?) be forbidden him because he is (1) a bourgeois, (2) a filthy intellectual, (3) a man belonging nowhere and objectively null who will never be 'involved', from the others' point of view, (4) an opponent systematically dedicated to endless contestation by his very condition, which excludes him from subjective as well as objective integration, (5) an outsider, a foreigner who would be thrown out for meddling in politics. And what attracts him to the CP (in South America, in India, in Spain) is precisely the temptation of the impossible; condemned to do nothing at all, he is fatally obsessed by the total incarnation, the complete return to the positive, as by a forbidden thing – just as the husband is obsessed by the image of adultery, the lover by the idea of killing the object of his love, the miser by that of destroying his wealth, the soldier by that of desertion, the criminal by that of becoming a stool pigeon, the policeman by the image of crime, the respectable citizen by the notion of sexual crime, the believer by mortal sin or atheism, etc. – an acceptance or betrayal which not only his condition but the way in which he values it forbids him.

He has said a number of things at once here, and he must recapitulate in order to straighten it all out, still content, for the moment, with this method of investigation which consists of letting himself go as far as his own momentum will take him in order to examine afterward, objectively, what this controlled abandon has brought to light. Hence:

1. The CP is a temptation, but a temptation for bad reasons; it is likely that a Marxist analysis will prove inadequate to disalienate an individual and permit him to recover his unity. For if you change the world for bad reasons that have more to do with psychoanalysis and moreover are unrealizable, you risk having your new world turn out badly too – a world in which you will not find yourself again.

2. The CP is a temptation because it is forbidden him by an objective exclusion, but also, he has just admitted, by a subjective one, which relates to the value he attaches to the former; he has made a vocation out of his condition and would feel he was perpetrating a betrayal by abandoning his vocation as an agent of contestation – and he is also incapable of doing so, knowing that he will not be able to integrate himself, that he will never even be a *condottiere* of the revolution (supposing that there were one) but, by temperament, a meticulous bureaucratic technician at best. Question: Is the temptation of the CP motivated by objective exclusion (temptation of the impossible) or subjective (temptation of betrayal)? By the latter, obviously. For the innocent man who is found guilty and condemned, escape is not a temptation but a task; if prohibition is imposed from the exterior, it is an obstacle. It is a temptation only if it is interiorized – the temptation to abolish a determination one has freely accepted (to be a husband, a lover, a believer, etc.), to betray. The temptation of the negative freedom which you are while at the same time you

suppress it, the temptation of being the nonbeing of your being, the temptation of nothingness, of nullity. He returns to this.

But first it is 1 which must be developed. If the CP can be a temptation for bad reasons (mine: which are to abdicate oneself by integrating oneself; to betray oneself while at the same time betraying one's class; to return to the positive while at the same time being the negation of what for him is positive and thereby detested – the 'Western world' which protects, nourishes, excludes, and has raised him; to be, as both negation and betrayal, guaranteed by the divinity of an orthodox order which believes itself infallible, an orthodoxy which, even while he serves it, he will immediately contest), then Marxist action, the social action, the project to change the world are not sufficient to disalienate and to recreate the unity of the person, at least not in this world of ours. But what do we know about another world, how even imagine it without having answered this question: Could the human reality ever become social and public to the point where the citizen's labour will resolve all the problems of the person and lead to his or her self-fulfilment?

For us, in any case, and for the generation following ours, this is not to be contemplated. Hence the legitimacy of this declaration: Social and political action is not the solution of all our problems, and though such action is absolutely necessary for that solution in the last analysis, it is also necessary for us to free ourselves from our subjective alienations (is this the right word?), which may warp our sense of the facts and our action. Hence psychoanalysis retains its privileges for us – and in saying 'for us' he is perhaps exaggeratedly timid, but he is not quite sure about his stand, and he is also afraid of disapproval from the Marxists, at least immediately.

## Psychoanalysis

Having discussed Marx and the meaning he attached to the human project, now he will try to determine what psychoanalysis offers. For psychoanalysis – and this is what Marxists reproach it

for – a person's subjective misery is not a result of his being alienated in fact by the social and economic world, or of the impossibility of his developing that world's praxis without alienating
himself still more, without entering into conflict with others and
himself, but it derives, above all and in particular, from an infantile 'complex' or – as he puts it – from an unhappy choice turned
against itself. He dismisses the Freudian interpretations, their
way of basing man on the libido regarded as irreducible; besides,
he does not know these interpretations in detail and does not
want to risk discussing them. What interests him is that there is a
frequently valid way of understanding a man starting from his
childhood, from his early history, from his family situation, from
the way in which, beginning with this situation, he has assumed
his body, his natural life, his being-for-others. The Marxists, of
course, can reply that the family is a bourgeois alienation and
that the complexes it gives rise to will disappear with it. He does
not argue this point. But it is not at all certain that other
complexes will not take their place, and after all, in his own case,
he has had a family, and it would be of no use, it would even be a
kind of speculative idealism, to claim he could resolve his
infantile and family conflicts by explaining them away as
bourgeois alienations resolved in spirit if not in fact by the post-
revolutionary disappearance (after how many generations?) of the
family.

    In short, complexes surviving from childhood are neither
explicable nor soluble by Marxist analysis as alienations like any
others, because the original choice functions at a moment and at
a period where there is still neither history nor conscious practice
nor possibility of reflective consciousness. And to take his case,
Marxism would not help him understand his prepersonal choice
of nullity and the way in which this choice was confirmed during
the course of his subsequent history, on the occasion of the
discovery of his mixed parentage and his exclusion. The Marxist
explanation always supposes that the world is the product of
man. It implies a moral criticism applied from the point of view
of an 'ethic of doing'; it starts from the highest requirement (that
man be his own product and that he recognize himself in his

product) and evaluates the ongoing praxis in relation to that requirement; it *exposes* the objective alienations and starting from them explains the ideological alienations as superstructures, substitutes for action, metaphysics of consolation, hoaxes – Freedom that cannot recognize itself in its product and cannot know itself as free and productive is necessarily hoaxed and has not the means to expose the hoax; it is alien to itself, in fact. According to Marx our task is not so much to understand the mystifications as to expose them as the pseudo-truths of a world concealing its actual truth (work). In other words, Marx addresses himself to the producers, the workers, the men of praxis who make the world and who must be made aware of what they are doing; he legitimately ignores – and cannot be understood by – the middlemen, consumers, capitalists, etc., who as men make nothing (save money) and for whom an ethic of making remains incomprehensible.

Now the man of praxis is necessarily an adult (he becomes adult as soon as he acts upon and is conscious of making the world). But before becoming an adult, he has been a nonacting child, and it is as a child that he assumed certain habits, that his affectivity was formed, his feeling for life, things, other people, his 'character' – that is, his original choice, which has therefore, necessarily, been first of all a choice *to be*, pertaining to psychoanalysis and radically incomprehensible from the point of view of an ethic of doing. In the earnestness of childhood, we have learned to consider the world not as the product of freedom at work, but as a theocratic order of which grown-ups were the gods. For the child, it was entirely a question of conforming to the laws, the norms and the uncomprehended, alien, absolute orders governing his existence from without; and though from the point of view of an ethic of doing there are only problems of praxis (that is, problems to be resolved by action), from the child's point of view there are only 'ontological' problems – for the child, it is a question of knowing what he is and what he ought to be. He receives *en bloc*, as a given value, the entire objective spirit of the society and is assigned the task of adapting himself to it (by apprenticeship, by training) even before he can have understood it, before he can establish himself within its reality as praxis. It is therefore legitimate to conclude that at this stage the child derives from the inculcated sociocultural heritage the only project he can be, a vital, subsequently religious project aiming at vital, subsequently mystical satisfactions, and that the social and cultural behaviour to which he is compelled has a strong tinge of affectivity and religiosity – that is, is understood solely in the light of his infantile experiences and desires, starting from his affective and material dependence on his parents, from his desire for metaphysical security, from his craving for approval and comfort. Things, people, actions are charged for him with entirely irrational affective values in relation to his situation of dependence and passivity. And these magico-religious values, if they can be liquidated, can also be developed even during adult life – are all the more likely to be so if the occasion of a rupture has not been furnished by autonomous work becoming conscious of itself as such through its product. Women, idlers, middlemen, bourgeois, members of the liberal professions, etc., will probably carry into their adult life the complexes and religious values of childhood for lack of occasions to liquidate them by the discovery that they make the world and that the world is the work of human beings. And this is particularly true of those societies which by their economic structure and their degree of technological evolution offer the human reality scarcely any opportunity to become conscious of itself as producing the social order and the world; in these societies, man therefore tends spontaneously to accord an ontological, religious, mystical value to the social order. The parallelism which Freud observed and mistakenly tried to base on genetic postulates is in reality based on analogous situations; the modern child, like the pre-historic adult, is dealing with a world and an objective spirit that are alien to him and which he values religiously for lack of consciousness of himself as its producer (having no effective technological and intellectual hold on it).

Notice that the preceding discussion has been conducted from a Marxist viewpoint. Psychoanalysis is therefore accessible to Marxist critique insofar as it is, in its classic forms, an accomplice of objective alienations; it interprets the human reality starting from an initial project *to be*, without explicitly providing it (save occasionally by manifesting its contradictions) the means of correcting and modifying this project, without demonstrating that the ultimate reason for subjective alienation is the objective alienation of freedom in a human world which, being estranged from freedom, must be changed. As a method of investigating the hoaxed consciousness, alienated in its freedom, psychoanalysis must confine itself to that mystified consciousness, cannot account for the man of praxis. Therefore there can be a Marxist analysis of psychoanalysis, bringing to bear a true and moral historical point of view, but there cannot be a psychoanalysis of Marxism, although there can be a psychoanalysis of Marx and of Marxists insofar as their Marxism still carries religious values, has not yet completely liquidated the choice *to be* and is still tainted with naturalism, fanaticism, religiosity, etc. And Marxism is likely to remain impure as long as Marxist action and thought remain alienated – today and for a long time to come, as long as Marxism's ethical requirement remains idealist, as long as the Marxist himself, in this period of political struggle and the construction of socialism's foundations, is unable to recognize himself in his action, to resolve by action all his problems and all his contradictions. When he can authentically *be* what he will *do* (supposing that he ever can), then psychoanalysis will no longer concern him. It will not, however, be pointless generally; that could happen only if men were to be born adult, already engaged in the social order, already masters of its praxis and its techniques. Now, in even a post-revolutionary society, men will still be born as children, will still relate to the world by an original choice *to be*, and must liquidate this choice in order to realize themselves authentically. Psychoanalysis can and must furnish men the method for this liquidation. It will therefore retain its privileges.

Evidence: There is no effective psychoanalysis, no possible moral conversion not accompanied by a Marxist criticism, not oriented by the Marxist ethical requirement that man be what he makes, and that he make man. This fundamental requirement, common to existential psychoanalysis and to Marxism, must establish the effort of comprehension and the existential conversion of the individual. The purpose of psychoanalysis must be to remove the psychological obstacles, to liquidate the choice-complexes of being which prevent both the consciousness of objective alienation (of which they are the accomplices) and the total realization of man in total action. Psychoanalysis, in other words, must lead to the comprehension of the necessity for freedom to change the world, to change its condition, to modify its situation, as it must also lead to the activation (or actualization – that is, to the recovery in the perspective of action) of every region of existence and dimension of the individual as so many possibilities to make oneself free, to produce a human world.

Now he feels he has nothing more to say; he believes he has gone as far as he can on the theoretical level, and that if he is to advance further he must refer again to experience, to himself: examine the interference of praxis with the ontological in his case; examine that share of failure which, for him as for any individual, the impossibility of total activity represents, the impossibility of the moralization of all dimensions of existence at once within a single synthesizing action. The share of failure – that is, the share of solitude, of lived contradiction which cannot transcend itself in action and constitutes the 'separating subjectivity'.

Before dealing with himself, he takes a brief respite. The satisfied sense of having covered a good deal of ground – this is the advantage of the method he has adopted, which renounces systematic exposition, advances hesitantly and elaborates his thought, modulating it and moving it forward, pencil in hand (instead of claiming to set down thoughts already worked out but which, because they are always insufficiently elaborated, are only incomplete thoughts, truncated, systematized before they have reached their conclusion, battering down open doors and passing by those that are still closed). He wants to run to Morel now and tell him, 'Don't judge me on the basis of that, I'm aware now of the inadequacies, the superficiality of what I gave you; I've made progress in three weeks, I think I'm on the right track now.' He had flung himself into his new work (an autobiography?) without knowing where he was going, after four days of despair; he had been caught up in it and now, suddenly, he feels involved, feels he is doing something new which he cannot let go of without feeling beaten. And he becomes conscious of this: he is in the process of pleading an appeal. This self-analysis – which initially aimed only at freeing himself from his anguish, at filling up an intolerably empty evening, at lessening the blow by anticipating how severe it was going to be – this self-analysis already amounted to more than fifteen hundred pages, written and rewritten over eight years. It has progressively become the proof – which he takes a dose of every day – that all is not lost; then his pledge of allegiance to his 'vocation' as a writer; then the perspective which he assumed in regard to an anterior product and which, by running now to Morel, he would already claim to have grown out of. His betrayal complex, discovered in a new form: his horror of letting himself be identified with his acts or works, his need (not the Gidean strategy of taking the opposite point of view) to escape the image of himself his acts establish, by declaring himself beyond them, insisting upon himself as their transcendence. But is it not characteristic of the writer's project, of any project that claims to create, that it cannot install itself within its creation once it has become part of the outside world, for it can exist only in action – and suffers this continual craving to express in written words a fundamental silence, an original solitude from which the writer escapes only by the action of writing (a bridge he passes over only once, for it collapses behind him as he advances over the section he constructs ahead) and which he always finds forever intact? The writer who has written a book is a dead writer whose book is of no help to him and who can only begin again, with the feeling (*his* feeling, now) that everything is still to be said, that the problems to be resolved have grown merely more complicated, enriched by new aspects.

He might continue in this direction, declare (or repeat?) that writing is the only way he can make himself a man (because there is no other action in which he can recognize himself and make himself recognized, because writing is the only way to recover the irrecoverable, to reverse the signs of solitude, silence, nonbeing – the failure every action represents for him); but this is not what he meant. Rather this: that writing is for him a purifying *ascesis*, a way of abstracting himself from the real, of becoming pure mind, of appropriating a world which is alien to him and in which he plays no part, by denying it, by rendering it useless, arrogantly putting himself at its origin by the very act of explaining it, of dissolving it into ideas and words. Writing is a kind of Black Mass he celebrates every evening (before, when he did nothing else, he preferred writing late at night, between midnight and three in the morning) when, alone in a room he thinks of as a hole in the world, a room silhouetted against universal darkness by the single pool of light from his lamp that reveals a white page, he annihilates the world and himself merely by the corrosive work of his mind, constructs out of ink a universe which is drawn from – outlined against – the real and which, in a bundle of pages greedily accumulated and counted, is the only one which belongs to him: the Non-Universe, the annihiliated universe.

There is this greedy labour of abstraction, and there is the image of the hole (he has discovered that one of his affective themes is the image of the animal huddling in its lair, the oyster in its shell), as well as the theme of destruction (for a long time he used to put himself to sleep by imagining that he was firing a cannon out of his window, or even through the walls; or else that he was besieged and using a battery of machine guns to down people in the streets; or again that he was in a car or even a tank and running down great crowds of people) and his unconfessed claim to create absolutes which he noticed the other evening when he was so annoyed that Jacques wanted to discuss a passage he himself had insisted Jacques read. Too impatient to listen to Jacques's remarks (impatient, in general, when other people talk; that's why he never listens to what is said around him, preferring to read or to become absorbed in himself; impatient again when Kay tells him something, only half listening to her, actually outraged that she should dare burst into his silent

mental Non-Universe and trouble its geometry by her real
problems 'of no importance' for him, everything that comes from
outside himself and bears the mark of the accidental is of no
importance; and when he simply cannot avoid it, when he feels
caught in reality, feels real himself – when someone shouts at
him, for instance, or gives him orders he cannot avoid by merely
going away – that is a catastrophe for him, a shake-up of his
whole being, creating a longing to escape, even by death, to find
as soon as possible that peace he is granted by the neutrality of a
world whose asperities familiarity attenuates; and he hates
having his habits questioned, his routines disturbed), he waited
until Jacques finally stopped talking, waited for him to admire
his own product instead of being forced to come back down to
earth.

Here he has stumbled on a veritable gold mine: It is not the
theme of *ascesis*, of destruction or of mental abstraction which
proves so rich, but the theme of impatience, of the *behaviour* of
abstraction which he has hitherto not noticed and which is his
way of *making himself* abstract, absent. As if he had touched a
nerve centre, a swarm of instances of such behaviour now come to
mind, all motivated by his project of abstraction, of retreating
into himself, so that he begins wondering if he is not dealing with
what is really fundamental in his behaviour, and with what
explains (that is, makes intelligible as aspects of the same project)
the following kinds of behaviour:

*His avarice*, his way of preferring *specie* to the things he likes,
choosing the abstract, universal equivalent of every possible
possession and enjoyment; renouncing the enjoyment of life in
favour of an abstract and disincarnated possibility, objectivized in
money, of living and enjoying himself. By economizing on his
pleasures and what others regard as need (to eat well, to live in
comfortable rooms, to be decently dressed) he economizes his
life, 'sets it aside' as an abstract possibility quantified in money.
And not only that; he has a tendency to hoard foodstuffs – he
once dreamed of having enough to live on for a year – and to
ration himself stringently when surrounded by mountains of

supplies. Even as a child he was like that; when he was five his mother, before going out one morning, set in front of him a dish of cherries swimming in pink juice, and since there weren't many, even before he started eating, he began to regret the inevitable moment when there wouldn't be one left. So he ate very slowly, licking his spoon, and since his mother was in a hurry she asked, 'Don't you like it?' And he answered, 'Yes. I want to enjoy it.' She thought that was very funny and told the story to everyone. Then when he was seven his grandmother gave him a big box of chocolate liqueurs for Christmas. And since he liked them, he locked the box in his drawer of the chest. He counted how many chocolates there were in the three-tiered box and decided that by eating only two a day, at four in the afternoon, he could make them last eighteen days. Eighteen days: an eternity. And every day he counted the number of days he had left for eating his two chocolates. And then, one day, he discovered that the second layer of his box was almost empty and the third already broached. He wanted to cry; they had robbed him – his sister and the maid – they had taken off the top drawer of the chest to get into his, and had stuffed themselves on the chocolates. They had made fun of him, and he wondered how they could enjoy what they were eating at the very moment they ate it, and why everything was spoiled for him by the mere fact that it was transitory. Everything, really, was spoiled by this anticipated regret. At five, he was already regretting the fact that his grandmother and his mother must die, and he would pray, 'Dear God, let my mother and grandmother be immortal – and my sister and my father too', he would add conscientiously. And since he doubted that God would be willing to work this miracle, he prayed, 'Dear God, let me die before my mother.' That everyone around him was mortal obsessed him for a long time. Then he began to collect things, everything – his sister's old blotters, pieces of paper, pencil stubs, chalk, used erasers – refused to discard anything, hoping to preserve the period of time incarnated in this eraser, this pencil stub. Then at ten, when his father began giving them pocket money (a schilling each week), he put his own schilling in his bank and allowed himself only one

ten-groschen ice a week, and a ten-groschen sandwich in winter
(with some Liptauer and a caper) while his sister spent her schilling on ices in two days and came whimpering to her father for
another. At the year's end he had a little fortune in his bank, so
he bought Christmas presents for his mother, his heart heavy at
having to spend his fortune. Then he ruined his vacation count-
ing every day how many days he had left and telling himself,
'Enjoy the day that's passing, you blockhead', but he couldn't
enjoy it, already he looked regretfully at this landscape, this
house, these stairs that he would have to leave. And for some
time now he was tempted – but he resisted the temptation – to
count the years he had left to live, the years that still remained
before he became impotent, senile, and if it had been possible he
might have economized on his expenditure of energy in order to
live longer. He dreamed of being a *rentier* with a capital always
preserved intact; he would live, meagrely enough, on the
dividends alone. He had a horror of waste, of material generosity; when Kay used more gas then she needed to warm up the
bottom of a pot, when she boiled more than enough water for
their tea, he flew into a rage; when he was alone, he would
measure three cups into the pot, just what he used; when Kay
wanted to throw away stale bread, he would immediately gulp it
down with hard cheese, so that nothing would be wasted.

*His manias.* But already, probably because of his fundamental
tendency toward escape, toward abstract and quintessentialized
self-possession, this inventory begins to bore him. What importance, what interest can his real person have? Can he still
progress, when the investigation suddenly loses all attraction for
him? He hopes so, returns to his manias; wonders for a moment
what the imperious evidence was which several days ago made
him think his manias were so indicative; catches himself scratch-
ing at the skin around his nails. That's one. Others: although he
lives in disorder, his possessions have a secret arrangement for
him, an order, a 'me-ness' as Morel called it, by which he insists
on being surrounded. He wants to be able to move, to orient
himself easily in the world by virtue of calm and collected habits:
invariable routines and schedules whose disturbance he reacts to

with recriminatory bad humour; invariable topographical dispo-
sition of his universe, 'everything in its place', and when it's elsewhere, as is often the case with his pen, he accuses Kay – 'Where
have you put my pen?' or, in a whimpering, panic-stricken tone,
heavy with reproach, 'You haven't seen my pen?' 'I can't find my
pen; I suppose it's disappeared.' Kay watches this exhibition with
incredulous scorn. Perhaps not scorn. His mother, yes – she
found it despicable. 'My toothbrush has disappeared!' 'Look for
it,' she replied, 'or I'll come and find it.' And when she came, the
toothbrush was 'right under your nose'.

This was an old impression: that the world was a hostile order
full of traps and set in motion by the Enemy God. Even as a child
he detested the world where you had to show yourself in broad
daylight, naked, without a protecting shell, judged by your
behaviour. 'Show what you can do.' He didn't know how to do
anything. He was paralysed by invisible eyes, caught in snares he
did not see; the world belonged to other people, was 'the Other'.
He had never been good at gymnastics, at sports (except for
swimming – in the water he was comfortable, it was the
nonworld, the unorganized, he splashed about in it as in a liquid
freedom). In the world, he was literally lost, dissolving into space,
confiscated, seized with dizzy spells (he is always subject to
vertigo), on the point of falling into the sky, into the hole gaping
around him. Perhaps that's why he was always looking for hiding
places under draperies, in dark holes – trying to plug up the
world into which he leaked away by an agonizing haemorrhage of
his being, to wrap himself in its protecting limits as if in a quilt.
His manias were an attempt to neutralize the world by making it
a habit, an extension of the body, the basis of a familiar gesture.
He always liked taking the same itineraries; he likes what he is
used to. He realized this when, in relative prosperity, he
continued eating the same food, oatmeal, that he had chosen
during the years of dearth; when he was hungry, he was hungry
for oatmeal. The centre of his universe is his room, and as soon
as he moves he arranges a corner with his familiar objects:
fetishes to protect him against the irruption of the world and its
open spaces. Once, in Switzerland, crossing the market square,

he realized that he had never *seen* this city he had been living in for seven years; it was a familiar décor, as though painted on canvas, weightless, with neither density nor reality, and after eight years he was astonished to discover that the landscape was without a doubt the kind you could call 'beautiful'. It was Kay who after six months in the city made him take walks that would never have occurred to him. Walks bored him; everything not related to the interminable labour of abstraction, which he incarnated in his manuscripts covered with his tiny handwriting, was an intolerable loss of time. The slightest event in his draught-proof universe assumed gigantic proportions, was immediately digested, neutralized, expelled from his life by the written account. His only contacts with what is generally called life were (1) books, which he sampled very slowly, rereading each paragraph until he had the sense of having grasped the entire implicit meaning; (2) films, which he permitted himself five times a week and where he lived intensely the actions and situations rendered harmless by the reassuring limits the screen and the writers assigned them. Then he came home to get rid of his existence by transfusing it into literature until three in the morning. His work, his room, were the walls of the fortress he was raising against the world, and whoever entered his life was an intruder he immediately put in irons; he kept the intruder under observation until he came to rest, sitting on the couch, then swiftly overcame him with a few questions, then with silence, and finally bound him hand and foot by reading him long passages. The intruder, thus anaesthetized, was inserted by force into his unreal universe, caught in his spider web of abstractions. As well as I can imagine him, the intruder probably finds him a distant, inattentive creature, unapproachable, bringing each conversation around to his curious intellectual speculations, dissecting every declaration in order to classify it in a category of attitudes, rendering dialogue impossible by turning it into a reflection *about* this dialogue. An elusive man, certainly, who had cut himself off from reality, including his own, by becoming the surgeon of the awareness of all reality; an absent man.

But I've digressed. Safe only when he felt cut off from a reality he could dismiss as a spectacle, outside himself, he was disabled as soon as he had to turn and confront it. Once, having left for Italy for two months, he returned after ten days, relieved to get back to his den after having made himself miserable; overcome with boredom, hunger (for he dared not eat in restaurants, the waiters terrified him), solitude, nullity in the streets of Milan, Venice, Bologna, Florence, Rome; finally spending the days on his bed rereading *Man's Fate*; crossing half of Venice (from the port, where he had a room in a *pensione*, to the station) on foot (he would have had to speak to take a *vaporetto*) to buy two *panettoni* and a tomato stuffed with rice in the same *rosticceria* he had discovered the first day and to which he subsequently returned in order not to have to deal with a new set of people, already relying on habit. Appropriating the world by force of habit, concealing reality with routine, abstracting himself from his own life and systematizing it into literature, in order not to have to live it any longer; tempted, finally, by the invisible, nonproductive, nonfunctioning activity par excellence, theft, withdrawing some object in a shop from the concrete richness of the real, annihilating it first by becoming the clandestine owner of a clandestine object (that is, having become clandestine for him and, for the former owner, absence of the object) and then by reselling the object (sacred now because it belonged to a transcendent order) and by receiving currency in exchange. The ideal essence of commerce, to steal is to transform concrete wealth into abstract wealth without having done anything; it is to be the invisible agent – that is, wholly negative – of this abstractive destruction, conjuring away the real by an action which must conceal itself, a null action which makes nothing happen except nothingness. Theft is poetry, the poetry of mercantile economy. And from this point of view, Switzerland is certainly the most enjoyable country to rob.

*His cowardice* (and timidity, of course). After everything I've just said, it would be surprising if he weren't a coward too. I'm coming to that. This notion of theft, however, goes further than I thought. It is the concealment, the whisking away, the 'out of sight, out of mind'; and that reminds me how ten years ago,

impotent with a woman offering herself, he used to have necro-
philiac daydreams and even started a story about a man who, in
order to make love to a girl, first anaesthetizes her with a wad of
cotton soaked in chloroform and placed, so as not to burn her
skin, on a napkin ring: a horror of being seen, a craving to be the
invisible voyeur; a sadistic temptation to kill or to anaesthetize the
Other to escape his (her) paralysing gaze. The theme of abstraction, the project to interiorize his existence altogether, proves to
be so fundamental that it seems to open all doors. This is why he
must regard it with suspicion, look further: How was this project
conceived? What else does it manifest? What conditions
provoked it? That is still to come.

Avarice, hatred of the world and of self-realization, cowardice
– it all belongs together. Cowardice: not exactly fear, but horror,
the emotional refusal to exteriorize himself, to lose himself
outside, to be conscious of himself in the world as a being of
vulnerable flesh – vulnerable precisely because he refuses to
exteriorize himself in actions and to exist by them alone. This is
clearly shown by his demeanour; he appears to be a thin fellow
with hollow cheeks and eyes, receding forehead and chin, a long
neck poking forward over his slightly hunched back, with the gait
of a heron and parsimonious gestures, as if he were trying to
contain his being within himself. When he meets someone in a
hallway, he stands aside awkwardly and murmurs an excuse
which passes unnoticed, lowers his eyes as though caught doing
something wrong. In the metro, he lets everyone get ahead of
him, even if he himself has opened the door first, and stands in a
corner to take up as little space as possible. If he talks, it is in a
low, muffled voice, as though frightened by the vibrations his
own throat creates in the surrounding air. He avoids the staircase
or the lift if he risks encountering there someone he knows
even vaguely with whom he would have to speak and who might
begin an 'ordinary' conversation. A tendency to jumble his
words together in his haste to finish what he has to say as quickly
as possible, to fall back again into a rapt silence. Great deference
and formal politeness, always embarrassed, toward people with
whom he has no personal connection – and often he has none, in

fact, just because of this. This behaviour gives him a preoccupied, abrupt manner (for in his concern to be brief, to reduce contact to the most impersonal level, he speaks in a tone of categorical declaration), a distant expression that intimidates interlocutors – they find him arrogant and assume he avoids them out of contempt. Furthermore, he always leaves others the initiative of setting the tone, of creating the atmosphere, of defining the relationship's nature, of formulating its rules and requirements, to which he immediately adapts himself, only too happy to so efface himself, adopting a different game with each interlocutor and, when involved in an argument, trying to show that each side is in the right.

I have emphasized 'ordinary', for any personal conversation, especially when someone asks his advice, finds him receptive, even beaming, all too pleased to be consulted, to be regarded as worthy of a question. Overflowing with gratitude, he answers the man asking directions, astonished that *he* could give something, could pass for a member of the collectivity as good as the rest, could be integrated with the others rather than excluded, regarded as null. Matters grow more complicated here, and even before dealing with the clue the word 'ordinary' provides, two others appear (on the one hand, his voluntary conformism with regard to all groups or representative individuals, never contradicting the man who takes him into his confidence or calls him to witness, even the worst kind of person; on the other, the gratitude he feels toward those who mistake him for a commonplace person when he is certain of not being one and revenges himself for such a mistake by what he calls his betrayals, his affective prejudice for the group opposed to that which calls upon him) which we will soon have to deal with afterward.

*Ordinary*. The ordinary conversation about the weather terrifies him, paralyses him; he never feels up to this interlocutor who expects him to be a man like any other and asks him to manifest himself as an ordinary member of the race. The exteriorization of these commonplaces is impossible for him. His terror is particularly intense when confronted with the tribe of salespeople, waiters, flunkies of any kind. This is important. There is a new key here. For a long time he thought his panic in the company of professional servitors was a moral disapproval, the horror of a system like capitalism which obliges some to sell and humiliate themselves for money. A noble explanation. What strikes me now is that he was panic-stricken before the very individuals whose job it was to satisfy his own requirements; these individuals wordlessly ask him to formulate desires, to state rules to which they will humbly adapt themselves, they precipitate him into a situation with no other rule than what he himself is willing to declare; they force him into autonomy. Yet he is horrified by autonomy; his fundamental attitude consists of scrupulously obeying a Rule forged by the Other (has he not admitted as much with regard to Morel? Has he not just written that 'he always leaves others the initiative of formulating the rules and requirements to which he immediately adapts himself, only too happy to efface himself', a notation whose importance has escaped him at the moment?), of formally, ritually performing the Other-requirement raised to the absolute – an absolute to such a degree, in fact, that he often rebels in order to feel its solidity and extent, his rebellions being violent recriminations (arguments with his superiors whom he rubs the wrong way and whose intransigence he magnifies on purpose; and his accusation that Kay leaves him no other alternative except to change himself radically or to 'jump out the window', so imperative, he says, are her demands). But in dealing with flunkies there is no longer any Rule. At loose ends, defenceless, not knowing where to turn, he hesitates in order to oblige the flunky, gently, politely to manifest his requirements. He assumes the duty of serving this servant who asks only to serve him. He is tempted to push consideration to the point of buying the product the salesman extols, just to avoid having to ask for some other; tempted to order the dish the waiter likes; tempted, too, to leave immoderately large tips to reverse the roles: to be the waiter's servant instead of the person who has been served.

His gratitude to those who permit him to 'give', to manifest himself as a man among men, is actually something different: he is grateful to anyone who inquires about something because the request can be satisfied according to a precise form and fixed rules, because within these rules he feels secure, comfortable, the instrument of a trancendent requirement into which he need only let himself flow as into a mould. And the other day, groping for a salient point by which to apprehend himself, he was complaining – significantly – that no rule, no law had been made for him, that he was a reject of society and nature alike. And some years before he wrote (but this is still valid) a sketch about a couple in which the girl is constantly asking, 'What would you like?' and the boy answering, 'I don't know, how about you?' and the girl replying, 'I don't know, I asked you.' And when Kay asks him what he wants to eat: 'I don't know, you decide.' Then there is his delight in filling out questionnaires that wrap him in their web of precise questions, permitting him, merely by obeying the printed requirements, to create an objective identity for himself that is perfectly adapted to an anonymous order, to flow into an impersonal world that is nevertheless prepared for him.

Here I am at grips with characteristic psychoanalytic material. And in a better position to interpret this attitude of abstraction which just now seemed so fundamental to me. A second approach to his total reality would be approximately this: avarice, mania, cowardice, systematizing intellectuality, all as a constant total means of existing as little as possible. Everything happens as if, since his earliest childhood, he were trying to suppress himself as a subject, stop living (*erleben*) in order to stop realizing his lived contradictions at the same time. He applies himself to neutralizing the world, his own existence and every signification, to replacing the lived project, the obligation to live, with rules, schedules, rigorous systematic tasks which are always gratuitous because stripped of any real and internal necessity – gratuitous, that is without real motivation and having neither internal basis (in some urgency, desire, felt need) nor external basis (in the empirical reality of which they offer him no grasp, but to which they juxtapose themselves and which they conceal by theorizing about it) – rules by which he tries to mechanize his existence. His compulsive behaviour, his attachment to habit, his

avarice are all attempts to replace the activity of living and of
realizing a human world by a mechanical activity affectively
neuter (that is, without lived signification) arrived at by a coldly
rational calculation (to eat the minimum amount necessary for
survival, to calculate the daily rations in advance, to banish from
his life all gratuitous enjoyments and expenses) and to perpetuate himself in existence by virtue of this mechanized, ritualized
behaviour perfected once and for all and thanks to which he
would definitively rid himself of the world and of himself. To
neutralize the world and himself (to 'designify' it, in Hesnard's
term) in order to replace it with the immutable universe of logical
madness; to reduce to a minimum the lived contact with reality
(he persists doggedly at this task in gaining his livelihood; as a
journalist he puts the world into files, builds up interminable
dossiers on every subject, claims to exhaust and petrify a
country's reality by statistics, declares that by consulting his files
he can give a view more exact than by an on-the-spot investigation; he has a weakness for world demographic problems,
statistics on the world's resources, strategic theories, five-year
plans; he would make a good official of the Planning Ministry or
the Population Service), in order to avoid the conflicts, contradictions and anguish which the slightest crack in his carapace of
routines produces. Upon the death (sometimes disbelievingly
imagined) of his wife, who prevents his complete escape into autistic madness, he imagines living in a tiny attic where he would
lead a cloistered life still more isolated than his existence in
Switzerland.

The impression all this leaves upon me: a schizoid personality
whom Kay's constant, sometimes desperate struggle to rescue, to
deflect from intellectual rumination, to invite into a human life
has perhaps saved from madness.

Thus I am in possession of a compendious diagnostic which
accords too large a share to psychoanalysis. I have defined the
profound intention which organizes his behaviour, I have shown
that it is a behaviour of escape, that he *is*, basically, a total escape
mechanism. This is perhaps useful; it is still not much, and I am

now going to try (how solemn it sounds to be writing in the first person) to list the questions this first investigation raises.

1. What is he trying to escape – that is, what is the motivation of his escape? An entirely abstract answer which indicates an impasse to come: he is escaping the intolerable contradiction he would have to live if he assented to his profound situation; he is avoiding a contradictory situation by removing himself to a fabricated situation which, having no other profound purpose than to reject the first, remains artificial for him, threatened with collapse, marginal to his lived reality; therefore he never recognizes himself in what he does because his actions remain without any relation to what he is. What is he, then, that he is trying to escape?

2. To this question, psychoanalytic investigation alone cannot provide the answer. It can explain, for instance, his inferiority complex or his sense of guilt as the nonliquidation of parental prohibitions and, as a consequence, his perseverance in an infantile attitude of affective dependence on the theological values of childhood; it can add that in relation to this infantile ethic his adult reality seems a sin, and that he therefore attempts to avoid it by escaping into autistic behaviour, an autistic universe. But why hasn't he liquidated the infantile behaviour? Here two explanations are possible, which, although they seem to complement each other, do not exhaust the question:

a. because he has been powerfully traumatized during his childhood and has not had the necessary patience, courage and resolution to free himself;

b. because occasions propitious to this liquidation have not presented themselves, or, what comes to the same thing (and this interpretation rather attracts me), because the liquidation, already begun, of his infantile universe has again been thwarted by unfavourable circumstances: by exile, exclusion, the impossibility of working, isolation, circumstances which have reactivated an anterior situation, already partly overcome, and occasioned a regression.

This interpretation would account for the 'miraculous coincidence' remarked on above. His situation of exile presents itself as a particular fact – an intentional fact – miraculously foreseen by the 'nullity complex' of his earliest childhood, not because this nullity situation was immediately chosen and valorized by a fundamental nullity complex, but (1) because the infantile nullity complex has been developed and enriched by means of this situation; (2) because, having thus resumed the affective atmosphere of his childhood, he has also recovered the recollection of that atmosphere as a kind of premonition; (3) the historical, Marxist explanation of his attitude, starting from his objective condition as an exile doomed to nullity, thus retains its validity; but it is complicated and enriched by psychoanalytic significations which the lived experience of this objective condition has assumed, for on the occasion of this objective condition he has reactivated certain infantile significations. Therefore, his attitude situating itself on two levels which are historically distinct (on the level of objective necessity, for it is true that his present situation is untenable, that he is doomed to alienation and can surmount it only by assuming his objective nullity in order to transcend it by intellectual effort; and on the level of the infantile nullity complex, which does not correspond to an objective necessity, has no further rational motivation, but reaches back to the prehistoric past of a choice of being), his liberation must be won on both these levels at once – as liquidation of the choice to be null and of the guilt complex (that is, as subjective conversion), and as the practical transcendence of his total situation, which instead of avoiding he must act upon and thereby transform.

This is not new (it has already been given some forty pages back), but it confirms me in my conviction that, after having acquired an approximative total view of the Marxist critique which can suitably be made of his mode of commitment to the world, he must begin not with that critique but with a psychoanalysis that would be circumspect as to its basic postulates. In fact, his 'dialectical process' now looks as follows to me (and in tracing its historical development, perhaps I shall succeed in grasping the instruments in which his choice is incarnated and which have been furnished to him by events): There was a child

who was marked in his early years by the repressiveness of
bourgeois education and by the particular values which his
parents attached to it. They gave him an inferiority complex, a
guilt complex. Yes, 'gave him'. For an anxious moment, he
wondered if he wasn't taking advantage of a determinist formula.
Shouldn't he have said, more accurately, 'He was urged by his
surroundings to choose himself as inferior and guilty'? That was
what he should say, of course, in principle. But the introduction
of the notion of choice at this point would raise endless difficulties. It would assume that the two- or three-year-old child might
have chosen himself differently under the same conditions; and if
this were true, he would have to return to that age and relive it in
recollection in order to seize once again the first basis of the
choice. Which is impossible in practice. I am quite willing to
assume all responsibilities but not that of the child I was made
into. In practice, determinism (that is, the explanation of
behaviour by external pressures) seems to me a process that must
apply to earliest childhood; under given conditions a child is
necessarily the way he is, and anyone would be the same in his
place, at his age. The child is conditioned like a plant that is
made to grow straight or in a spiral; he is provided with certain
instruments, all others being excluded, by which to relate himself
to others, to the world, to himself. He is given a certain image of
himself, of others, of his value, his place in the world. It is in the
frame of this first conditioning that he will later choose himself.
He is already marked, already in gear with certain forms of
fundamental behaviour which, whether he knows it or not, he
has been obliged to adopt (not because discipline has forcibly
imposed them upon him, but because there is no other behaviour
available) and which constitute his mode of initial contact with
the world, the original structure of his behaviour, on the basis of
which his person will be established. The child is an almost
entirely fabricated being; his fundamental behaviour is created for
him. There is as yet no question of choice; the child gets along
by the means available, does his best to escape punishment, to
reconcile himself with the categorical and incomprehensible
requirements of those around him. The behaviour he adopts to

this end is a behaviour of magical exorcism; it has no meaning
for him save that of magically making the grown-ups smile. The
child finds himself in a situation which is beyond his means;
obliged to play a game whose rules he does not know, he
advances hesitantly, exploring the path that will rouse the least
reprobation. Urged on by slaps and rewards to adopt attitudes
which correspond to what is incomprehensibly demanded of
him, he alienates himself in a role, develops the possibilities
which correspond to it, assumes a 'character'.

What is happening here is a mimetic adaptation to the
requirements of the milieu, a montage of automatisms which, for
the child, are devoid of all meaning. He is living beyond his
means; his behaviour, which he feels to be mysteriously significant
for others, is not so for himself; his training affords him the
means of signifying these significations which escape him. And
that is why he is doomed to act a part; he spends his time playing
roles he does not understand though he sees they are understood
by others; his resources as a deceiver are being developed, and
yet everyone is surprised to discover he employs these same
resources either to hoax those around him or to play any role at
all with equal ease. The fundamental role, however, the
inculcated role, is in the image of the clothes and the boots he is
given: they are too big for him, he doesn't manage to fill them, he
swims in them, but that doesn't matter, 'It'll fit you later on,
when you get bigger.' Like the sleeves, the laces, the trousers that
are too long, the gestures go beyond him. This is just what the
discipline intends; he is provided with cultural behaviour whose
cultural signification he is unaware of (who can boast of grasping
it?), he swims in oversize manners; he will end up by filling
them, like his clothes; he will end up by living the only significations he is given the means to signify; to the exclusion of all
others, he owns in advance the means of the person he will be
'when he grows up'. He will become the character whose habits
he has been obliged to develop; he will end up by producing the
intention of his gestures, of the roles he has learned how to act;
the objective will react upon the subjective; he will interiorize his
role. At first he didn't know what he was doing or even that he

was doing it; later he does what he knows how to do. At first he plays with words and speaks without knowing what he is saying; later he speaks and thinks only within the limits of his verbal habits. Constituted language, the instrument of thought, is at first only a body that is too big for him, a body in which he swims; later he will assume this body and will make his own the intentions the latter permits him to produce – he will signify what he has the means of signifying. The child becomes the subjective accomplice of a behaviour structure which is objectively determined and which is his familial, social, cultural role. To be otherwise, he would have to invent different means from those he finds at his disposal. Normally he does not invent them. The humble, obedient, obliging, polite behaviour inculcated from the age of two reveals other people as terrors; producing intentions corresponding to his behaviour (adopted at first without express intention), he now is terrified. And he will become still more profoundly terrified as his field of vision widens. Starting from his conditioning and his basic possibilities, he transcends himself toward new possibilities. He is marked. There must now be a crisis in his life, a rupture of continuity, a displacement in order, for the child – incapable of coping with his arsenal of habits and constituted means of perception – to be forced to modify his infantile choice, to revoke it in rebellion. Adolescence may be this occasion; but the occasion may also not present itself at all.

Whether or not it does, however, one never altogether rids oneself of one's childhood. It remains as the initial given situation. It does not explain everything; it explains only the affective colouring of the present. From another aspect, it must itself be explained, first of all because it is a particular image of my social situation (family, education, surroundings, and so on) and refers back to the society and the entire world whose imprint it bears, later because a man is explained just as much by his adult condition as by his childhood.

His past conditions the way he relates to the world and situates himself within it; his childhood qualifies the goals he assigns himself and the significations he perceives. But inversely, the real world, with its perspectives and its possible objectives, conditions and qualifies my relation to the past. The question now is to know (1) if the past can be put to use and integrated with the present possibilities so as to enlarge my grasp of reality – if the truth of the past serves me to extend the objective truth of my actions and is confirmed by it; or (2) if the past is a handicap, a conditioning which disadapts me in relation to my present condition – if the truth of the past contradicts the truth of my actions and introduces a moment of apparent irrationality into my behaviour.

In the first case, the person will be simple; the totalization of his temporal dimensions will present itself as an immediately available possibility. He will be inclined to believe that 'the first impulse is always the right one', that the past gives him certain rights over the world – and he will be blind to the truth of his conduct as seen by others (the citizen of Auteuil *never* goes to Aubervilliers).

In the second case, on the other hand, the person will be caught between contradictory significations and truths (being both proletarian and bourgeois, son and orphan, Jew and gentile, urban and rural), his past contests his present objectivity and, inversely, there is too much play in the gears, the person can be nothing wholly but must integrate incompatible structures by transcending them, feels alone because he never signifies himself when he employs the means of signification of a group to which he does not wholly belong, doomed to the contestation of whatever he does. For the person in this case, there is nothing 'natural' or immediately evident; he must continually think, reflect, question; he must base his behaviour on reasons that are universally admissible; he cannot make himself real (recover an objectivity that might be his own) save by inventing personal means of signification in order to perform his personal unity.

To understand a man you must therefore deal with him in terms both of his present condition and of his – for him – prehistoric past (that is, of a past anterior to *his* history). His way of dealing with events, organizing his world and putting it in perspective is realistic, rational, objectively conditioned (he formulates it according to the material and intellectual means he invents, at a moment's notice, starting with those which are already at one's disposal), but it is also and at the same time dense with a past, with passions, with prejudices contracted in childhood, all of which qualify his behaviour, give it a singular quality, an individual savour that is not always fortunate.

The past conditions the present and the future, but present and future act dialectically on the past and give it variable significations. It is in any case unlikely that my childhood will survive in me as such, as a raw determinant, that it will not receive from the present a signification justifying the fact that I retain it within me; and the justifications I find for it now cannot be pure make-believe: they necessarily correspond (unless I go mad) to a present truth. It is absurd to believe, as Hesnard does, that 'infantile behaviour can continue to survive on its own account in later life', that 'segments of infantile life can occur separately in the existing adult'* as 'nonintegrated structures'. If infantile behaviour were merely this, merely facts, fossils bequeathed by childhood, without present meaning, how easy it would be to liquidate them! In reality, if infantile behaviour has enduring life, it is because it has assumed, in the present situation, significations no longer infantile. It is because it is anything but alien to the person or automatic or accidental; it is because it permits the organization of the present situation and, confirmed by it at the same time, seems to be requisite to it. Such behaviour is 'over-determined' – conditioned by the past and the present at the same time. Its infantile origin (the materialist–psychoanalytic explanation of the person by his past) cannot account for the present motivating power of this past and of the value (or antivalue) accorded it.

Yes, 'segments of behaviour' of infantile origin survive in us; but there infantile motivation has been lost, an adult motivation has replaced them, behaviour originally accountable to an infantile intention is now accountable to a deeply personal intention, not at all accidental, oblivious to the contingent condition of its reappearance. An example: The sexually inhibited person who

*L'Univers morbide de la faute, p. 308.

avoids contact with women, laying down an ascetic and virtuous morality for himself, not only avoids his sexual existence but by doing so avoids existence itself; his bad faith is not confined to the sexual realm, it is complete; his inhibition, which originally was perhaps only the effect of education, without profound signification, has cancerously invaded his entire person, has been developed and personalized. It is now not only a sexual behaviour, but a total behaviour with ontological motivation; this man is afraid not only of his sexuality but of himself, his freedom in all its aspects. And it is impossible to distinguish the sexual motivations in this fear from the ontological ones, impossible to attribute a sexual signification rather than a moral one. The former is nothing more than a partial aspect of the latter, enveloped by it. And although there was originally an infantile motivation, you can never change a man only from the waist down; his morality now conditions and justifies his sexual behaviour, although the latter originally conditioned the former. It is his entire person which he must now modify in order to modify his sexual behaviour; his psychoanalytic treatment will succeed only insofar as it will incite him to this total modification, through his sexuality, for instance; it will be successful, in short, despite the psychiatrist's theoretical error, an error which all the same risks retarding his cure indefinitely.

Another example: A man has an antisexual complex, becomes a mystic, justifies his puritanism by his mysticism (a moral choice) and forgets its real conditioning. How can he demystify himself? By becoming conscious of the infantile conditioning of his choice – that is, of its accidental origin? But all choices are contingent and conditioned, and if you tell me my Marxism is a result of my condition as a half-caste doomed to contest the existing order, you will not thereby deconvert me; for my convictions produce their own autonomous motivation (there is a specific cohesion of the 'superstructure'), and I will not relinquish them if they account for my condition and afford me some grasp of it, if they establish an authentic correspondence between intention and action. Psychoanalysis finds its limit in authenticity. Making a moral choice relative by explaining its conditioning therefore proves nothing, either for or against that choice; I am a mystic 'because' of the antisexual morality of my milieu. And then? And suppose this mysticism were, under the circumstances, in that milieu, the best possible attitude. But is it? Here is quite another question, to which the psychoanalytic dissection of my infantile conditioning furnishes no answer; the conditioning is a fact, a mediated fact which has become significant, an instrument of signification, indissociable from the way in which I assume it in order to situate myself in the world.

In conclusion: The infantile condition 'survives' in us only insofar as our present condition confirms us in it, insofar as this behaviour inherited from childhood permits the organization of a situation which seems to require it and thereby establishes us in a truth based on the facts. His nullity complex, to return to that, survives in him because an objective situation of nullity has caused it to revive – has permitted it to survive – just when it was being liquidated. He has not simply regressed to this infantile attitude, he has recovered it in a new light, with new significations, as his truth; and it is not by attacking the infantile origin of this 'sentiment' that he can hope to rid himself of it. That 'sentiment' does not exist; if it is not based on a lived reality which confirms it, it will vanish by itself. But on the other hand, if he had had a different childhood, he would doubtless not have assumed the events of his life in the same way, would not have accorded them the same signification.

The supposed conflict between the materialist explanation and psychoanalysis is therefore a false dilemma. Both, although they are on different levels, explain man by his condition (material, infantile). This explanation is always true, but that is also its weakness; since every choice is conditioned, you can always prove it was 'given in advance' as a possibility or an objective probability, but you can never prove it was fatal or necessary, or foresee it – you can foresee it only after the fact, by showing how and why it was possible.

The psychologist explanation, on the other hand, is always false; feelings are not in the air, unmotivated or purely 'subjective'; they always have an objective basis (the condition of fact) which should not be considered as a neutral reality the 'subject' fits out with his subjective tastes, but as a web of significations and potentialities from which we can retain and make effective only some to the detriment of others. What is called the 'subjective side' has in fact nothing to do with subjectivity; it is merely the fact that, in confronting an objective situation, we behave in a manner which is not to be explained by this situation alone and which seems to activate motivations that cannot be grasped objectively, irrational motivations. We always seem to be situated below the level of objective reality; this is because at the moment we confront it, we are already instruments of perception (habits, knowledge, aptitudes, mannerisms) acquired in the past, under different circumstances.

Up to this point, there has been no question of freedom; everything has been explicable by present or past conditioning. But what is no longer explicable by conditioning alone is:

1. That we should cling to a past situation (to our past) when it disadapts us for dealing with the present reality, and that the latter has less reality for us than what we were in the past. If man were merely the product of the circumstances which condition him, why would present conditioning weigh less than past conditioning? The difficulty of modifying the instruments of perception inherited from the past does not suffice to explain the fact that we cling to attitudes whose present value is obsolete; if we still cling to them, it is because they incarnate significations and ethical values we adhere to absolutely, values which are the norm by which we exist and without which we are afraid of going beyond our depth, of sinking into nothingness.

2. That we should be capable of modifying the instruments of perception we already are, of adjusting them to the circumstances, of transcending ourselves toward an enlarged grasp of the given. This perpetual modification, this power of initiative and transformation is freedom.

The question now is one of knowing whether the total instrument of perception which we are (what he has elsewhere called the 'original situation'), the way we situate ourselves in the present reality and establish its signification and truth, reveals the potentialities most valuable for us, affords us the widest possible grasp; or if it deceives us as to our condition, disguises the most important potentialities, raises obstacles to our grasp, abuses our assessment of our opportunities. In short, must the original situation be modified or is it a sufficient means to realize the real, to match our intentions, our opportunities, and the objective signification of our actions? It is this question which is the first moment of moral conversion; and again he finds what he has said ten pages earlier: The subjective conversion must begin by an objective investigation. And this objective investigation (which applies to my total condition – that is, to the whole world as a tangle of possibilities and significations, constituted or potential) *is* the conversion at work. To know myself, to know what I am and can be, to understand if I am sufficiently equipped to do what, in my condition, is most effective and valuable, I must put in parentheses my habitual way of assuming my condition, I must suspend my original choice and its prejudices. But this contestation and suspension is not an instantaneous subjective operation; it is further work. You can suspend a commitment only by making another commitment; but in the present instance it is not a matter of another commitment but of taking stock of the contingency and the limitations of my means of perception, of contesting the tendencies incarnated in them – by elaborating different means, by interrogating the world about the opportunities which it offers and which I let pass because I have neither the means nor the heart to grasp them, by making myself 'unquiet' by groping along until I find a new way of seeing this arbitrarily familiarized reality.

To relearn how to see. Because the solution of the problems of existence is outside (if it exists at all), freedom is outside, along with the instruments by which it can make itself free and without which it does not exist. (The unity of society and a civilization, *à propos*, is also outside, in the instruments of perception and action elaborated by and conditioning praxis. They furnish us the possibility of certain ethical choices, to the exclusion of all the rest. Which does not mean that all ethical choices are of equal value; it is precisely because they are not that wanting to change the world has a meaning.) Being concerned with what is inside yourself, trying to find yourself within is the surest means of not finding yourself at all, of futilely hashing over immutable psychological problems. You would be more likely to find yourself if you were concerned with the world, undertook something, forgot yourself – if you no longer craved for an identity that conformed to some norm.

He says this, but has still to prove it. 'All the same,' Jacques said, 'you're looking for fame, aren't you?' 'No,' he answered quickly, 'no' – with a tiny sense of superiority – 'to be recognized by those *I* recognize.' To be recognized by Morel and those who recognize Morel; no longer to be a nocturnal scribbler lost in the darkness between the Chemin Vert and the Rue Saint-Maur, covering sheets of paper with blue specks and producing nothing, like the thousands who hopelessly parade their mediocrity, filling their desk drawers with rejected manuscripts by which their human reality has been refused them. 'It comes down to the same thing,' Jacques said. 'Fame among a coterie of the elect means more to you than glory among the great mass of fools.' This is not certain. He honestly believes that he is not in search of a coterie life. He believed that in '47, imagining Paris was the centre of the world, supposing he was exiled from truth because he was not in Paris, and dreaming he would be at the heart of the world and of truth if he could go to bistros and have discussions with Morel's circle. That if he could do this, of course he would be admitted among the gods and acquire an absolute importance in all eyes, including his own. But he no longer believes this. He has known for some time that having a book published, even having it recognized by Morel's circle, is not a metaphysical revolution; that a book doesn't get you very far (just a little way), because afterward you have to begin again and keep abreast of where you were; and that merely not falling behind means you have to advance constantly, and constantly invent; and that there is nothing gained for good. Fame does not interest him (that is, fame for its own sake), perhaps because it has been available to him anyway and because, measuring its mediocrity (pontificating bores him and he's no good at it), he has already refused it. If it still counts, as recognition, it is because of the possibilities of action, even the obligations to action it can provide; recognized, he would be in the world, it would no longer be indifferent whether he did this, that, or the other thing; he would really exist as doing what he does, he would be obliged to continue under pain of abdication and betrayal. While whether he abdicates, betrays, accepts money from the Fascists or sells out to the Americans now, it matters to no one and he refuses to do so quite gratuitously, out of *amour-propre*, out of love of austerity, without effect, since there are many in his position who sell out, and to whom his pure refusal – not opposition but merely refusal – simply leaves the field open. If he wants to be recognized, it is so that to write will some day become an action, not remain this futile and ascetic gesture of a man who works himself up every night and who, alone in conferring a staggering importance on what he says, is inevitably tempted to think that he is indulging in nothing more than spiritual exercises. How could he believe in his responsibility and his task, since what he thinks rouses no echo anywhere and produces no consequence, since, without a public, he has no possibility of action?

*To things themselves.* For weeks now he has postponed getting down 'to things'. Having grasped some fundamental attitudes, he is already tempted to think he is through, supposes he is cured of his abstract madness, enjoys the idle moments before getting down to work and tells himself, 'You see, you're changing, you're enjoying things'; and he wonders if this euphoria isn't merely the stupid satisfaction of the schoolboy who thinks he's put himself right with Heaven because he's done his homework.

But try to find the signification of this kind of feeling – what is the right one? And where? Nowhere. Stupid satisfaction or awakening to life, engulfment or progress – this intermittent euphoria can be all these, but it is nothing of the kind for the moment; it will be one or the other according to the direction he takes. For the moment, he is heading nowhere; he is feeling his way. For fifteen days he has been wondering where to start, where to begin unravelling the skein. 'Begin anywhere,' Jacques said. 'Once you've begun, it goes by itself.'

'Yes,' he answered, 'but where is anywhere?' He thought he could penetrate himself by starting with some real event and proceeding backward from there, illuminating the signification which this event has for him by its historical depth; then ridding the event of this individual signification, which perhaps obscures his assessment, in order to arrive at an interpretation of the facts which is not purely personal. Take Poujadism, for instance. His assessment of Poujadism is certainly emotional in part. He recognizes in the Poujadists the congested stupidity of big- and small-time profiteers who resent the society that keeps them from making out; he recognizes the drunken cowardice glorying in its self-exhibition, like the upheaval when the concierge, the grocer, the barber, and the newspaper vendor put out swastikas and dragged the Jewish woman and her daughter out of the building all the way to the SA car parked a hundred yards from a hydrant. (The crowd made a circle around them, spat on them. They were given buckets. 'Wash!' shouted the SA man, and the women started dragging the buckets full of water from the hydrant to the car, the grey hair hanging over the old woman's forehead as she hobbled along, panting. 'Faster!' the SA man screamed, and he tore the bucket out of the old woman's hands, flinging the water over the car in one great cascade; the car was a black Steyr 100; the crowd, frightened by its own audacity, watched in silence, and he himself, shaken by a kind of interior tremor, felt only that he did not understand something that was happening, something that upset him deeply, something lodged in the inexplicable contradiction between, on the one hand, the silent, idle crowd, the motionless silhouette of the husky SA man, his boots and belt gleaming – the incarnation of arrogant power – and, on the other, the two panting, terrified women, their weakness straining beneath the scornful eyes of strength. It was his first image of the pogrom, decisive because from that day on, seized with a slight nausea at the sight of this gratuitous hatred, he realized that those in power, the masters of the world, were on the 'other side', and that his own place, as a mute spectator sitting on his bicycle, was nowhere, that there was no way for him to pass into the camp of the violent and powerful, nor into the camp of the crowd, that complacent accomplice nervously enjoying its spectacle, nor into the camp of the victims, for whom he was not prepared to have sympathy – only a disgusted pity. Spectator: in the person of the two women, it was his father they were spitting on, his father whom he despised; in the person of the SA man was incarnated a virility he was beginning to hanker for; as for the crowd, its complicity was stealing his country from him, for he had no part in its silent communion. The world fell outside him; again he was alone; weak, and null, the bastard taunted by Strauss, kicked in the tar and not even fighting back, convinced of his own irremediable impotence.) He was surely overestimating the Poujadist danger and power, filtering out of the information he gathered about the movement what confirmed his alarmist assessment of the situation and then, conscious that he was inclined toward alarmism (worse, toward defeatism when confronted with the mounting strength of the new fascism; he could foresee opposition to it only as defensive), correcting this first assessment by a second, which was calmer and more prudent and which boiled down to an admission of ignorance: 'It might become dangerous, although it is not necessarily so at present.' Sensitive to a certain real aspect of Poujadism, he therefore feels that other aspects, just as real, might well escape him. Rather than trust himself to the 'first impulse, which is always the right one', he should therefore undertake a scientific study of the phenomenon – that is, apply a method so rigorous that his personal feelings would be put in parentheses from the start. Fine. But what good would such a study do? What if he learned everything about Poujadism, for instance? (Which was impossible anyway, for such a movement would most likely be altered or aetiolated before he had succeeded in examining it thoroughly, just as he fears that a man's lifetime, his own in particular, will be too short to permit him to grasp and change himself.) Now he has no particular desire to consecrate the years to come to the scientific study of the contemporary neofascist movements in France. That would be a false scent. He would do better to divide his task into two phases: (1) to understand himself (and here the study not of Poujadism but of the meaning he spontaneously accorded it can be precious, for his spontaneous reaction to this particular phenomenon is indicative of his total person, as is his attitude to women, friends, society, the bourgeoisie, money, Communism, etc.); (2) having reached an understanding of his original choice and his original situation, to see what grasp of reality and what possibilities of action this situation (which still remains to be explained) offers him in the world (which he must get to know better).

This much is beginning to be clear; and he now realizes that if he has been swimming so long to reach this conclusion, it is because he has momentarily relapsed into one of his most revealing failings: his taste for abstract and theoretical knowledge, the craving to conceive the world as a pure object entirely exterior to him thanks to an impersonal method of knowledge (his passion for statistics), instead of concerning himself for once with the place he himself takes in the world, with the way he himself can join it starting from his own situation – for it is understood that he will never rid himself of this situation (only modify it) or of the 'prejudices' (idiosyncrasies) it necessarily inclines him to, that he will never be an anonymous, prefectly transparent, reasonable consciousness, but that he can only try to take advantage of the fact that his situation makes him sensitive to certain significations, makes him live intensely a certain truth, though one with many lacunae, of course, and one which he must complete by a reasoned understanding of those aspects that remain alien to him. He still has to assume himself in his individuality in order to transcend this individuality effectively and to *live* some positive undertaking which will make his truth explicit to himself, instead of trying (convinced that his situation exiles him forever from the world and from humanity) to join humanity by abstracting himself from any situation, systematically annihilating himself as a person in the articulation of austere and abstract generalities.

Now he sees where to begin (his second exile, at the age he began to integrate himself, with considerable effort; the chasm that appeared between himself and the society of men starting on a spring day in 1938), although beginning in the middle (almost

arithmetically – he is twice as old now) is obviously not a beginning at all and must clarify itself by earlier experiences as it
proceeds. He will call this chapter relating to his exclusion from
the world of men 'They', and 'We' what he has written up to this
point, since by using the first person plural he has shown that the
'we', the community of the living, consists for him in the ascetic
accession of intellects to that abstract universality in which they
can proliferate their theories and lose themselves in the anonymity of the generic.

Then he will still have to take inventory of his reality as a
person in relation to other persons; and he will call this chapter
'You'. And finally, if he succeeds in his undertaking, he will
have the right to call the last chapter 'I' and speak there in the
first person; he would regain himself from his phantasms, the
subject at last of a situation claimed as his own, a situation in
which he will see the totality of *his* means to make himself a man
and free – instead of being, as he is now, their sad dupe and
complacent victim.

# *They*

## A. EXCLUSION

Covered with tarpaulins and full of soldiers, grey-green trucks
with three axles, flat radiators and vertical windscreens were rolling down the main avenue of the Thirteenth Bezirk at dusk.
Standing with his forehead pressed against the window – the
same window from which, four years before, he had seen two
men with Socialist Party armbands shooting rifles in the street
('Get away from the window', the maid had said. 'Why?' 'Because
of ricochets.') – he was admiring the interminable cavalcade of
trucks, and then, seized by the excitement in the air, he took out
his bicycle to go and watch them on the highway.

Something crucial must be happening, but he couldn't have
said what it was; all he knew for sure was his feverish desire to get
nearer the trucks, to smell the petrol and hear the rumble of
their motors. The crowd formed a hedge along the highway; as
each truck passed (bigger trucks now, uncovered, with the soldiers standing), the crowd shouted '*Heil!*' and raised their arms.
Pushing into the front row and raising his arm too, he shouted
'*Heil!*' with them, happy to be lost in the crowd and to see the
soldiers laughing as they returned – somewhat weakly, he
thought – the Nazi salute.

The next day, on his way to school, he went into the stationery shop, where the thin, ill-tempered woman greeted him with '*Heil* Hitler!' '*Heil* Hitler!' he said. 'I'd like a swastika.' She took out some little boxes full of swastikas, he chose a large one – it cost thirty groschen – and pinned it on the green lapel of his Tyrolean jacket.

He wasn't quite sure how he felt about it. Two years before he had decided to be a Nazi because the Nazis were strong and noisy, arrogant, virile, and with a great power behind them that made nonsense out of this petty, putty Austria (Dollfuss, rustic idylls, patriotic songs no one believed in, good workmanship, honesty and thrift); because the Nazis saw things 'big', talked loud, hated Jews and his father was a Jew. He would have liked to get rid of his father, with his business worries ('Your father has worries', 'Business is bad'), his eternal reproaches ('You're such a blockhead; you'd do better to learn your lessons; get something inside your head instead of worrying about your muscles; that boy will never come to anything; what can I do with a boy like you?'), his incomprehension, his narrow-mindedness, his Schaffhausen watch that gained five seconds a week according to a nightly check and that had to be regulated when it was more than fifteen seconds fast. He would have liked to get rid of such a father (even at six he preferred the garage mechanic), with his little potbelly, the vaseline he put in his nose every night, the liquid paraffin ('*Nujol tut wohl*') he drank from the bottle, and the greasy old Jews he brought home to talk business with. But when he pinned the swastika on his lapel, he felt that something was wrong, and whenever he met anyone on the street, he felt as if he were at fault. He stared at other people's lapels, and other people stared at his, and he wondered if he had the right to wear a swastika, and if it showed on his face that his father was a Jew. And when he saw someone without a swastika, he was torn between the sense of his own superiority (here was someone in whose eyes he must be a redoubtable Nazi, in his *Lederhosen*, his hobnail boots, his big swastika) and a hesitant admiration for someone who could defy the triumphant National Socialism.

In class that day, almost everyone wore swastikas, some even wore Hitlerjugend badges, but Felix wore the badge of the

Dollfussjugend 'because', he said, 'I'm Austrian.' The fact that
Felix (an old Catholic family from the Vorarlberg), the only boy
who was equally good in maths, Latin and gym, should claim to
be Austrian left him open-mouthed, and he wondered if it wasn't
really more manful, after all, not to wear a swastika. Perhaps it
was Felix who sowed the seeds of doubt that day (on the foot-
bridge over the level-crossing – they had hoisted themselves up
the beams while the priest, red-faced and sputtering, had brand-
ished his fist at them – it was Felix who had taught him the
'Internationale' and the 'Avanti Popolo', picked up God knows
where; in the middle of class it was Felix who had put his behind
on the desk and released an echoing fart which he fanned with a
sheet of paper until protests rose from the back of the room
against the stink, making him giggle hysterically and infuriating
the German teacher, a Monarchist with a distinguished Hapsburg
face whose virility was accentuated by a scar at the corner of his
mouth), making him suspect that not being a Nazi was not
necessarily 'less' than a Nazi but might mean 'more'. But what
was possible for Felix was not possible for him; for Felix was a
'whole' person with obvious rights on the world, with a Catholic
father named Thomas who was a government official and a
peasant grandmother who still baked her own bread. Whereas *he*
was only half, a half man, half Jew, half Aryan – two halves that
would never make a whole; he would have to get rid of one or the
other.

The German teacher with the sabre cut on his chin, an arrogant
patriot, Austria forever, love of one's country, duty and Chancellor Dollfuss always on his lips, had not come to class that day,
and the man who did come, a tall, bombastic, gawky fellow,
made them a little speech: 'I was blind, the scales have fallen
from my eyes, I confess the error of my ways, I believe in the
Reich and in the Führer.' But that didn't save him from being
fired afterward. Some teachers came in wearing party badges,
but the class didn't last long. They put bales of straw in the class-
rooms for the soldiers to sleep on. There was three weeks'
vacation because the school had been requisitioned by the army.

He asked himself few questions during those three weeks. The

universe had capsized into Nazism so quickly and so completely
that, caught unawares, overcome by the facts, he tried only to dig
himself a niche without attempting to understand or catch up
with the gigantic head start the facts had just taken.

From one day to the next, Nazism had burst into bloom, had
spread out over the city like a glue, had stuck to the walls, the
fences, the pavement, painted huge swastikas and slogans: '*Wir
kehren heim ins Reich*', '*Ein Volk ein Reich ein Führer.*' The tentacles could be discerned in the questioning look of the stationery
seller, the mealymouthed talk of fat Klima with his Czech accent,
his gold teeth, his hands folded over his belly, standing in front of
his barbershop, the window full of little German flags, shouting
'*Heil* Hitler!' as soon as he saw a familiar face. They had come
out of their holes like rats, swastikas in their buttonholes, servile
smiles on their lips – Klima, the baker, the dry-goods salesman,
the tobacconist, the milkman with the Polish accent, they had to
get into the good books of the new masters, had to show how
pleased they were. They vied to show their zeal, made calculations, for they mustn't miss the opportunity; after eight years of
hard times when they had had to bow to Herr Baron and Herr
Major and Herr Kommerzienrat to sell barleysugar or a tube of
paste or a shave, they changed sides, they were going to butter up
the SA man on the corner, smile knowingly at the major in the
Heimwehr, glance greedily at the Jew's shop across the street.
'*Heim ins Reich*'; they were going to sell their linen sheets to the
German businessmen who followed close on the army's heels
and who would give them synthetic fabrics in return, buy up ten-
year-old stocks; best of all, they were going to share the cake of
Jewish business – no, not share it, take it by signing up in the
Nazi Party and looking for protectors. 'Poor lady, what will you
do?' they would ask his mother with exaggerated solicitude, and
between one '*Heil* Hitler!' and the next they would lean over the
counter to whisper some filth about the Nazis and swear they
hated their guts, but if you let yourself be taken in by their confidences they gave you a sly look that seemed to say, 'It's our turn
now – after the *Juden*, we're the ones to make a penny now.' All
except for big Frau Bachrach, monstrously fat, disfigured by a

tumour on her left cheek, with her Yiddish jargon and her
chlorotic, velvet-eyed daughter – Frau Bachrach sitting
enthroned among her dusty sweets, destined for the cremation
ovens, greeting his father (how many customers did *she* have
left?) with a persecuted smile and moist lamentations, while the
sweet shop across the street sold out of its ice cream every day.

They grovelled, afraid someone would remember they had not
always been Nazis, afraid of missing their chance to get ahead, to
eat their slice of cake. And to spirit away their fear, they
discovered their Germanic souls; they listened to Germanic
blood shrilling through their veins; they said in voices like that of
the pleasant little minor official's wife, 'I can't help it, I simply
cannot *bear* breathing the same air as an Asiatic!'

For three weeks he took refuge in outdoor pleasures, riding his
bike around the school, watching the soldiers coming in and out
with cases of grenades, inspecting the 1930 trucks with their flat
radiators, asking the soldiers about the speeds they could make.
With Felix he climbed the Red Mountain, from the top of which
you could see most of the city, where suburban families went on
Saturday afternoons to fly kites (he had never had a kite) and to
ski or sledge in winter. He took breakneck bike rides along the
steep paths of the Red Mountain with Felix, happy to keep up
with this 'whole' man though he himself was only a half man,
confident that he had the muscles and the nerve of an Aryan,
speaking the crudest slang, the jargon of the toughs who lived on
the other side of the drill ground, a place that even Bradovic, a
gang leader who was two years older than they, his eyes blue and
insolent, his chin covered with blond hair, would not cross at
night unless he was armed with a long key 'to knock their teeth
out with'.

To be accepted by Felix and the big boys like Bradovic,
Kalmar, Urmann, Schoeps (whose father, a gigantic butcher,
declared that in his youth he could pull himself up three times
with one arm and that even now he could do five pull-ups on his
butcher's hooks), he had imposed a discipline on himself 'whose
severity deserved a better cause', his father said. He had learned
to spit considerable distances (from the pavement to the other side

of the first tram line), and on his good days he could beat
Felix. For months he rode off every day, alone on his bicycle,
clocking the time it took him to cover a certain distance, pedal-
ling as fast as he could, determined to beat his record, to beat the
weakness he sensed within himself, which he somehow identified
with his Jewish blood. He was determined to toughen himself,
running uphill (he had been teased once by a governess who did
not like him and who claimed, when he was eleven, that he
couldn't climb to the top of a tiny grassy slope), trying to run a
kilometre in less than three minutes, carrying heavy stones,
exercising every night by doing pull-ups on the cupboard, then
on a trapeze hung between two rooms. Overcoming his weakness, his own fear, and the continual criticism of his parents, he
acquired skills which made him acceptable among the strongest
of the other boys, and to be accepted by them meant more to
him than to be accepted by his parents. He did not want to be
the prodigy his mother hoped would be the decoration of her
family; just a boy like the rest, accepted by the rest; each triumph
he won from them gave him a liberating revenge over his family.

Accepted, acceptable, not loved, admired, followed. Accepted
by the groups that had formed at school according to the different roads they took to go home. Accepted by Bradovic ever since
they had fought a duel with T-squares one evening and his own
had broken and he had gone on with only a stump of wood, his
hand bleeding; accepted by Felix ever since he had learned to
throw snowballs far and hard and, hiding behind the rampart of
shovelled snow, had aimed so well that his snowball had
smashed against the windscreen right in the driver's face and the
furious driver had stopped to look for them with his car lamp.
Accepted, but without any friend or confidant; even Felix, whom
he liked more than the rest, took sides against him when anyone
began teasing him; even Felix, when he felt like it, called him
'Jew, Jew, lick-my-ass Jew!' a chant that put an end to all possible discussion, a definitive statement which Felix considered of
great subtlety and which he delighted in using instead of an
answer or an explanation.

They, and Felix above all, were the way they were; they had

their values and their certitudes; they had something like a nature (energies they used as it pleased them, muscles they didn't dream of increasing, a body they lived comfortably with). He, by nature, had none. What they were naturally he had become by having wanted to; he had chosen his models: to be tough, muscular and rough like Andreas Hofer, the Tyrolean hero of the resistance against Napoleon, a man who was one with his rocky country, to the point of having dolomite in his head probably; to be a piece of nature, united with it, insensible to everything except its own energies, participating in a cosmic force. He could become this model, the 'whole' man, only by a patient *ascesis*; in other words, he would never become it at all, he wanted it because he wasn't it – and he could only want it because what he wanted was radically Other than himself. He wanted to become Other than himself, and because he was never this Other *for* himself, he attached the greatest importance to the exterior signs of his transformation, to his appearance-for-others. The limbs and muscles others had he made for himself, teaching himself to walk on the outer edges of his soles to make his legs bowed (the Tyrolean peasant, the 'prolo', the football player are bowlegged), doing exercises to develop his thigh and calf muscles; rolling up his *Lederhosen* so that these muscles were quite visible, and rolling down his socks or better still not wearing them so as not to break the curve of his leg. His pastimes were never gratuitous; bicycling, running, swimming, sunbathing were not activities with pleasure as their goal, but work he deliberately imposed on himself to increase his capital of muscles and tan. He did not choose his bicycle routes for pleasure or for the beauty of the landscape, but to add a fixed number of daily kilometres to his speedometer; during vacation with his grandparents, at thirteen or fourteen, he left the house every day after lunch, not to explore the countryside but to cover the same circuit ten times – a circuit including a steep hill, then a descent spoiled by big rocks and bogs which necessitated constant use of the brakes.

His only satisfaction was in overcoming himself, and he felt defeated as soon as he indulged the slightest personal desire or preference. From his twelfth or thirteenth year, the beginning of his simultaneous conversion to Nazism and to a puritanical Catholicism, he had imposed a rigorous discipline upon himself, which consisted of systematically doing the opposite of whatever he was spontaneously inclined to do (taking the route to school he found most boring; not eating what he liked and eating what he didn't; praying for all humanity but not for himself or his parents, who, in the eyes of God, had no particular claim to grace, being only mortals like the rest) and offering to God the pleasures he refused himself, though without feeling exonerated even so. For to have any claim on the grace of God, he should be deep in prayer all the time and not only in the morning, in the toilet (the only place where he was certain not to be seen, where he said three Paters and three Aves in Latin until his father, suspecting God knows what practices, got in the habit of pounding on the toilet door as soon as he had taken refuge inside and shouting furiously, 'There he sits again like a brooding hen!' – a habit which provoked him to hide, when he wanted to pray, behind the wardrobe in the corridor, then, doubting the effectiveness of his prayers, to say them once more on the way to school), and at night, kneeling under his covers, to make sure he wouldn't be caught. At any moment he might wake up guiltily and remind himself, 'I'm not praying', so that instead of a prayer, for which he lacked serenity, he would offer God some expiatory act, like not looking at the cars in the street, keeping his eyes fixed on his feet.

Yet he loved God no more than his physical exercises. It was impossible for him to conceive God, who remained a terrifying and jealous abstraction (in short, the God of the Jews), and nothing he learned in catechism class established Him as a clement and smiling saviour. 'God sees all, knows all, judges all.' He was living transfixed by this judge's stare with its terrible and unknown requirements; before God he felt always guilty and about to be punished, unless he was imposing some privation on himself and overcoming his desires.

A religious *ascesis* (though not a mystical one – not loving himself, he felt despised by God and could therefore neither love nor communicate with God but only exorcize Him), a physical *ascesis*, the feeling of his own minimal value and the attribution of value to what was most alien to him; aspects of a fundamental attitude of refusal, as if, incapable of accepting himself for what he was (incapable of establishing his value in his real situation), he could reach salvation only by conforming to alien norms and rules, waiting for an impossible transfiguration; as if he had either to efface himself (as he did before God) or make himself radically Other in order to accede to some dignity, even a minor one, as if the fact of remaining himself despite these exercises were a failure, a kind of inner corruption.

So I was wrong to think I could say that in 1938, at the age of fifteen, he was on the verge of integrating himself, and that the Anschluss *again* flung him into exile. The truth is that the events of the period made him conscious of an exile from which in fact he had never emerged, obliged him to admit that the bridges between himself and the others were cut, to assume this separation which he was making such heroic efforts to overcome. That these efforts were futile precisely because of their voluntary nature he had always, deep down, suspected. He knew he could fool some people, imitate a prolo and, by the slang formulas, the guttural noises, the careless and sometimes shabby clothes, magically invoke a proletarian universe (that is, a universe exempt from bourgeois artifices and familial complications, a universe he would enter as an orphan, a child without known origins, therefore without a Jewish father and without an Aryan mother, therefore simply a man judged by his merits and strength alone), but he also felt he lacked something essential in order to deceive the prolos and himself: the boldness, the conviction, the confidence in the solidity of his role – that is, in himself. That a fault subsisted at the heart of his being, undermining the whole structure, he had realized whenever it was a question of employing physical force and the acquired slang formulas. He knew that in relation to his weight his strength was at least equal to that of the huskiest of his schoolfellows, and his agility, maintained by daily exercises, was probably hard to beat; he outstripped them all when it came to climbing poles of ropes

without using his legs; he was fifth, and first in his school, in the
school swimming championships; he could throw a stone or a
ball as far as anyone; and yet he was among the worst handball
players in his class, completely worthless in any team sport. (The
most popular of these consisted of throwing the ball at a member
of the opposite side; if you hit him, he was 'killed', eliminated,
unless he caught the ball in the air. This brutal game terrified
him; he made no effort to catch the ball and tried to take refuge
in the crowd that huddled against the radiator pipes or to
conceal himself behind good catchers. The ball frightened him;
so much so that several times it hit him in the face, and, his eyes
smarting with dust, his face burning, he felt on the verge of tears.
It hit him several times in the genitals too; he ran from it like a
rabbit from the hunter, feared it so much that often he was the
only 'survivor' and had to go through another torture: trying to
avoid a 'death' he knew was ultimately fatal. Lacking confidence
in his aim, he felt embarrassed by the ball when he managed to
get hold of it, and he thought only of getting rid of it as soon as
possible, throwing it in no particular direction.) He was worse
still in any exercise that demanded boldness. Brutal and cynical
prolos like Bradovic or Kalmar were particularly good at the
saddle jump – raised one notch each time the 'horse' was to be
cleared by a kind of scaring flight, clapping of both hands on the
cold leather to avoid hitting your coccyx against the farther edge
of the 'animal'. It was all right at the beginning, but as soon as
the horse was several notches up, his fear of hurting himself (it
had happened once) made his knees buckle and he leaped without conviction, landing on the horse beneath the contemptuous
gaze of the gym teacher. Failing where those weaker than he
succeeded, he knew that only his cowardice was responsible.
And he was so cowardly that his other performances passed
unnoticed; he was classified as a bad athlete. Only in the spring
of 1939 did the gym teacher discover his resources, the occasion
an exercise of pure strength: hanging from the bar, they were to
pull themselves up as often as possible – six for Bradovic, seven
for Kalmar and only five for Felix. 'Try for five', the gym teacher
said to him, probably suspecting his ambition. Then, under the

astonished eyes of the whole class, starting slowly in order to save his strength, while the gym teacher counted, he did thirteen pull-ups. He was in ecstasy. Leutner, who came after him, beat his record with fourteen. But he knew he could have beaten Leutner if *he* had come afterward. The instructor's remarks soon annihilated his triumph. He didn't say, 'First Leutner with fourteen, second G with thirteen.' He said, 'The big surprise today is that G did thirteen pull-ups.' The big surprise. They hadn't expected so many from him; he was not particularly admired for his prowess and more was not asked of him later on. It was really surprising that someone as mediocre should have given such a performance. And he knew that the contempt such surprise implied was justified. He had the strength but not the guts, the matter but not the spirit of a good athlete; his athlete's body was paradoxically inhibited by a timid soul. His strength could only *be*, apply itself reflexively to his own body, in exercises without danger; it could not act, it was turned in on itself, narcissistically, but without a basis in the world, without a hold on it. A strength turned back on itself, ascetic and voluntary, perfectly summing up the fundamental sterility of his person. Rootless strength, abstract as his thoughts were to be later; what he lacked was transcendence, or, if you prefer, life. Such strength could function only by holding the world at a distance (like his intellect later on) but could not embrace the world.

He was tempted to say then, and again recently, that this deep inconsistency, this cowardice consisting of a lack of courage rather than any real fear, was inherent and inevitable in his situation. Caught between a mother and a father incompatible not only because of their origins, their religion, their 'race', but particularly because of their temperaments and values, he had no foundation anywhere, no point of view he could adopt as profoundly his own; he was tempted by all the roles the world offered, while at the same time being unable to commit himself to any of them. In this false situation, false from every point of view, he was condemned to invent an individual truth at the same time as being incapable of inventing one. This is the explanation of his inconsistency, but not his excuse. For others in an

analogous situation (Mauthner, Weiss, Hoffmann, later on)
were, on the contrary, noisy, combative, energetic, and therefore
cynical, but they overcame their contradiction by ambitions
(social ambitions – to 'arrive' and impress others – in Weiss and
Mauthner, ambition to be a better Nazi than the Aryans in
Hoffmann, who was killed in 1941 on the Russian front) which,
though they resolved nothing, provided them with a façade, a
solidity, a surface which he lacked. And before searching, by
means of a deeper analysis, for the origin of this lack of surface, I
want to describe the events after which he finally renounced all
attempts to acquire one.

   The summer of 1938 went by rather well. And he had not had
the eyes to see what was going badly. His father had worries and
his mother referred to them, said business was bad, but that was
usual enough. Someone with the badge of an old party member
began coming to the house at night for conferences with his
father, whose 'partner' he was going to be to keep the business
from being 'Aryanized' (that is, appropriated by an Aryan). He
went swimming in the public pool with K, a little red-headed
boy who wore a Hitlerjugend uniform and who, of modest
family, had developed a crush on him ever since he had seen
their living room. With motives that were doubtless ulterior, his
mother had one evening asked K, in his velvet shorts and Hitlerjugend belt, to sit in one of the deep salon armchairs, had offered
him a glass of something and begun making conversation. K was
disturbed and, Hitlerjugend though he was, began saying that
the racial laws should be taken with a grain of salt. With K, Felix
and the others, he swam two hundred yards in the pool one day,
after which he made a bet, out of breath as he was, that he could
still do a certain number of push-ups. They took him up on it, he
won the bet, and K told him he was quite a guy and it was too
bad he couldn't join the Hitlerjugend.

   Just before the vacation, the Conservatory student who gave
him piano lessons showed up one afternoon in an SA uniform.
He spoke to his mother, gave him his harmony lesson and told
him this would be their last session. After the lesson they went
out into the street together. The young SA teacher seemed

uneasy, and as they passed a fence he said, 'In here', and pushed him through an opening into a sunny empty lot. It was warm, and the young teacher (his name was Opitz or something of the kind) put his hand on his shoulder and said, his blond forehead dripping with sweat, 'I'd like to go on teaching you – you're a talented boy. I think you could become a good musician. I'd like to teach you counterpoint. But you have to understand, I'm in the SA, I can't let myself be caught giving lessons to a half-caste. I'm really awfully sorry. And promise you'll go on working at your music. You promise?'

Keeping his hand on his shoulder, he made him promise. They shook hands, 'between men', in silence. 'Go out first and walk ahead', Opitz said. 'We shouldn't be seen together. Goodbye.'

On the way home, he really felt sorry for that nice Opitz who had looked so embarrassed. And he decided he should try to become a great musician. Because there would be no more lessons, he began practising quite regularly for a few weeks; his piano had acquired the signification of a challenge. He played (badly – he never acquired the minimal agility to interpret in the true sense of the word) during a few warm afternoons instead of going swimming, and the music he wrung from the instrument, staring at the maple leaves that shimmered in the sunshine outside the window, was like a triumphant affirmation against the world. Afterward he stopped playing; vacation came, and after the vacation, no more piano.

He spent that vacation in the village where their maid had been born, in the house of some farmers. A tiny village some twenty kilometres from Salzburg; when you came out of a woods there was a road, and on each side of the road some low brick houses, a few fields, and some peat bogs that were no longer worked. The farmer had a clubfoot (a war wound), a squint-eyed wife, a senile mother, three children, a one-story house, a little barn, six hens, two hogs, perhaps an acre of peat bog, two of poor wheat, and a pasture. He arrived on the farm just as they were bringing in the wheat (cut by sickle) and the next day he offered to help thresh it. For three days, he threshed the wheat with a

flail, an astonishing tool that turned in his hand and over his
head and made his palms smooth and calloused. Three days of
threshing, one of winnowing. Then a week of transporting peat
in a wheelbarrow over ditches full of water bridged by shaky,
narrow planks. The first time, he dumped the whole barrow into
the ditch; later it went better, the farmer was pleased with him,
and he happy because of it. After the peat, there was the hay
which he cut with a scythe, careful not to nick the legs of the man
cutting in front of him. A few kilometres away there was a little
lake to which he bicycled to swim, some woods, some abandoned brickyards, wagons that had once been used to carry the
peat and on which, after pushing them up their still intact rails,
he could coast down with amazing speed. For a long time he
remembered such things with great happiness; he had virtually
forgotten himself and by manual work exteriorized himself in a
product (wheat, hay, peat; food, fuel, wealth) whose indisputable
value would permit him to re-enter the society of men in the
simplest, most direct way.

I know, this dream of simplicity was sheer romanticism and
his 'great happiness' of the period was not unalloyed. He could
have escaped into field labour only if he had been born a farmer,
and the uncertain joy he derived from it was more nostalgia than
anything else. Threshing the wheat and carrying blocks of peat,
he discovered the elementary needs which make all men alike; it
was a way of returning to a human generality beyond morality.
He wanted to be the servant of elementary man in his generality,
a labour force producing indisputable vital wealth, a power
unquestioned as to its origins or its destination because all men
are equal before fire and bread, equally cold in winter, and
hungry without food; to work toward the satisfaction of
elemental needs. (A temptation he has not dismissed to this day,
since he often dreams of working as an agronomist, as a brick-
layer in a Communist country, since he can fascinate himself
with the statistics of national and world production, of five-year
plans, big dams and the problems of American surplus; since the
least quantity of food is something sacred for him, an image of
wealth connected with an incident that crystallized whole visions

of the world: at the age of nine or so he had made a little ball of bread crumbs and flicked it off the table after a meal. 'What's the matter with you?' his father had shouted. 'Food is not to be played with! There are millions of men starving all over the world!' He didn't play with bread after that, and when he saw American films where people broke eggs over each other's head and threw pies in each other's face, he grew furious with the film and the stupidity of the laughing audience, his heart pounding with indignation at all that food wasted, with all the millions of men starving all over the world.) Starting from humanity's elementary needs, starting from the naked body, emaciated or gleaming with sweat, starting from the body's labour, its power and its wretchedness, without decoration or clothing (for with them begin the differences and the hierarchies, the myths, mystiques and exclusivities, the rules and social values), directly at grips with *things*, stripping men with his eyes and wondering what they would look like naked and judging them consequently ('Did he have a potbelly?' he asked his mother when she came home from a lecture by Amundsen. 'A little.' 'What do you mean, a little – like Papa?' 'A little less,' she said, 'just a little stomach.' He couldn't respect a man, no matter how great his prestige, if he had a potbelly, and his admiration for Alexander of Macedonia was due to the powerful musculature of his statue), his was a way of putting in parentheses the whole social and cultural nexus, the origin of his complications and his exclusion, getting rid, through the naturalist or materialist perspective, of the social, racial and religious moralities, the sources of his alienation, his laceration and his guilt feelings.

Elemental needs, elemental works: a way of making a *tabula rasa* of history and the distinctions between man and man; hunger, sweat and toil: means of access to a forbidden fraternity, the nostalgia for which ultimately led him to the extreme left. But even then he already felt that the elemental humanity whose destitution he would share – being destitute of any sociocultural roots himself – existed nowhere, that the wretchedest members of the proletariat were more impregnated with culture than he (that the ideal proletariat existed no more than the man of perfect

simplicity, Gide's quest for whom was to appeal to him to
greatly), that the farmers of Salzburg judged him and scorned
him by norms he would never satisfy – out of scorn for 'city
people' and especially for people from Vienna, because of his
very excess of good will, and because of his education. He could
do a farmer's work as well as he liked, but in the farmer's eyes it
wasn't *his* work, and because he hadn't been born here in this
village, didn't have it in his blood, didn't love it in the same way
as the natives, he could never be one of them.

He felt this, and when there was no more work to do he began
imposing tasks upon himself again: to bicycle to the next village
every morning and then back up the steep hillside without putting his feet on the ground; to read five pages of Nietzsche every
night (*The Birth of Tragedy*) without understanding a word and
getting through one English lesson of the Langenscheidt
method, which consisted of learning a story of Dickens' by heart.
In short, every task he accomplished was changed into an escape,
became a struggle to attain a result that was entirely objective
(muscles, impersonal knowledge, elemental wealth), whose
objectivity became a source of separation, since he no longer
recognized himself in his work and could project himself in it
only by virtue of a rational will hardened against itself.

'Should I get a divorce?' his mother asked, when they were
back in Vienna. She embarked on a long explanation: that the
business could be put in her name if she got a divorce; that she
could keep the apartment; that she could even declare her
husband not to be the father of her children if she could find an
accomplice. 'I wouldn't want you to reproach me some day for
having stayed with your father and not having tried everything to
save the Business.' Of course he and his sister had said, 'Stay
with Father.' The Business meant nothing to them except
endless boredom and bother, and they were quite incapable of
imagining the future. Their father had grown thinner; one night
the man with the old party member's badge came to the house;
there was a long discussion; the man had decided to take over
the Business for himself, and their father, his face grey, had
collapsed on the sofa, gasping for breath, on the verge of a

syncope. A week later, they were evicted from the apartment; a party official coveted it, and since a non-Aryan couple was living there, he had priority.

His father's illness and expulsion did not particularly affect him. He watched it all as a series of events that didn't concern him. He was incapable of taking sides with the weak or the strong because, wanting to be strong, he despised the weak and, rejected by the strong into the camp of the weak, he detached himself from the latter in order not to feel weak and lost and secretly allowed himself the chance to change camps, in spite of everything, by the force of his perseverance. He had still not broken with the Nazis (this rupture was a late one and occurred under conditions which hardly had the value of a choice), he maintained a troubled complicity with them whenever it was a question of taking sides, as if putting himself verbally on their side could free him from being, in fact, in the opposite camp, as if his subjective complicity magically kept open a path toward 'salvation' or at least maintained an escape from his true condition. He was pleased to see his uncle on his mother's side wearing the swastika of the *Reichskulturkammer* in his capacity as director of a theatrical agency that procured engagements for performers, and by this avuncular badge he contested the Jewishness he inherited on his paternal side.

This one-way contestation (for he never dreamed of contesting the maternal Aryanness by the paternal Jewishness, thus choosing to endure this Jewishness as an external curse which was often identified with this misfortune of having this particular father) requires a commentary already too long postponed. This odd family, which was divided against itself and whose divisions he had had to internalize, must be described. Described objectively. Having told himself this for some time already, he is struck by the egocentric character of his account, each impulse toward description breaking off or dissolving at once into considerations about himself, as if he were quite incapable of extending his consciousness outside the magic circle in which it confined itself, incapable of coming to grips with empirical reality. This is quite significant; his memory provides him only vague, pale recollections, not that he has a bad memory (quite the contrary), but because he has never been able to live events without reflective mediation. He has always watched himself living; he has never taken things for what they were. The reason I have just offered for this (or one of the reasons, for there are certainly others) is this necessity to contest: to contest his father by his mother, his Jewishness by his Catholicism, his Catholicism by his Jewishness. There was nothing simple or immediate for him, each moment always referred to its opposite, nothing was what it was but remained divided from itself by an elsewhere he had to shift into in order to be facing whatever it was. He lived events by his interrogative meditation on the attitude he was to adopt toward them, as when he watched Hitler's triumphant entry into the city from the balcony of his father's office, seized by the fever of the hysterical crowd he would have liked to join, at the same time infected by the anguish of his father, who already felt like a stranger in his own office and stared at the big safe as if his enemies were about to empty it; as when he watched the Jewish woman forced to wash the SA man's car, hesitating to feel sorry for her and hesitating to hate her torturers, wondering if his pity wouldn't make him into the cowardly and weak 'Yid' he refused to become, and if his hatred wouldn't prove he lacked the stuff to be strong.

I don't know precisely what occurred between the mother and the maternal grandfather at this period. But the latter, surnamed Yaroslav because of his adoration for Czechoslovakia and Prague ('Learn Czech, my boy! Wherever you go, when you say, "*Nazdar!*" there will be people to answer, "*Nazdar pane*", and you'll be accepted'), had urged her to get rid of her Jewish husband. 'Think of your children', he had said. 'What will you gain by hanging on to your scruples about Jacob? Jacob's ruined. Take my advice, believe me, or you'll regret it.'

Yaroslav had never liked Jacob much, and he fought a series of epic battles with Maria. He was full of resentment against this proud daughter who claimed to 'raise' herself above the family milieu, and Maria, in order not to have to blush for her father, always claimed he was endowed with fathomless wisdom.

'There's no one better than Yaroslav. Remember what our papa told us – if you find something that doesn't belong to you, even if it's only a pin, don't touch it!' 'Just as my Yaroslav says, don't worry, one way or another things always straighten out in the end.' These commonplaces were offered as though they were the pinnacle of wisdom and ended in Grandfather being called 'Saint Yaroslav'. He had been born in some village of Bohemia and with his tiny, chubby wife to whom he had given four children (one had died in infancy) he had led the most ordinary *vie de bohème*. He had been a singer ('an opera singer', his mother said), a third-rate one to judge from his continual wanderings between Dresden, Leipzig, Nuremberg, and provincial engagements, often living with his whole family in one room that sometimes had a ceiling so low they could reach up and swat the cockroaches swarming across it, sometimes near a railroad viaduct under which his mother had played in the stream.

Yaroslav had settled in Vienna in 1918 as 'director of a theatrical agency', for, having made his debut as a tenor and retired as a bass, he had finally lost his voice. 'I went to work as a secretary,' his mother had told him, 'and God knows I was a dutiful daughter. I brought home every penny I earned, and even in winter I walked to the office to save the ten groschen the streetcar would have cost.' She had been a pretty, dark girl, with strong legs and severe glances despite the inviting smile that revealed two rows of regular white teeth. She must have had her fill of not taking the tram and of eating bad food, and she certainly had a devouring ambition to rise above her modest station in life. In short, she married her boss, fifteen years older than she (she was twenty-four), after violent scenes with her Yaroslav, who shouted, 'You can't marry that Jew!' Maria was a stubborn girl. Not only did she marry that Jew, a timid man with few social gifts, a niggling, scrupulous 'agent' in his rich brother-in-law's crate-and-barrel business, but she even persuaded her Jewish husband, despised by his Aryan in-laws, to put money in Yaroslav's 'theatrical agency'; the Jew owed them that to deserve Maria.

Convinced she had bridged the gulf, had entered a superior

social order, Maria began by getting some culture: she read
many of the books people talked about and studied works on art
as well; she took piano lessons in order to be able to play for her
guests. And she refused to see her horrible Jewish in-laws
(especially fat Anna, who had a partnership in the business), who
on their side spoke bitterly of this pretentious *Goyin* who was glad
enough to take their money but who put on her contemptuous
airs before the *Juden* ('Jacob, why are you still hanging around
with those *Juden*?'). Jacob must have soon realized that he would
regret this marriage. Youngest son (or almost) of a numerous
family of Moravian landowners (property, houses, trucking), he
had been sacrificed to his brothers. He would not inherit the
property because it was being given to the oldest brother; he
would not be allowed to study because Oscar was more talented;
he would not go into the trucking business because Bruno
wanted to. Finally, to be got rid of, he was sent to Sister Anna
(rich, fat, beringed, covered with pearls and lace, brooding over
her wealth amid her flabby flesh like a mollusc in its shell,
married to a tiny, sickly, wizened man the war had apparently
made rich). Weak, unsure of himself, conscious of his limitations
and his ignorance, Jacob needed to be protected, respected, and
tenderly encouraged as well. It was probably the advice giver, the
counsellor in Maria that attracted him; in this young and
energetic woman who never hesitated and seemed ready to
swallow the whole world, he must have sought a moral support.
And she probably saw in him an instrument of her ambitions to
rise socially.

Spineless, dedicated to his routine out of fear of the unknown
('I don't care about what I don't understand', a saying magnifi-
cent for its naïveté and its complacent timidity, characteristic of
the man Jacob, resigned to his mediocrity, making it into a virtue
by claiming it was modesty and defiantly opposing it to the too
urgent or intelligent interlocutor before whom, in reality, he
desperately tried to put on a good front, especially with regard to
his son), vulnerable, having decided once and for all that greatness and ambition were other people's business (so much so that
he believed the great and the ambitious were of a different

essence, professed his respect for the old nobility, remained attached to the Emperor and the Empire, addressed nobles by their titles and bowed before them, distinguished the ranks of the Army and humbly admired his 'intellectual' brother, Oscar, an intolerably arrogant man), Jacob probably dreamed of some quiet corner and a life without incident when, at thirty-nine, he happened to meet this young woman who won him by guile.

I shall describe elsewhere what their relations were or might have been on the personal level. I'm not sure I can explain their behaviour in detail, particularly the motivation of Maria's icy ambition, always tricked out in excessive bursts of sentiment. Having known her only as an adult and receiving only from her what he knows of her childhood, he sees her as an iceberg of which the greatest and heaviest portion remains below the surface, while that which shows gives the impression of a density, an opacity difficult to comprehend. Maria was convinced that her place was at the top of the social pyramid and that consequently the world owed her such a place. During the first years of her marriage, she insisted on dazzling her parents and her brothers and sisters with her opulence every Sunday, as if by exhibiting this wealth, exaggerating it, she took revenge upon the 'ordinary' family she had come from, the family which had begrudged her tram tickets. It was from a need to feel 'superior', a member of the same race as the ancient nobility whose values must have dominated her childhood, that she too respected titles, ranks and manners, invented a grandfather who was a count, perpetuated her father's anti-Semitism (fundamentally a resentment, the wretched singer Yaroslav being convinced that his career had been spoiled by the Jewish conspiracy), and persuaded her husband to quarrel with his own family in order to take over and enlarge the Business.

Annoyed by twenty years of boasting and by the arrogance which, from the pinnacle of her 'success', Maria paraded before her family, the latter probably took its long-delayed revenge in 1938 when it retorted, 'Now you see what you get for marrying a Jew. Get out of it by yourself.' It was doubtless out of pride that Maria failed to ask for a divorce, in order not to confess her defeat to her family. But all the same she requested a legal separation, and while she took her children to live in her sister's apartment, Jacob was relegated to a verminous rented room where she visited him one hour a day.

Humiliated, confused, stubborn, Jacob felt that he was being done an absolute and undeserved wrong; consequently, since he was within his rights, he would not budge. To defend himself, become an exile – such actions would have been beneath his dignity; he had no taste for adventure, spoke no foreign language, was terrified by novelty, preferred to be a wreck 'at home' rather than an *arriviste* abroad. To Maria's months and months of pressure to make him go to Brazil, Jacob opposed a child's stubborn refusal. In his hierarchized and formalist universe, Right was on his side ('I have done nothing I cannot answer for'); therefore he would wait with lowered head ('with your Judaic rigidity', Maria called it) for whatever blows were to fall, blows he could scarcely credit, moreover, for the changes occurring around him were so incomprehensible to him that after the war, in 1951, he was still saying, 'I have nothing against this Hitler, and if it weren't for his anti-Semitism, I'd probably vote for him tomorrow. The man restored order, did something for his country.' Respect for titles and ranks, love of order, the necessary basis of the hierarchy which Jacob and Maria had been striving all their life to be admitted to, made their daughter a neurotic girl as convinced as they were that success consists in cutting a figure among 'respectable people' and prompted her (at the price of unknown humiliations and agonies) to frequent throughout the war Nazi bosses, dignitaries and diplomats, from whom she begged impossible positions.

Even as late as November 1938, they were still living from day to day without believing in the catastrophes occurring all around them. Not that they doubted the perversity and the administrative effectiveness of the persecutors of the Jews (the Dachau concentration camp was already sending little boxes of ashes to wives of Jews seized in their own homes); rather, like the persecutors themselves, they were convinced that 'this sort of thing couldn't happen to me'. And why? Well, because when your name is G, when you have 'connections', when you're 'respectable people', you aren't treated like some *Juden* from Galicia; because, when you think the world owes you something and you've always been on the side of order, then you can't be persecuted by a regime of order; because the Nazi persecutors were from among those 'little people' who always tipped their hats to you and with whom you could always settle things by a tip (and Maria was particularly good at impressing her successive concierges by condescending kindnesses and coins pressed into their palms); because, finally, if the rank-and-file Nazis made trouble for you, you could always speak to the big shots of the regime who were not 'of the people' but belonged (or were ambitious to belong) to that same level of 'respectable people' with whom Maria excelled in establishing a flattering class complicity. ('*Entre nous*, Herr Doktor, I know you don't think the way all those hysterics do.')

All the same, by November things began to look bad. At school one day, classes were dismissed at ten o'clock in the morning. Kalmar ran to get wooden bats for the gym and handed them to Urmann, Bradovic, Kamleitner and others. Accompanied by a gang of boys who guessed something was up, they left school and headed toward a square five hundred yards away. Here stood a low yellow house that looked like a farmhouse, and an apartment building put up around 1900, with a dry-goods shop on the ground floor. In the house was a knife grinder's shop run by a man with the interesting name Amadeo Amadei, but it was toward the Oser dry-goods shop that they were headed. It was at the corner. They hesitated for a long moment, then Kalmar rushed forward and smashed his bat against the window. It refused to break. Bradovic and Urmann entered the shop and came out armed with the kind of poles used to pull down the metal shutters at night. Kalmar dashed forward, banging the iron hook of his pole against the glass, fell flat on his back, quickly got up, furious now, and began smashing the shop window with great whacks. They were starting on the second window when the shopkeeper, his face pale, appeared on the doorstep. 'Keep your trap shut or I'll tear your guts

out', Kalmar said threateningly. Two sales-girls came out and
lowered the shutters over the ruined displays. It was only as they
were leaving that he began to suspect that Oser must be a Jew.

It was early, it was snowing, and he decided to walk to Yaroslav's where he had been having his lunch ever since they had
temporarily moved to Uncle Oscar's – the latter was leaving for
Boston. As he came down the Mariahilferstrasse, he saw a
column of smoke on the right, and he headed toward it. In a little
square with low, dirty, peeling façades (looking like the entire
neighbourhood and four fifths of Vienna, stuck here for no
good reason, smelling of poverty, fleas, leaking gas and futility,
with suspicious faces, motheaten coats, uneven pavements, a look
of failure and indolence), a building with a cupola was burning.
It was a funny-looking building with a big portico in which only
one little door was open. Smoky flames were coming out of the
roof and licking the cupola, against which a short steeple
appeared to be leaning. There were some twenty idlers, no fire-
men (what was the Fire Department waiting for, he asked, but no
one answered), and a policeman who said, 'Stand back, the
steeple's going to fall!' but no one moved. He waited a long time
for the steeple to fall; it was only when he got bored and decided
to leave that he noticed two SA men with petrol cans and
suspected that the building was a synagogue and that they had
set it on fire themselves.

The next day he heard that synagogues all over the Reich had
been burned down, Jewish shop windows broken, Jews rounded
up and made to scrub pavements, and that Yankel (his maternal
aunt's boy friend, an antique dealer who wrote pornographic
stories) had been forced to scrub too, and that many Jews had
been arrested and deported. He also heard about the Nuremberg
laws, according to which his father had a vaguely privileged
status as a baptized Jew and the husband of an Aryan mother of
Christian children, who, because of their religion, were half-
castes of the first class (the second class included individuals with
only one Jewish grandparent), whereas they would be classed as
Jews altogether had they not been baptized. His mother took
steps to obtain new birth certificates for her children, for their

father had been baptized in 1930 (upon Maria's insistence; she even had Jacob change his name so that his Jewishness should become less apparent, and paid the sum of one hundred schillings for this service, a considerable amount since they had argued for months on end before paying sixty for a secondhand radio and since he had had to wait years before they bought him a bicycle costing a hundred and ten) and new documents had to be made out on which his father figured as a 'Roman Catholic'.

Jews deported had not come back, wives had received little boxes full of ashes and marked with their husband's names; he no longer had any contact, in class, with Bradovic's gang or with the others, since he now had to cover over eight kilometres on his bicycle to reach school, and he began to regard the militant Nazis as a hostile race capable of smashing his skull because of his two Jewish grandparents. The Nazis were on the other side, the bridges were cut; he was tolerated at school, but grudgingly, and the English teacher, an old party member, 'impartially' asked him sticklers in order not to have to give him the good marks he would otherwise deserve. He began to suspect that the injustices of the history and geography teacher (this dated back two or three years; his face showed that he had called him to the blackboard only to send him back to his seat with a furious look of scorn) had had racial reasons too, and with the teachers changing every week he began to realize that his inadequacy in so many subjects (physics, chemistry, history, geography) was doubtless due in large measure to the ignorance and the mental confusion of his instructors.

A puny wretch, furious and pathetic, regularly bombarded by erasers, chalk, explosions of cherry pits, stink bombs and sneezing powder, until, on the verge of tears, he begged them to listen to him, gave them a course in racial edcation (*Rassenkunde*), showing them dolichocephalic, brachycephalic types, Nordic, Frisian, Baltic, Alpine and Latin races (in hierarchic order), and explaining that Hannibal, since he had proved to be a great general, must have been a blond, blue-eyed Druse; similarly that Christ, since he had blue eyes and blond hair (in German paintings), was Aryan; and so forth. The rural, Alpine, artisanal,

peasant and family values of the Catholic regime (the so-called
New Era of Dollfuss) gave way to the heroic values of Germanic
mythology, blood, force, the clan, the Wagnerian grandeur, the
cult of the leader, discipline, and the hierarchy, the 'useful' (and
not Promethean) sacrifice to a nation whose superhuman greatness was reflected upon the sons it was devouring; the hollow,
exalted style (à la Goebbels) became obligatory, and the compo-
sition richest in pompous commonplaces passed for the best.

Only the Greek professor, Sacher, a greying, clubfooted giant
with a jagged nose, resisted this inflation of words and senti-
ments; his severe grey eyes showed what seemed to be a secret
benevolence when, sitting on the edge of his desk, he made G
conjugate irregular verbs or translate a passage from *The Iliad.*
The incarnation of justice, inaccessible to persuasion, impertur-
bably advancing through his Homer, more methodical and
demanding than any other teacher (he insisted they know every
verb and vocable learned during three years), Sacher was the man
he liked most without ever having exchanged a word with him; he
dreamed of calling for him as he left school if he ever was rich
enough to have a car when he grew up. But he already doubted
that a man like Sacher could stay in school for long, opposing his
equitable rigour to the prejudicial treatment the leaders of the
Hitlerjugend enjoyed, being excused from classes when it served
the 'responsibilities of their charge' and given good marks by the
other teachers.

He felt the world closing over him and, alone now, absorbed
himself in three activities: his bicycle, music and reading. The
bicycle had become his chief instrument of penetration and
domination. Astride it every morning at seven-twenty with the
same delight, he was alone and victorious, cutting through the
city for over eight kilometres and at a speed he never let fall
below twenty-five kilometres an hour, absorbing the jolts from
the bad paving by inflating his tyres to something less than
capacity, and reaching school at seven-forty, exhilarated by the
speed and the risks taken at the crossroads, at the red lights and
on the snowy highway where the motorcycles and the military
trucks made the laws. These solitary rides were a revenge on the

city, on the sparkling chromium of the Luftwaffe daggers, on the
black daggers of the SS and their shiny, echoing boots, their fearful elegance of men Aryan to the seventh generation, entitled to
scrutinize everyone's life with the fixed, impassive eye of a robot;
the masking of their flesh (and therefore their humanity and their
consciousness) entirely in black made them into unforeseeable
and sacred instruments of a secret and supreme power. The
earth which they arrogantly strode across he barely brushed over
with his tyres; and unlike the Wehrmacht motorcycles and cars,
he took possession of the streets by the work of his muscles,
realizing in their effort the configuration of a city they only knew
at a distance and on the surface. The *ascesis* of his own recreation
changed its meaning. It was no longer a victory over himself and
the voluntary construction of a new being with neither race nor
origin on the ruins of the old; it was also a challenge to and a
victory over the people, a conquest of this city which, crossing it
so often, he began to love, a way of getting rooted physically in
the very soil that was being morally alienated from him, an
acquisition of a carnal citizenship constituting a kind of antidote
to the Jewishness that he knew circulated in his veins and that he
imagined as an invading germ swelling his flesh, sprouting black
hairs and fat at the joints, thickening the noble parts of the body.
Jewishness, for him, was essentially passive, the dead weight of
facticity – that chancrous proliferation – paralyzing his transcendence. He did not imagine that a Jew could be slim, agile,
graceful, athletic; he identified Aryan values with the highest
vital values, with the nobility of the body charged with energy –
not because he had ever met a single Aryan who incarnated all
the values of this ideal type (they sometimes approached it, and
even when they were far from it they could claim these qualities
by the mere fact that they could invoke their Aryanness against
him), but because he had learned to assimilate Jewishness to
unredeemable facticity (and this by virtue of his refusal of his
own Jewishness, a pure obstacle, a dimension of being he could
in no way put to advantage) and Aryanness to vital value. It
seemed to him that everything he refused in himself was
besmirched with Jewishness and everything to which he aspired

was aureoled with Aryanness. He had permitted a dichotomy to establish itself within him, where the Aryan crossed swords with the Jew like God with the powers of darkness. It is tempting, of course, to explain starting from this his puritanical and frigid ways: refusing Jewishness, an aspect of his facticity impossible to assume, he would have to refuse his entire facticity, since you cannot refuse yourself halfway – rot cannot remain only partial, but necessarily pervades the whole being and must be hunted out in all its dimensions. Though tempting, this explanation cannot be a final one; the discovery of his Jewishness as an original stain might not have poisoned him altogether and motivated an *ascesis* dedicated to overcome it if, at the very moment this discovery occurred, he had not already placed himself in a situation of inferiority and vital non-value. Rather than as an original motivation, the discovery of his Jewishness through the derision of others complicated and confirmed a choice of inferiority and culpability already made, a choice which rendered him receptive to that derision – he felt it was well founded. So his drama had to be as follows: Derided for his Jewishness because of his real weaknesses, and derided for his weaknesses because of his Jewishness, he chose to impute the weaknesses to his Jewishness and thereby to give them a sub-stratum that was both biological and metaphysical. He decided at a certain period (probably around twelve, an age when he began seeing a good deal of a Nazi pederast who provoked in him an ambition for virile values and made him regard his own weaknesses with horror) that he could shed his inconsistency, his cowardice and the inferiority in which he had established himself only on condition that he suppress his Jewishness at the same time. This was to render the conversion impossible from the outset and to bar all paths toward salvation; it was to postulate that he could change only by becoming Other, to strive for a metaphysical metamorphosis pursued by an ascetic will which did not affect the profound basis of his choice and therefore remained exterior to him, in no way capable of accomplishment, condemning him forever to renew the experiment of his failure. Rather than the determining motive of his isolation and his weaknesses, his Jewishness thus became their alibi; he had done everything under the sun to get rid of them, without success. The very manner – quite voluntaristic – which he had adopted from the outset rendered success impossible. And it was no good wondering if he could have integrated and asserted himself under different historical conditions, with a different racial origin. Would he have even tried to change himself in the direction of self-assertion if his bastardy had not guaranteed the failure of his undertaking and assured him that he would always be inferior and subject? Supposing he had been Aryan, would he not have found other biological obstacles to his emancipation? An idle question, but one which illuminates the meaning of my remarks: Jewishness and the experience of Nazism were occasions which confirmed him in an original attitude and which he exploited to the latter's benefit. Historical objectivity was deflected to the advantage of a prehistoric choice in which its truth* was reflected, its signification accounting for him, for its objective meaning. He was not a victim of the event. The event was the occasion for him to victimize himself.

A reactionary theory? It is no theory; this time, it is a certainty. And to prove that the truth is never reactionary, I shall add this: Objectively, a wrong was done him; but he had chosen to deserve this wrong subjectively. The reactionary is not an

---

*Morel later suggested this idea to me: The first infantile attitude ('the constituted', as Morel calls it) might be the 'blurred reflection' of the bastard condition. And would that not be why this first attitude, motivated by the situation of objective bastardy, confirmed itself upon the discovery of this situation – even more, seized upon the situation as the objective truth of an attitude which had hitherto seemed quite individual and contingent? This would constitute the explanation of the feeling of 'miraculous coincidence'.

Indeed, until the age of seven, he had felt null and inferior and guilty without quite knowing why (because, in particular, of his mother's exorbitant requirements). Then, with his Jewishness, he found a solid basis for this feeling. But if this reason suddenly seemed determinant, it is because it was indeed the real one even before he knew it.

– His mother had married a Jew whom she did not forgive for being Jewish;
– the fact of having married a Jew opposed her aristocratic ambitions while at the same time it permitted her to satisfy them in part;

individual who recognizes that it has been thus and so; the reactionary is an individual who believes he deserves injustice and
who is thereby deserving it in fact. In order to combat injustice
effectively and to recognize its arbitrary quality, he would have
had to avoid being its accomplice. Yet he *was* its accomplice.
Effectiveness in combat requires belief in the possibility of
winning; he did not believe in this possibility; he was beaten
before he ever began to fight.

This truth, of which the above is the subjective aspect, has
also, however, a historical aspect. I have said that his revolt
against his weaknesses was made in bad faith, because it was a
revolt against an ineffaceable Jewishness. I have said he was
beaten in advance, by himself in the first place, because he had
chosen the very victory which was, of all those possible, the one
victory forbidden him. But what other victory could he have
chosen? Vienna between 1934 and 1938 was a city heading for
catastrophe, first amputated of its empire, then from faith in its
own possibilities of survival, finally from its democratic liberties –
therefore from the possibility of giving the present a meaning.
Feeling itself sliding toward the abyss, toward nullity and
oblivion, it tried to keep itself from living, as if that could also
keep it from falling in ruins. It clung to its own remains and
desperately tried to warm its corpse by the cult of memory, by

---

 – this Jewish father was, in his own family and in his own house, the 'poor
relation' despite his relative wealth, continually harangued, shoved, nagged at;
 – the law, at home, was his mother's law, and his father represented failure
and forfeiture.
 And for those reasons:
 – his mother monopolized her son to make of him a virile aristocratic super-
Aryan whose handsome bearing would satisfy her own social ambitions and
relieve her of the compromise she had had to accept;
 – the son, incapable of satisfying his mother's requirements, felt guilty and
null;
 – he spontaneously identified his nullity and his guilt with his racial impur-
ity – that is, with his father's share in himself.
 His mother's attitude was therefore motivated by the conflict between her
aristocratic ambition and the fact that she had married a Jew. And it was the
way his mother tried, through her son, by her attitude toward him, to surmount
this contradiction, which conditioned her son's original complex.

the simulacra of a time gone by. That was Dollfuss – a bourgeoisie clinging to privileges it knew to be ephemeral, renouncing life in order to survive, crying, '*Peccavi*'. Work, Family,
Nation, Church. In this context, Nazism was like a great wind of
regenerative barbarism, the emanation of a country which
declared itself headed for the future, headed for expansion; it
offered him both a way of revolting against the chauvinist and
clerical asphyxia and a means of freeing himself from maternal
conformism and from the narrow-mindedness of a detested
father. To become a Nazi was to rise up against his situation as a
mediocre student in a condemned country and against that of a
misfit, dishonour of his family, of whom it was predicted that he
would 'come to nothing'. No other instrument of liberation was
available to him at the time. But here historical objectivity made
his revolt into an abortive attempt. His only instrument of liberation was rotten, and by having tried to employ it he had thrust
his nose in his own filth; he learned that salvation was impossible. There was no way toward himself, even with the best will
in the world; he had no choice save a choice between false situations, and by proletarianizing and Nazifying himself he had at
least chosen the way which best attested to his desire for autonomy. What could henceforth be surprising in the fact that this
desire, stripped of all means of realizing itself, remained purely
*voluntaristic* and that his actions never resulted from his own
conviction, that he remained inconsistent, weak and vulnerable
even in his attempt to change himself? There was no place for
him in the world or in his family (unless he resigned himself to
joining with his father and accepting a future as a crate manufacturer with money and business worries), nor outside it (unless he
succeeded in shedding his Jewishness, to which he futilely
applied himself). His condition was one of exclusion and weakness, it inevitably maintained him in the attitude that had been
his since his earliest childhood; and he could not even regard this
as abnormal.

Events had therefore furnished him only so many occasions to
confirm his original attitude; he exploited them in the direction
of the latter, but no other was offered to him. His condition had

an objective meaning of weakness, inconsistency, self-division, against which the best intentions of unification, or self-affirmation and of strength remained necessarily inoperative – subjective and voluntaristic good intentions deflected, by the logic of his objective situation, in the very direction he was trying to avoid. It was this condition he would have to change in order to correct his weaknesses. But he had no control over his condition; he could merely struggle against himself, against his way of living his contradictions, leaving those contradictions themselves intact. His attempts to make himself a man were doomed to sterility and bad faith; they amounted to an agonized revolt against a condition which, seizing him from behind, became a destiny submitted to, a destiny whose permanence he discovered in himself by the permanent awareness of the inconsistency and the inauthenticity of his own efforts.

His attempts at self-affirmation and integration were doomed, since, even supposing that the possibility of suppressing his Jewishness existed, they could succeed only by changing him into someone else. But this bad faith of his escape project concealed an objective truth: The whole man, in accord with himself and with others, was Other, and no way could lead to him. The defeatism, cowardice and masochism he accused himself of as subjective weaknesses (his conviction that no one loved him, his readiness to feel dismissed and insulted, his way of regarding other people as necessarily stronger and more valuable than himself and of accepting exclusion) had an objective basis, accounted for a situation of fact to which his infantile choice had made him sensitive and against whose meaning (that he was insignificant, had no future and no place in the world) he could not protect himself without bad faith. Doubtless there were other possible ways of living this truth. But were they better? His own was tinged with masochism; he interiorized his exclusion as a biological fault at the same time that he saw it as the deserved punishment of his cowardice and his sins. Mauthner and Weiss made aggressive choices; resolved to compensate for their racial blemish, they made themselves noisy, greedy and scornful, ambitious to gain their revenge by social success – wealth, the power wealth confers, and the respect it imposes upon the Aryan bourgeoisie. As for Hoffmann, he had made himself a fanatic Nazi to beat the anti-Semites on their own ground. *Arrivisme* and fanaticism, were the only other ways immediately open to the half-caste. I contend they were worse still; avoiding their contradiction without transcending it, repressing it but conserving it (as an incurable wound), fanaticism and *arrivisme* led these half-castes to alienate themselves in roles that conformed to bourgeois norms and requirements, that 'collaborated' with the mystifications this class secreted. More conformist, more avid of honours than even those of whom they wished to become the equals, they were all the more insatiably eager for victories of prestige which no victory could convince them they had really won. Doubtless they were combative, but their values, phony positives, were merely the reverse of the nothingness that fissured their arrogance and whose corrosion they vainly attempted to conceal. They were excessively positive and rigid, while he was excessively negative and soft. The inauthentic half-caste seems doomed to excesses by which he tries to end his laceration, to repudiate one of the terms of his contradiction. If I prefer an excessive negativism, it is not because I dream of giving him any credit for it; he was brought to it by his infantile masochism – *arrivisme* and fanaticism were not within his range. It was by virtue of the contingent choice developed since his childhood, and not by some moral option, that he had cut himself off from the possibility of an excessive positivism. If I contend that he made the better choice thereby, it is because the consciousness that continues to reflect on its contradictions in humiliation and suffering remains better armed to assume its condition and some day to attempt a liberating synthesis than the consciousness which claims fulfilment by alienating itself among the fetishes of its time.

## B. PERSECUTION AND TREASON

Objectively based on his half-caste condition, the conviction that he could become a 'whole' man only by becoming Other and that consequently man was Other and he himself a misfit – this conviction is rooted so far back in his childhood that its objective signification does not suffice to account for it. I can doubtless say that for any child adults are fearful divinities legislating in the absolute, and that any child is held captive by the prestige emanating from the Other; the Other has the metaphysical superiority of seeming exempt (because seen from outside) from the secret inconsistency and doubt which every subject bears deep inside himself. I could doubtless add that because of his half-caste condition, he simply overenlarged the prestige originally attaching to the Other, and that this condition therefore extended longer than is customary the inferiority feelings characteristic of infantile dependence, delaying their liquidation. However, this explanation does not satisfy me, because it explains too well; it describes as a necessary and therefore immutable effect an attitude which was not really so necessary (for instance, had he not found himself continually at fault with regard to parents, the discovery of his Jewishness would have assumed a less serious and less definitive signification for him) and from which he believes he can find a way out.

One of the aspects of this attitude is the constant attribution of value, throughout his life, to the types of humanity who are most remote from himself and whom he admired all the more as they differed from the people around him. Man, for him, was always the Other, not only Other than himself, but Other than those whose situation he shared and whom he might have called his equals. At the age of nine or ten, he wanted so much to become Chinese that he prayed for weeks that God would change him into a Chinese boy, even for only a few days. At seven he convinced Halama, the tailor's idiot son, that he was a Jew and that instead of leaving the catechism class he was going to stay on as a spy. He was quite ignorant, at the time, of his Jewish origins and their possible signification. He was merely trying to pull Halama's leg and distinguish himself in other people's eyes. 'Sir', Halama screamed as the father came into the classroom, 'G's staying in class even though he's a Jew.' 'Who said so?' the father asked. 'He did', Halama answered. 'Is that true?' the father asked, turning to G. 'No', he said. 'Then why did you say so?' 'It was a joke to make him think so', he said. 'You must not play jokes like that', the father said gravely. And when he came home that day, he found out his father was a Jew who had converted to Catholicism.

To be a Jew, a Chinese, a Negro, a Nazi – he had always wanted to incarnate the negation of what he was as one among many others. He wanted to be someone disturbing, scandalous, and admirable too. To be Other than himself while remaining himself; to be himself and his opposite; to be a girl for a day while continuing to be a boy (a favour he had also asked God for at ten, after inventing at five an imaginary playmate he pursued among the roses of the wallpaper during his afternoon naps – the androgyne 'Rini', a little girl with a penis).

Perhaps this tendency toward contradictory singularization, acquired long before his consciousness of the Jewish-Aryan dichotomy, dates back to the period of Ninon Vilmorin, a governess from Nice with negroid features, her cheeks pitted with smallpox, her black hair oiled and flattened, repulsively ugly according to most people but beautiful in his eyes. Back to the period of Ninon (who, when he was five, told him frightening and fantastic adventure stories), because she was at the origin of a misunderstanding: vacationing on one of the Carinthian lakes, he had acquired so dark a tan that he was taken for a Negro child. Since, thanks to Ninon, he also spoke French better than German, he was assumed to be her son and people went into ecstasies when they learned he was his own mother's son. To be admired because he seemed to be what he was not may have made a deep impression on him; for the moment I can see no other origin for this tendency toward difference which subsequently became one of the dominant themes of his life.

This taste, moreover, was not stamped with vanity, dandyism, or that mania for 'distinction' he so loathes in the bourgeoisie. It was simply a question of escaping the common measure and also of protecting himself against the persecuting forces of reification. By wanting to be a Negro, a Chinese, a hermaphrodite, a squirrel, a lemur (or some other animal, as when he hid under the

sheets, under a sofa, in a closet, or walked on all fours barking or
mewing), he was trying to escape human supremacy and its
coercion. This coercion proved so strong that he acquired the
sense of systematic persecution quite early and preferred identi-
fying himself with persecuted animals (tiny creatures cowering in
cages, Bambi pursued by hateful hunters), sympathizing with
anything that crawls and risks being stepped on, to the point
where at even the age of three or four he was picking up beetles,
slugs and caterpillars from the pavement and tenderly setting
them down where they would be safe (his mother: 'Leave those
nasty bugs alone!' he: 'Why? They too are God's creatures!')
from human wickedness. Men were on one side, animals on the
other; he was on the animals' side. He burst into tears when his
sister threw his teddy bear against the wall; it had got hurt. He
played for hours on end with his painted plaster menagerie; but
he stubbornly refused to put his animals in their cages. He had
them parading across the whole room, except for the monkey.
This monkey, hanging his one arm from a tree, his pink mouth
open, provoked a stubborn antagonism in him; the monkey not
only looked mean (he was not the only one) but gave evidence of
an all too obvious human presence – because he walked upright,
because he was hung from a branch and couldn't move around
the room, because this green branch introduced a vegetal disson-
ance into the animal harmony.

The correct interpretation of his tendency toward difference is
surely this: to exchange the human world for another in order to
protect himself against the constraints and norms of the people
around him, and, thanks to this desertion, to take refuge from
various persecutions and judgments. This is the key to that
treason complex whose history he wanted to recount: his wish to
desert all collectivities which applied their constraints to him,
beginning with the human race.

There are two possible reactions to disproportionate coercion:
revolt and masochism. But a child of three has no means of
rebelling; he feels guilty and in danger of abandonment. I am
not sure what 'disproportionate coercion' is and whether a more
combative child would have reacted differently to the pressures

brought to bear upon him. I am sure, however, that Maria's requirements were such that no child could have satisfied them. His sister, moreover, also became masochistic. Maria wanted to be perfect; just as she had passionately committed herself, after her marriage, to her household, to culture and 'Society', so, after the birth of her first child, she decided to be a perfect mother with the happiest child in the world. This child, a girl named Helena, was a golden-haired 'treasure'. Maria nursed her herself, determined to sacrifice the beauty of her breasts (a relatively easy sacrifice: Maria was frigid; her ambitions with regard to respectability, her passion to be a great lady demanded that she be a good and faithful wife, well informed, orderly and energetic – it did not require her to love her husband). She decided that this daughter satisfied her every wish, that she was the happiest mother in the world. To prove it to herself, she devoted a huge notebook to Helena in which she set down her happiness every day. Her daughter was the 'ray of sunshine in her life', 'a radiant creature'. After this daughter, Maria decided she wanted a son. I can see her calculating the most opportune date for his birth and deciding that of his conception in consequence. Helena was born in June, summer being the most comfortable season for maternity; but a second child within twelve months was bad for the health and an interval of two years between children was too great for familial equilibrium. So she decided that her son would be born eighteen months after her daughter, that his virile strength would be as perfect as the girl's feminine charm, and that he would be named after an actor she admired for his virility. From the moment of her son's birth, Maria's maternal passion began to slacken; it fell off still further when she discovered that instead of the radiant being his name seemed to require, her son was ugly squalling and dark-haired ('You had black hair growing down to the bridge of your nose and when Yaroslav saw you he screamed, "But what's that black jellyfish"'), and that Helena's sun miracle had not been repeated in his case. Probably less loved than his sister, the son felt inferior to her and incapable of competing with her for parental favours. They left his black curls, they said he looked like a girl, they thought he

seemed a little soft – except for his nurse, whom he hammered
with his fists because it made her laugh until he hurt her and she
became angry. He wanted to be a girl because everyone found
his sister prettier and more interesting than he was. Then, at
about four, his curls were cut off; they told him that he was a boy
now and that he should behave like one. He wept for his curls
and refused to be a boy. They discovered that he squinted and
lisped, and they took him to doctors. They gave him glasses and
made him do *s* exercises with his tongue held in a kind of tiny
metal brace. They decided he was not growing fast enough and
he was given cod-liver oil and brains every morning. But,
perched on a high chair, the tray that was lowered over his head
holding him prisoner, a bib tied around his neck, he would not
eat, and every meal was an interminable tantrum his mother and
sister finally refused to sit through.

He felt he was being persecuted, asked to be what he didn't
want to be, or couldn't be: to be 'a man', 'a big brave boy', to eat, not
to drink, to defecate at fixed hours, to wet neither his pants nor
his bed, not to touch his *pipi* ('or it'll get inflamed', and when it
was inflamed because he had phimosis, his mother said, 'That's
because you've been playing with your *pipi* again'; she sent for
the doctor, they spread him out on the big table in front of everybody, and the doctor 'pushed back' his *pipi*, which hurt a lot and
he thought it was a punishment for playing with it), not to dirty
the white gloves he was to wear even in summer, not to walk in
puddles, not to soil his clothes, not to pick his nose, not to run on
all fours, not to tease his sister, not to play with scissors, not to
play in the living room, and so on. 'Put your hand on the table,
close your mouth, don't stare at the lady, it's not polite, say hello
to the gentleman, say thank you to the lady'; then he had to kiss
Mme Martel's hand (Mme Martel was an old Frenchwoman
who gave his mother lessons and whose false teeth fascinated
him), speak to people at his mother's parties to show off how
much he knew, to greet them one by one when he came in and
when he left, not forgetting to kiss the ladies' hands, so that they
could see how well brought up he was at the age of four. And to
bow to the gentlemen, clicking his heels, and to take off his cap

when he met someone in the street, and not to unbutton his
gloves or his coat ('What will people think, they'll think Frau G's
little boy is badly brought up, Frau G's little boy doesn't even
have white gloves, I'm ashamed of you, I don't deserve it after
everything I've done for you, after all the money we've spent'). In
the evening, when his father came home, he asked, 'Has the boy
been good?' or 'What has the boy done now?' and then, according to the answer, he held out his rough cheek which smelled of
tobacco or said, 'Go away, good-for-nothing.' When he was bad
(once he broke a windowpane in the vestibule with a tennis ball,
that was one of his worst crimes), his father gave him two slaps in
the face, one with each hand, called him an imbecile and a good-
for-nothing, shouted wonderingly, 'How can anyone be so
stupid?', told him that he would have to pay the damages out of
his pocket money (one schilling a week), and declared he
wouldn't talk to him for three days; he kept his word. The child
would have welcomed all the slaps and punishments in the
world, would have punished himself if that would have helped
expiate his crimes. But there was no immediate expiation possible; tears and pardon humbly begged from a man pretending to
be unaware of his existence were no good whatever; he had to
purge his guilt and for days on end endure a silent moral
condemnation.

For him such moral condemnation – a hard, silent, arrogant
reprobation focusing on his guilt, which, since it was inexpiable,
was absolute – constituted the worst punishment of all. There
was no possible atonement. He was guilty, which meant that no
one loved him any more, that he had no place in his family, nor
any rights to existence. It was as if he no longer existed, since he
wasn't the son he was supposed to be and what he was they no
longer wanted. Guilty without appeal – that is, not conforming
to his being-for-others, to that image of himself which alone had
any right to tenderness and protection; not conforming, deprived
of being, reduced to his inner shadows, he experienced a kind of
catastrophic landslide – the universe collapsed, he fell into an
abyss; his body was being stripped of his conforming and
protecting identity, reducing itself to a heap of guilty flesh; self-

conscious, virtually annihilated by his failure, he retired into a corner and longed for death.

He was perhaps three years old when, having broken a light bulb with one of his building blocks, he first thought of avoiding moral condemnation by punishing himself; to annihilate his guilt in anticipation of his condemnation, he lay down and knocked his head against the floor. His mother ran in, picked him up and asked what had got into him. She supposed it had been a tantrum and, annoyed by his attitude, forgot about the bulb. After that, he punished himself secretly: biting himself, pulling out his hair, kneeling in the corner of his own accord after he had been exiled there several times ('Go kneel in the corner!'), or, when he was sent into the dark vestibule at night ('Stand in front of the door'), throwing himself at the wall head first, until he saw stars and could hear terrible cracks. Since the expiation of his guilt was refused, since even after punishment he continued to be subject to universal reprobation, there was nothing to do but invent his own expiations in the hope of simultaneously destroying his badness and of proving, by his struggle against himself, that he was perhaps not so bad after all. But no sign indicated that he had obtained this proof.

He felt he always had to deserve parental favour and that he lived in the continued postponement of condemnation and abandonment. It soon became clear to him that the role of son was perhaps beyond his ability; that his mother had wanted a son, but perhaps not the child that he himself was. She would say, 'I want to be proud of you', and she encouraged him to dream of a heroic future: explorer, aviator, captain. 'Will you take me up in your plane?' she asked. 'Oh, yes,' he answered, 'and when I'm grown up I'll marry you.' Then she laughed and told her guests what he had said. She called him into the living room and asked him in front of everyone what he wanted to be when he was grown up. 'And you'll leave me all alone?' He knew she was asking him to play his role and obediently recited it. When she took him visiting or saw someone she knew coming down the street, she would indoctrinate him: 'Stand up straight. Don't forget to take off your cap. Don't look self-conscious. Look

people in the eyes when you talk to them. Don't mumble, open
your mouth. Look like a little man.' He was convinced that all
grown-ups were judges; each meeting was a test he had to pass;
he had to behave with others according to a host of rules she
reminded him of each time. Human relationships were regulated
by a complicated ritual and he felt he would never be equal to all
the requirements of Good Behaviour. Maria chatted loudly with
other people, and he noticed she described him, to them, as
quite different from what he was for himself – as intelligent,
good-humoured, brave and inquisitive. 'Only he's a little shy',
she added. 'And naughty.' He discovered that naughtiness was
set down to his credit for other people (probably as a sign of virility) and that shyness excused his silence and awkwardness. To
cure him of it, she forced him to answer the telephone, whose
ringing terrified him (behind the black instrument someone was
waiting, he was spied on from afar without seeing anything, and
by picking up the receiver he would have to become someone, a
voice able to inform the invisible interlocutor, would have to fill a
role defined by strict and mysterious rules). The first time, he
had merely picked up the receiver and then run away, trembling
with fear, to call his mother. She had insisted that he say in the
future, 'Hello. This is A.G. Who's calling?'

When he was five years old he asked her, 'Why did you want a
little boy?'

'So I could love him.'

'But you couldn't tell that your little boy would be me, so how
could you be sure you would love him?'

'A mother always loves her children.'

'Even when they're bad?'

'Even when they're bad', she said. 'Mothers have big hearts.
They suffer so much they can't help loving their children.
They're like the Virgin Mary. The Good Lord gives them chil-
dren only when they have warm hearts.'

So he decided she loved him, although he was himself,
because she had a warm heart and couldn't help it. But he still
wanted to find out if it was himself or only her son she loved, and
if she wouldn't have preferred another kind of son, and if she

would have had him for her son if she had married another man;
or if, in that case, there would be another boy to call her 'Mama'
whom she would love as much as him; or whether she might love
him more; or whether she would simply love him without
noticing that he wasn't himself.

The impression that he had been brought into the world for a
specific purpose ('Why do people have children?' 'To have someone to love', they told him first; and later: 'To have someone to
lean on when we're old', or even: 'You'll see, when I'm an old
woman you'll abandon me for some girl'), that he owed his
parents a debt and that he was an ingrate for not giving them
more satisfaction, was consolidated by his second year at school.
At the age of seven, his term report card showed a 2 in drawing (1
being excellent, 2 good, 3 adequate, and 4 poor), and at the end
of the year a 2 in arithmetic. These 'failures' assumed catastrophic proportions for his mother. Not only was he not the first
in his class, he was bringing home Bad Grades. 'God knows I
spare nothing on your education! When I think of all the money
we've spent on your governesses, your French lessons, your
music. . . . And Frau G's son is a mediocre student! Look at R's
son! He has no governesses, he hasn't learned French, his father
is an ordinary engineer, but he's first in everything! And my son
brings home twos on his report card!' At nine he had a third 2 –
in conduct. It was just before his birthday. Beside herself, his
mother announced she would send him to a boarding school
where they'd teach him how to work, and she rushed to the telephone, where she pretended to speak to the head of the school.
'Yes, Herr Direktor, and be sure to pound something into his
head.' 'With a hammer, if you have to', his father added. It was
only after he tearfully promised to try much harder and begged
forgiveness several times that his mother agreed to let him stay at
home. Reprieved. The threat of boarding school remained hanging over his head.

In a situation of insecurity and guilt, he loved and feared his
mother as the dog loves and fears his master, quivering with joy
when she caressed him, overwhelmed when she rebuffed him,
dreaming of some law he could permanently obey which would

guarantee him against her reprobation, and discovering that
such a law, if it existed, was capricious and required not only
obedience but initiative, audacity and ambition, which he
became still more incapable of as the certainty of his mediocrity
and inadequacy grew. Continually at fault in a universe swarming with rules and imperatives none of which was within his
power, he felt illegitimate, and to make a place for himself within
legitimacy he laboured long and hard, doomed to failure by his
very attitude of submission. Having lost faith in his chances of
success (if he had ever had such faith), he struggled without
conviction. He was doomed to mediocrity because he believed in
a formula for success, and he believed in this formula because he
was convinced of his mediocrity – that there was nothing in him
on which to base success, and that this success could therefore
have only an exterior basis. To improve, he would have to
become Other and regulate his behaviour according to alien
criteria. But the more he forced himself to do so, the more mediocre he became, feeling that he would never equal those who set
these criteria and of whom he could be merely the pale and
servile imitator.

When an individual respects legitimacy yet cannot come to
terms with the world and succeed according to its norms, mysticism offers a tempting solution: By God he can raise himself
above all particular rules without contesting their legitimacy; he
merely transfers himself to another level, that of the absolute
Law, in regard to which all particular rules reveal their contingency. He exchanges his relative illegitimacy for an absolute
illegitimacy; absolutely guilty and inadequate, he rediscovers a
relative peace in the conviction that success is impossible and, in
any case, does not depend on him. The judgment of God, even if
it is terrible, protects him against the judgment of men. Persecuted by the latter, he betrays them all; by praying for them, by
invoking, for him and them alike, a divine pity without dis-
criminations, he makes all men equal in the nullity common to
them in God's eyes. But he, praying for them twice a day as for
himself (because, he says, he has no particular claim to divine
pity), *he* knows this nullity; and from this particular knowledge

he becomes conscious of an absolute superiority. He is superior because he understands what others conceal from themselves, he is nearer to God because he knows himself irremediably and absolutely separated from Him, while the others, who think they can touch Him with their little individual misfortunes, are ignorant of this separation.

Progressively, he has learned to see the world upside down, from the Eternal's point of view. He began quite simply, one day when he had been scolded, by praying while he was still crying – praying without conviction, merely to ease his conscience, telling himself that God, if He existed, might give him the intelligence and the courage he lacked and that in any case he could lose nothing by asking for them. This lukewarm prayer by which he tried to come to terms with God, lacking the ability to come to terms with men, developed, in the space of several weeks, into an instrument for the total annihilation of all humanity. He had been told that God sees all and is all-powerful, judges each person according to intentions, not deeds. Feeling absolutely guilty and devoid of the qualities that might have saved him, he needed a miraculous transfiguration. But how could he approach this God of miracles who saw further into him than he himself, who perhaps discerned some basely egotistic motive in his prayers, such as the fear of blows and blame? He could imagine only neutral and ritual means; God was the absolutely distant, and only formulae consecrated by Him could reach Him. Therefore he chose the most neutral prayers to invoke Him, the Pater and the Ave, prayers in which there was no place for any personal, that is, any suspect solicitation. He did not believe the problems of a mediocre child could move the Eternal, who had the entire creation to worry about, especially since this child was probably mediocre because the Eternal felt offended by his sins and his lack of fervour. 'Pray, faith will come after', he was taught. He prayed in German first, then in Latin, for he was told that God, though he understood all languages, had chosen Latin in which to be glorified. 'Make me improve and forgive my presumption; it's for my parents' sake and not my own that I ask it', he added at the end of his prayer. But he decided later that

his parents were merely individuals with no special claims to
divine grace, and he modified his formula: three Paters, three
Aves, and at the end a 'Help us, my parents and myself, as well
as all men.'

Thus, with the help of religious logic, he began to see humanity upside down, from the viewpoint of the Eternal, as a heap of
wretchedness and nullity, an ash falling back into ashes, its cares
and agitations merely the mask of nothingness. Moving from
spontaneous to reasoned humility, he discovered the pride of
knowing his nullity better than others and therefore being superior to them by the fact that he was inferior to them. Such pride
had nothing exalting about it; its only benefit, a dubious one at
that, was the resulting all-pervasive discipline. To please God, he
must permanently abase himself, for everything he refused
himself in this world would be set down to his credit in the next;
the finitude of the creature is what separates him from God (the
nondivine in him, his nonbeing with regard to the Eternal), while
the negation of his finitude (by mortification and *ascesis*) is what
brings him closer to God and, diminishing him on earth,
increases him in heaven. The less is more, the more less, pain is
good and pleasure bad, true faith is infinite remorse, loving God
is suffering from life. But he did not love God; he wondered how
saints dared love God; who was he to give God his love? The
creature, before God, was merely a heap of offal whose love could
only stink in the Lord's nostrils. For him, faith was abjection, fear
and trembling; love of God was systematic hatred of himself. At
about twelve he therefore descended into hell, blaming on
himself as so many sins and weaknesses the desires he surren-
dered to, systematically opposing his spontaneous tastes. Achieving a kind of drought and vacuum after several months of such
exercises, accomplishing the agreeable and the disagreeable with
equal facility, inured to the point where everything became
indifferent (where cold showers no longer made him cold, where
dry bread no longer seemed dry, nor tea without sugar bitter, nor
lukewarm water stale), he reached the limit of mortification,
devoid of inclinations to oppose. Having no pronounced tastes,
finding nothing repugnant, he had only his routine prayers to

offer God, spoken with a dry heart and an empty mind. All he might have sacrificed to Him was annihilated. He had vanquished his pleasures along with his faculty for suffering; his victory – indifference – was a defeat which left him empty-handed.

Empty is too much to say, for from this very defeat he derived a kind of pride. Like the women lining up in front of the Laennec Clinic, each bidding for the glory of having suffered more than the others, he silently prided himself on his ability to endure, his capacity for sacrifice; he had stripped himself of everything others clung to, he had conquered in himself the humanity by which they remained enslaved. (Something like the pride he felt at the age of three, sitting beside his sister on the commode where his mother washed them, being cited as an example to his whimpering sister. 'When she says "Ow" I don't flinch, and when she screams and cries I say "Ow".' He had been the first to venture jumping down from the commode, and he stared scornfully at his sister, thinking, She's afraid. At the same age he proved his resistance to pain by pulling out handfuls of his own hair.) Feeding on his masochism from the start, his faith had dialectically led him to the experience of humility, and from there to resentment and pride. Starting with the intention of improving by divine favour, the logic of his original attitude led him to abase himself still further; and once conscious of his greater and irremediable abasement, he had claimed it as his dignity. The humanity that trampled upon him was the instrument of his abasement; but he was the only one to know that this abasement was deserved (and deserved for reasons known to God and himself alone), and that his executioners were fundamentally worth no more than he; therefore he suffered for them all, experiencing a wretchedness they should have felt; he let himself be crucified and indeed crucified himself, praying for his executioners. He exiled himself from the human world, passing imperceptibly into the Lord's camp, as seven years before he had passed into that of the animals. He was seeking in imposed exile a religious signification, and in so doing tried to make a virtue out of it as if he had chosen it; he felt he was the best because he accepted being the lowest.

The world had already become external to him at this period. The religious *ascesis* had taught him to accept it as an instrument of mortification. But mortification has a logic which dialectically leads you where you had not dreamed of going. Used as arbitrary baffles to facilitate self-mortification, rules became alien objects; he discovered that they were contingent and therefore contestable. Mysticism was therefore a machine for contestation; it made him see his companions from the outside, his unbelieving parents who sinned and who would also die, their imperatives and their scarcely holy preoccupations. These parents who did not go to mass, did not take communion and did not pray – he was no longer sure that their will was identified with the will of God. Religion provided him a discipline more demanding than the family discipline and therefore liberated him from it.

What I like about this mystical period is that it illustrates the complexity of the dialectical process. He had not chosen himself as a mystic (and in fact he never found faith) any more than he had chosen himself as inferior. He had found himself in a situation of inferiority and in order to escape persecution he had asked religion for a miracle, a ready-made structure consisting of an ensemble of rites and magical practices. It was in its ritual and objective rigidity that he tried to incorporate religion into himself. And it was only then that religious objectivity assumed significations for him, significations which were, moreover, extrinsic to that religion (his 'faith' being Judaic or Puritan rather than Catholic). The objective spirit of religion got rooted in a prereligious attitude of inferiority and despair which now animated a faith of dogmatic dryness. It was his infantile complexes which made him accessible to the religious experience and deflected the latter from its ordinary meaning; but subsequently, the religious experience deflected the attitude with which he had addressed himself to God from *its* original meaning (masochistic submission) – it furnished him an instrument of contestation and opened a way toward possible liberation.

What strikes me in this dialectic is the rooting of a structure of objective behaviour charged with a certain historical signification (obscure for the individual who adopts it) in an attitude whose motivations are extrinsic to this 'superstructure'. Is this not always the process when the superstructure is an aspect of man's alienation? Marxism teaches us to see the superstructure in its causal relation to praxis, as if religious mystification, for instance, were deliberately instituted by the ruling class to conceal from the oppressed their alienation and to help them endure it. Actually, of course, there is no question of a deliberate stratagem, of an explicit intention. Marxism imputes to the oppressors intentions corresponding to the objective signification of their behaviour, in which it is properly cathartic: it describes men in their involuntary actions and thereby requires them to assume actions which they have not willed and cannot justify, it requires them to deny themselves or to become cynics; it holds up the cynical image of themselves which they conceal from themselves. Yet the resistance to Marxism's demystification process does not derive only from the material interests and the socioeconomic structure which the superstructure sublimates as far as it can; such resistance also derives from the anchoring of this super-structure in the individual complexes. Without psychological basis, the superstructure would be much more fragile than it is; yet it owes a part of its solidity to the fact that it can satisfy psychological needs which are not entirely determined by the existing society and which call into play an infinite diversity of contingent circumstances and individual choices. This is why it is always possible to explain an attitude such as anti-Semitism or religiosity by the objective situation which it necessarily accounts for, since it rises out of it and is motivated by it; possible to say, for instance, that anti-Semitism results from the obstruction of opportunities for social ascension among thousands of *petits bourgeois* who, unable to grow rich, to rise socially in a recession economy, compensate their desire for ascension by disenfranchising a group of citizens, appropriating the wealth of Jews and 'foreigners', and 'raising themselves' by the contempt they show for them. Yet this explanation, if it illuminates the objective implications of anti-Semitism, does not account for it altogether; it fails notably in explaining its emotional basis in some people while others remain exempt from it, though willing to profit by it. Appearing at a certain economic juncture, with a precise objective signification (as a means of palliating the contradictions of capitalist society), the fact is that anti-Semitism is also based, emotionally, on sexual repression – for instance, permitting the frustrated Aryan woman to believe herself in danger of rape, permitting the inhibited Aryan man to feed his images of violence and lubricity – therefore flourishing by preference in societies or milieus that are repressed and puritanical, and unable to achieve its most virulent form where sex is exempt from remorse. Economic motives are therefore not enough to account for it; in fact, anti-Semitism subsists independently of them in a latent state and does not disappear with them. The economic juncture occasions the appearance of attitudes which precede it in latency, furnishing them with a positive content; but the attitude itself, although it is of course conditioned by the social praxis, is rooted beneath the latter, in the penumbra of vital prehistoric motivations (called 'psychological'), and is thematized only when the state of affairs offers it a signification and a social relevance justifying by an appearance of rationality what originates in the irrational, etc.

For him, who needed a miracle without believing in one, religion became interesting only from the moment he discovered it was a way of cancelling out other people – of considering guilty those who made him guilty, of considering inessential an existence that was scarcely endurable, of considering essential its obverse, the side God sees. I am returning to these sophisms of faith only to say this: that faith betrays the society of men, that the believer, like the traitor, is a man who, while you think you are dealing with him and seeing him in his reality, treacherously escapes into a superreality and deals with the now from the alien perspective of the Eternal, judging those men who regard him as their equal by norms unknown to all men and to himself. Socially excluded or maladjusted, he bails out of 'his' society and takes his revenge by symbolically destroying it.

It makes little difference whether this symbolic destruction functions through mysticism (a means of regarding the real as

illusory with regard to the superreal Being of God and his Kingdom), through materialism (a means of regarding human significations as the illusory man-made nothingness shimmering on
the surface of an unqualified Matter) or through treason properly
speaking (a means of denying the society to which one actually
belongs for another, opposed society which one prefers to it
because it contests one's own society and with which one
mentally allies oneself because this mental integration in the
alien society need never submit to the test of reality – one is not
*in* that alien society – and permits the contestation of one's own
society without any positive rejoinder); mysticism, materialism
and treason are the three possible forms of a single fundamental
attitude, the escape from and negation of reality in favour of an
abstract, absolute reality acceptable only insofar as it permits
affective reality to be regarded as inessential. And to these three
forms a fourth should be added, which he is to discern later on:
the activity of writing, which abolishes reality in favour of an
abstract and merely signified reality to which the writer sacrifices
his life, continually annihilating in thoughts and words the
reality of his existence in the world.

*Not to be here*; to be only a transparent, ineffable and therefore
invulnerable presence, a transcendent scrutiny sliding over the
surfaces of events without taking hold, impervious to reproaches,
disengaged from all commitments toward others because absolutely committed toward the absolutely Other – this is how he
began to be toward his twelfth year, this is how he still is today.
To exchange religiosity for Nazism after a year's *ascesis* was an
easy matter. Like religion, Nazism permitted him to integrate
himself mentally in another realm, that of the Reich, which
would never be the realm of his fellow beings, which denied
them, which he himself could never achieve, and which permitted him to disdain the world around him.

And he just said reality was an entanglement of significations!
Here is the third interpretation I have given of his conversion to
Nazism, and it is as valid as the preceding two. Virile protest;
desire to be Other (that is, Aryan) and to exterminate in himself
the Jewish 'weakness'; religion of Strength, Race and the Reich,

by virtue of which he could transfer himself to a Germanic Elsewhere from which he would scornfully contest men and events as a lesser reality – Nazism was all that for him, and this too: a Rule like a religious discipline, similarly intransigent, which no one had tried to impose upon him. A Rule by which no one would have dreamed of gauging him, and which he had chosen for just that reason – precisely because this Rule (as religion before it, but to a greater extent) was not made for him; because no one asked him to excel according to its norms; because even the least compliance with it was a supererogatory act; because, even if he were last among the Nazis, he was still first, for the virtues which were supposedly inherent in the 'Germanic race' were lacking in him, and to possess even the slightest trace of them was already a victory over his abjection.

Perhaps this interpretation contains all the others: unable to excel by the family rule, unable to be what he should have been, he chose to conform to alien rules, to do what no one expected of him, to answer for requirements not personally intended for him in order to conceal his failure to satisfy those which were. The good Catholic no one asked him to be, the good Nazi no one could have expected, later the good Frenchman when France no longer existed nor did any real Frenchman within four hundred kilometres – so that was it: to disguise himself in a borrowed being which made no attempt to fool anyone, to mask his nullity by an Otherness which frankly admitted itself as such, to overcome his fellow beings, absolutely this time, on grounds completely alien to them (as to himself), and also to impress the strangers who would say of him, 'This Jew is a good Catholic, a good Nazi; this Austrian speaks French perfectly; this Frenchman knows more about Germany, England, the USA and India, than the Germans, English, Americans and Indians.' To be what he is not, though not in order to stay that way and accomplish something positive, but only to deny what he is (incompletely), what he cannot entirely be, and therefore compensate for his infirmity by an excellence no one would contest, for there was no God, there were no Nazis, no Frenchmen, no Germans, English, Americans or Indians to put him to the test. A choice, therefore,

of grounds on which he was unbeatable because no one dreamed
of competing with him, a way of astounding other people by
showing himself to be so different from the sort of person they
were expecting – injecting into his relations with others a corrosive dose of negativity, presenting himself as the negation of the
world he ought to have in common with them, therefore of them
and of himself.

I am going to try and trace the genesis of this negativism, but
before that I should like to clarify the above theoretically (a
praiseworthy ambition, of course, but how characteristic of the
attitude he has just described, for, having spoken of himself,
having allowed the reader to think for a moment that he can
finally come to grips with him, here he is, rushing to confound
the reader already; creating the theory for his own interpretations of himself, he presents himself as the pure theorizing
mind of a 'himself' he suddenly abandons like an empty skin,
leaving it in the reader's hands, overpowering the reader with
abstract digressions that will prove, by the distance from their
object, that he is who he isn't, that he is the undefinable and
ineffable scrutiny focused on all things, himself included).

Starting from a child feeling persecuted and trying to escape
the constraints of the human world, I have reached an adolescent
feeling of being if not continually persecuted, at least excluded
and the object of contempt. The original inferiority situation has
subsisted, hence also the conviction that he is inferior; but this
original attitude of inferiority and alienation has been complicated, as it has developed, by a negativist attitude of resentment,
pride and treason which will remain dominant for a long time.
He has chosen this attitude no more deliberately than he has
chosen inferiority; he has fallen into it by a dialectic whose basis
cannot be found in his conscious intentions, but in the instruments of perception and behaviour which circumstances have
offered him and which, set in motion to the advantage of his
original attitude, have reacted upon it by their inherent logic – a
logic which can reveal itself only by this motion. I mean that the
law of the development is not in events any more than in the
intention which makes use of them; but that, utilizing certain

instruments of behaviour (systems of thought, beliefs, stereo-
typed attitudes), the original intention was led beyond itself,
discovering significations and reasons which were entirely alien
to it at the start and which it nevertheless finished by assuming as
its own. He came to religion, for instance, out of despair, and to
Nazism out of virile protest, and continued with them for quite
different reasons (to raise himself above deriding humanity and
to reject it in favour of an absolute Otherness). Has he been the
plaything of some logic immanent in these beliefs and in his
situation? That would be too much to say. But the original intention had to assume the factual condition and articulate itself
against it by a certain (finite) number of possibilities thematically
unforeseen – by certain 'objective possibilities'. So the individual,
having adopted this attitude for reasons he is soon to forget, finds
himself actually living by these objective possibilities, first unconsciously, then gradually discovering them as his own – that
is, discovering in his attitude new possible significations (discovering 'temptations', unforeseen possibilities, significations to
which he will attribute value and which he will choose as subjectively determinant when, by thematizing them, he will claim to be
the subject of behaviour which was at first his own only objectively, and as if in spite of himself).

This is to say that, in fact and historically, we merely choose to
be what we can already be without having chosen it (or, as Marx
said, that humanity raises only the issues it can solve), that the
choice assumes, thematizes, and attributes value to significations
which offer themselves to the individual without his having
wanted or foreseen them, but which he is living unknowingly as
the objective significations attaching themselves to his behaviour
intact with the empirical world and other people. The most
reassuring thing that can happen to a man is that the behaviour
by which he rationally deals with events allows of only one signification and that his freedom can choose itself through the attribution of value to this signifying behaviour. To be the man of a
single signification and a single intention – that is what we are all
nostalgic for, because this condition is refused us and because,
intellectuals or not, we live in contradiction, incapable of

summing up our existence in one clear, positive, effective action, gnawed by bad conscience or guilty of bad faith when we claim to do so against all the evidence. Today our behaviour always signifies more than we would like it to signify in order to live in peace with ourselves and with others; peace can be achieved only as the price of deceptions, abusive simplifications, and amputations of ourselves. Honesty would require us to assume the contradictions in which we live, but we can do this only by agreeing to confess the dark, negative, ineffective side of our action; and this confession itself cannot be an action, since it admits the share of failure which action implies. This confession, an attempt to recover the share of ourselves which cannot be realized in action, which action reduces to silence, which, as our irremediable solitude, separates us from our positive image, this confession can be only literary – that is, simultaneously individual, public and ineffective (though not necessarily inoperative).

Nostalgia for a simple and effective action is something I understand very well, for everyone wants to escape contradiction and solitude; but at the same time I am ashamed of it, for it is impossible to escape these conditions (and that is why I regard his case as significant of the common condition). This nostalgia, if we yield to it, is cowardice, for it desires a world where objective signification, attaching to the only possible and rational behaviour, would impose itself with a clarity so imperative that we could stop choosing it without our behaviour being modified by it; we would be inside truth 'by the force of events', protected by the laws of a historical process (which would no longer deserve the qualification of 'dialectical' – it would be a providential 'way of the world'), sure of making real the human world whether we chose it or not; we would *be chosen* ('elected') *by* history and would go 'in the right direction' even without wanting to. Saved from the start, we would be condemned to being and doing what we would do, as the Swedes are condemned to happiness – as the immortals, if they existed, would be condemned to perpetual life. But that is not possible, and that is why I refer to a cowardly nostalgia secreted by individuals whose historical good fortune, despite and because of

its agonies, is this: they are condemned to thought, to doubt, to
contestation, condemned to freedom, to the certainty that man
cannot *be* anything. Torn by the contradictory significations of
their behaviour, protected against themselves by no grace of
state, they are faced with the necessity of choosing; and because
this condition is so difficult to bear, they engage in occasional
crusades with eagerness, dogmatizing anti-Communism or
Communism, rendering absolute the opposition between East
and West, between formal democracy and socialism. They
project outside, upon the other camp, one term of their contradiction which they identify as absolute Evil, claim to be proof
against its temptations and thereby reassure others like themselves. And they have great need of reassurance; as bourgeois
infected with Marxism and haunted by the decline of their class,
they rattle their swords against it, predict the great catastrophe,
preach the great purification, because for them the annihilation
of the Marxist devil haunting them is the only hope of being able
to endure their bourgeois being without shame or remorse; as
Marxists infected with *bourgeoisism* because they come from the
bourgeoisie and must live side by side with it, they try, unable to
destroy it or to eradicate it from themselves, to cut themselves off
from it by religious dogmatism which humiliates their bourgeois
intelligence, exorcises the temptations of their origins, raises
them to the dignity of the elect, the heralds of history (a role all
the more tempting because history, for the last ten years, has
been made without them and because their impotence to make it
and to live according to ideas encourages ideological absolutism).

But he does not want to talk about this now, for fear that hasty
generalizations might weigh upon the methodical examination
he promises himself to make later on. His intention, for the
moment, is to show how his original condition, in the course of
various 'prefabricated' attitudes, has assumed various objective
significations; how each of these significations permits a true
interpretation of his existence, for each has been a temptation for
him; but how each of these interpretations offers only a partial
truth, for the total truth, accessible only to historical description,
is this: that he could not unify himself by any one of the contra-

dictory objective significations which were offered to him, that he spent his life seeking a signification which would permit him to subsume them all, that the choice of this signification has never been able to avoid the consciousness of its revocability, the evidence that it was only one possibility among others equally tempting, and that what was fundamental in him, his ultimate truth, was this necessity always to be seeking the activity capable of transcending towards their synthesis the objective significations offered to him. Yes, his truth is that he must seek, must invent an activity which unifies his individual 'Diaspora' and leads its scattered members into a new country, one over which his rights would inevitably remain precarious. But for this activity to become even conceivable has taken a long time – he has discovered it only after already committing himself to it. It is again an undertaking begun for other reasons, in the dark, which has progressively assumed an unforeseen signification, afterward discovered to be perhaps his only possibility of salvation. For at the start this undertaking aimed only at showing that there was no undertaking, no salvation possible, that he could only crucify himself upon the double impossibility of being and of being nothing, of choosing a single signification for himself and of choosing all that were offered to him. But that will come later.

The train on 20 July 1939 ('Date of entry into Switzerland: 21 July 1939', question and answer which have recurred over ten years on dozens of questionnaires and forms), boarded at the West Station, his father pale, thin, exceptionally upset and saying, 'This may be the last time we'll see each other!'; but he wasn't thinking so far ahead, they were going to spend the vacation in Montreux. They stayed at the Pension Beau Séjour, which cost eight Swiss francs a day, a strangely empty Byzantine villa with too many servants and a casino he had to take his sister to in the afternoons so that a handsome Chilean could dance with her between cups of chocolate. Departure for Zurich fifteen days later, staying first at a hotel, later at a pension, then in the same pension but with the three of them in one room and with one meal a day, then only breakfast. The miserly prosperity of

Zurich, overabundance, stinginess, anti-alcohol self-righteousness, League of Women, Protection of Young Girls, Zwingli, clean blue trams, cabarets and bars hidden in the Old Town where gusts of tobacco smoke and the smell of beer suggested vice, prostitution, Forbidden Pleasures. A complacent opulence assuming the expression of modest contentment, poverty (regarded as shameful) relieved with scornful pity, as one might treat a disease. For him, his mother and his sister, the apprenticeship of hunger before shop windows full of food while the past fell from them like scales, and with it the future. The Nazi-Soviet Pact, the invasion of Poland, his mother's feverish manoeuvres to 'settle' them in Switzerland, a letter to the Pope, interminable financial calculations, the discovery of a German-Swiss boarding school up in the mountains approved by the German ambassador and costing 650 Swiss francs a month – a fortune. For Maria, who had hesitated three months before deciding to get him a bicycle that cost 110 schillings, who bought a radio only in 1936, and secondhand at that, who had every month struggled to set aside two hundred schillings for French lessons and piano lessons which Jacob disapproved of – for Maria, finding 650 Swiss francs a month to 'save the boy' ('By saving you I lost you, and I knew it') was a challenge. The kind of challenge which the thrifty bourgeois who has been saving for twenty years in hopes that his stinginess will permit him to 'improve his position' accepts only on very great occasions, when he feels that all is lost already because the opulent future he dreamed of has fallen away and the meagre remains suddenly burn his fingers – 'Let's take advantage of it while we still have something.' Jewels sold, secret funds changed into dollars at a wretched exchange in bars where she met suspicious characters (an old American woman with a Polish gigolo); purchase of his first suit with long trousers, which he wore for three years, having no other; arrival in Graubünden, where his mother confided to the head of the school that her son was half Jewish, that she wanted to save him, that she could not pay the entire tuition (which would be sent regularly, each month, from Germany) and that she hoped he would give her a reduced rate; she obtained it (a cut of fifty francs) thanks to her power of making people feel it would be unworthy of her high opinion of them not to yield to her, but she did not guess that the director whose Swiss patriotism she appealed to was a Nazi drunkard who would take his revenge for her victory over him.

Institut Montana: a huge yellow building towering over a little village in a narrow valley, five thousand feet above sea level; tiny separate rooms whose windows overlooked the granitic mass of a grey mountain that crushed him beneath its immutability. At first the mountain thrilled him, then it weighed on him; he dreamed of the sea because the sea inspires dreams, while the mountain, unchanging, daunts imagination. Men crawl in its shadow, their thoughts short as the horizon, narrow as the valley, greedy as the rocky soil; because human activity does not affect it, the mountain is discouraging, nourishes introversion, conservatism. History washes over its feet without affecting it, and men of the mountain do not believe in history; for them there is only a lunar eternity, boredom articulated by the barber, tobacco and wine.

The perfect exile. Some sixty children, rich Dutch, German and Swiss boys banded together in vague cliques secreting the snob values (jazz, movie stars, exotic cigarettes, whisky) of spoiled and abandoned adolescents, yearning for their emancipation. It was as if he had landed on a new planet, accustomed as he was to virile values (vigour, sobriety, contempt for decadent artifices), armed with a Bruckner symphony (which infatuated him by its forbidding length and its polyphonic elaborations) and records of Ravel (chosen because of their relative hermeticism for an untrained ear), a bicycle and one rough grey suit. They made fun of his Viennese accent, his ignorance of jazz, alcohol, tobacco and racing cars, as well as of his naïve seriousness. There were eighteen months to get through until graduation. Shut into his cell of six square yards, where he was permitted to play music only on Saturday and Sunday afternoons, he began to realize he was terribly alone.

Winter 1939–40. His window steamed over, his brass lamp casting its yellow circle on the raw wood table. His mother was

working at Yaroslav's to pay his tuition and Yaroslav dealt with
her haughtily, taking his revenge on this stubborn daughter. Sitting at his table, he stuck his nails into the raw wood and stared
at nothing for whole evenings at a time. The nothingness gradually rose from his stomach, then filled his whole chest. He
wanted to lay his head on the desk and sob, but the master
prowled the corridors on crepe soles and might walk in without
knocking. He said, 'My God, let me die', but he didn't believe in
God any more. Then he put his forehead against the steamy
glass and stared out into the darkness. There was nothing to do.
Nothing to hope for. The world was like the great granite mountain; he could only look at its mass, he was nothing but this looking on the surface of an alien world which had no use for him.
That was when he began feeling that life was unlivable; that man
is a wound in which the world turns like a knife; and that
between man and the world there was one term too many.

Wondering later what this terrible desire to cry meant, this
impulse to huddle in a corner in his own body's warmth, what
name to give this blankness, which he had experienced before
(the first time, at the age of five or six, when he had fallen in love
with a pale, silent little girl with long brown hair; later, listening
to a Chopin waltz; still later, when he fell in love again – this
time with two girls; and after that, whenever he encountered the
specific atmosphere of loving), he discovered that 'sadness is self-
tenderness'. Self-tenderness: nostalgia for a world whose textures
and limits merge with those of the body, because the body
becomes the only home, both Promised Land and Paradise Lost,
when it is the only endurable thing left; desire to wrap his arms
around his own body, last refuge of life's sweetness, last barrier
against a hostile world; and after this desire, the appeal to
another body to make him conscious of his own, a body he
would love and press himself against as against his own sweetness objectified.

For the man confined in an alien and hostile world, there are
three possibilities: to attempt to escape, to resign himself to his
lot and escape in dreams, and to adapt to the imprisoning order, to
conform to its requirements, even at the price of self-distortion.

Among these three possibilities, I have elsewhere set up an absolute hierarchy: I have attributed to the first (the effort of liberation) a moral significance, to the second (the creation of an imaginary world to live in because the real world is unlivable) an aesthetic significance, and to the third (a behaviour of conformist heteronomy) a vital significance. Now, since these three possibilities are the three objective meanings of the confined man's situation, it is more than likely that he will discover each of them, one day or another, as a temptation. If the word 'alienation' is to have a meaning, this alienated man cannot live in either the third or the second attitude without suffering, at least secretly, from their contradictions and their inauthenticity, and therefore without being tempted to escape them by the first (his success is another question). It is this dialectic that *his* history seems to me to illustrate.

To attempt to escape.... There could be no question of escape in the winter of 1939–40. For outside his cell his prison was the whole world. This world was at war; the camp he belonged to according to his origins repudiated him because of his Jewishness, suspected him because of this repudiation, and rejected him into the other camp; but the other camp repudiated him in its turn, first of all because he had a German passport (brown, with a black swastika; it revealed his half-caste nature only to the initiated by underlining the first name once, the last name twice), then because he was not Jewish enough for his hostility to the Reich to be trusted. As for Switzerland, its citizens mistrusted him as a German, and the authorities (anxious not to offend Germany) suspected he was not German enough. So there was no effective escape possible, nor any way of conforming to the local order, which set up unrealizable requirements: that he be Swiss and 'think Swiss'; that he be German (he wasn't German enough; after 1943 he would be too German); that he be a carefree lover of jazz, cigarettes and American film stars. There remained the second way.

This way, escape into imagination, was imposed upon him in fact, without his having to choose it. But precisely for this reason he followed it at first against his will, without recognizing it as his own. He could do nothing but dream of the possibility of living which had been refused him; but dreaming had to be learned, too, and he had still not discovered (invented) this possibility which, objectively, was the only one he had. I want to emphasize this possible gap between objective and subjective possibilities, for it shows a limitation of the Marxist explanation. As a matter of fact, it is only historically that men always choose their objective possibilities; not because the history of collectivities deals with huge numbers that verify statistical probability, but because it deals with long periods. Shrink history to a few days or months and it will evaporate into the diversity and indecision of collective as well as individual behaviour, the ways which upon methodical examination reveal themselves (and therefore exist objectively) as the only possible ones rarely being the ones chosen from the start; acts come first, the meaning only afterwards. And when society refuses the objective meaning of the situation, when, subjectively, it is not prepared for its objective possibilities, then what happens to it is the same thing that happens to the individual in the same case: it goes mad. It disguises reality, preferring its chimeras, it yields itself up to a terror that aims at expelling reality from its heart; it pursues this reality which it refuses to know, in the persons of the 'traitors'. Society must have traitors to pursue, for it feels betrayed, since history confers upon its behaviour an objective meaning which robs it of its intentions, weakens its meaning in order to substitute another meaning for it. Traitors, for this mad society, are quite simply those who recognize what it does not want to see: the unavoidable toward which it is advancing, walking backward. This refusal of reality, and therefore of the 'only way objectively possible', can last days or years. If it lasts a long time, society's schizophrenic behaviour secretes a kind of secondary reality; the world of madness tends to objectify, the notion of what is really possible and of what is not is lost, the meaning of history fades, and groups of lunatics appear preaching that truth is violent (of course, since such 'truth' must repudiate reality), that atomic bombs must be dropped on the forests of Dien-Bien Phu, that the Algerians must be slaughtered and M. Duclos hanged.

All this to say that in 1939 he was not subjectively ready to

choose and therefore to make his own the only objective possibility available, and that he advanced toward it backwards,
unawares, only to discover that after many long months he had
in fact adopted it while he was looking for – and thought he was
doing – something entirely different. That he had discovered it I
nevertheless set down to his credit; others, in the same situation,
continued to avoid their effective possibilities. The individual,
like Marx's proletariat, appropriates his vocation, the objective
meaning of his existence, only if he chooses it, attributes value to
it, makes himself its responsible subject; he can miss it
indefinitely.

And he began by missing it. The radical solitude which
excludes us from humanity, which obliges us to invent our own
values because other people's are irremediably alien to us – this
was the solitude he was not prepared for. At sixteen he was not
inclined to dreaming, nor to philosophical contestation, nor to
creating his own way. Discovering his solitude, he decided he
must be guilty, for you must have a strong mind to believe you
are right when everyone around you says you are wrong. He
decided he was wrong to be a Jew; he decided he was wrong not
to enjoy jazz, cigarettes, film stars (lovingly drawn on big sheets
of paper by Kunz, to the applause of his confederates), and, with
his pathetic good will, began to make it his duty to understand
these infatuations. Only there was nothing to understand (except
that this infatuation was the manifestation of an intellectual
vacuity masking its boredom by snob distractions, parochial
squabbles as to the superiority of the paternal Buick or Chevro-
let), which is why, instead of producing edifying answers to his
ingenuous questions, they suspected he patronized their 'values'
and, incapable of justifying them, made them into a superiority
system: derision of his incomprehension; incomprehensible
allusions or silence as soon as he came into their rooms; and,
despite this boycott, Kunz every Saturday borrowing his phono-
graph ('Pierre wants to know if you'll lend us your victrola'),
which was better than theirs and which he would not see again
until Monday, when he couldn't use it again until the following
week.

His nails dug into the raw wood of his desk where the brass
lamp projected its circle of light, the nothingness swelled within
him – the feeling of being nothing. And just to hold on to something, he began to pay attention to his studies for the first time in
his life. He had two terms to make up, and private lessons to help
him to do so; a challenge the chemistry teacher (a German Nazi
who intrigued him, with whom he engaged in a sporting rivalry)
flung him: to learn the courses he had missed in fewer lessons
than had been set for him. How beguiling was the aridity of the
natural sciences which fill the mind and by their apparent rigour
protect it against anguish and doubt; how reassuring was the
precision of laws, figures and theorems which, once learned,
permitted you to annihilate the contingent diversity of the real;
the world could be spirited away by an intellectual gymnastics
which, occupying the mind, maintained your being in hiber-
nation. To see the world scientifically: to kill off its significations,
to detach yourself from the concrete, to stop living and feeling, to
intellectualize your affective contact with it, to mechanize it in
obedience to a Rule, no longer anything but impersonal Reason.
Scientific discipline replaced religious discipline; the *ascesis* was
almost the same. He played dead. It was the only kind of conformism accessible to him – conforming to scientific discipline since
he could not conform to the norms of those around him. But this
conformism was also a treason. Against the human world he
took sides this time with the mineral world; man was chemistry.

This was not enough. The rudiments of science taught in his
school were not sufficient for mechanizing the whole world. And
then, it is not true that the sciences are exact. Perhaps he would
have excelled in them if intellectual gymnastics, obeying rigorous
rules, were the last word of the scientific spirit. This was not the
case. Mathematics in particular, detested from the start,
demanded a high-wire boldness (that the reasoner release the
thread of his linear logic, seize the multiple aspects of the question at a glance in order to choose a different thread) of which his
mind, fearing the void and seeking security, was incapable. None
of the scholarly disciplines provided a law he could submit to in
servile obedience, a means for him to die to himself, entirely

defined by exterior requirements.

So he invented something else. He decided that the 'whole man' was French, that the body of true thought and reason was the French language, that the country where life was still and par excellence possible was France. France, which was the Other of all that he was and knew, the Unknown par excellence, since it was a forbidden country where not one of his ancestors had set foot; but an *existing* unknown (unlike Brazil or Africa or China, so absolutely alien that they couldn't even be Other; lacking any relation with them, he couldn't reject himself in their favour) whose Otherness he could explore, by means of the language, in order to lose himself in it.

A passionate, disciplined, ascetic attempt: One day during the winter of 1939–40 he resolved to make himself French and to expel from himself everything by which he was Other than the Other. From that winter day on, he read only French books – at night, on the raw wood desk, in the circle of the brass lamp, marking in the margin each line of text containing a new word and after some thirty pages jotting in his yellow notebook all these words, each in a phrase to indicate its meaning; discovering that thirty pages were enough to appropriate an author's vocabulary (with the exception of Giraudoux and his fireworks of exotic words). His yellow notebook swelled from week to week, amassing the French substance, which he ingurgitated with methodical patience; methodically he read his way through all the French authors of any interest at all in the school library, quickly discarding the members of the Académie Française and other bores (Bordeaux, Estaunié, Cherbuliez, Bourget) for Marcel Arland, Proust (proud of following his meanders but with no enjoyment), Giraudoux (who disconcerted him; did his 'profundity' mean anything?), Malraux (misunderstood at the time), Maurois, Baudelaire, Valéry, scorning the classics, convinced that thought had progressed since, that what was most recent was most valuable.

He assimilated the French substance as, before, he had prayed and developed his muscles, with the same voluntary insistence, but this time with the sense of total involvement, compelling himself, in this German school where no one spoke French (except the teacher, in class) to think only in French; speaking to himself in French, making up dialogues, poring over the dictionary whenever he came up against an obstacle, discovering the nonequivalence of languages – the fact that knowing one means you no longer refer to the other; moving within French, as in a closed system (his jubilation when he began to dream in French, then his weakness for sprinkling his German compositions with Gallicisms). He was totally engaged in this work, for the first time in his life; this undertaking gathered up all the significations of his previous behaviour, realized all his complexes, contradictions and possibilities, starting with his masochism.

For at the start his 'French *ascesis*' was a masochistic project, and only accessorily an attempt to escape. He postulated that man was French as he had previously admitted that man was Aryan. But he gained by the exchange; he was no more French than he was Aryan, but in relation to France he was only one foreigner among others, while in relation to the Aryans he was an individual essentially inferior. He had no possibility of appropriating Aryanness, which was denied him as the very basis of human dignity; but he could at least try to appropriate French thinking, since to do so it was enough that he think in French. He did not think of it as the thinking of a particular race of people (carrying within it, like German, clots of mystery and irrationality, its very vocabulary corrupted by value judgements: *Blut, Volk, Deutsch, Führer*, blond Siegfried against black Hagen, *Reich, Rasse, Volksfremd, Kraft, Reinheit*, 'disintegrating' Jewish intelligence, *Wein, Weib, Gesang*), but as thought itself, the exercise of reason, transparent and universal. To become French, for him, was to abandon the swamps of Teutonism for universal reason; the universal was French. But French was Other.

Which is to say that he converted to French as you convert to a religion – the religion of the French language which required a totalitarian discipline, the renunciation of his entire past, of everything which had been himself, and the mystical submission to an alien Rule which (like the exercises of religious mortification) permitted him to enter into communion with the universal. A discipline more radical than all those he had hitherto imposed on himself, because it required that he refuse everything (including the present – his school, his mountain, his teachers, his fellow students) and because it promised him everything (the abstract universal) if he succeeded in this autodestructive abstraction.

So here he is praying again, as four years before. But instead of saying three Paters and three Aves morning and night and doing the opposite of what he likes the rest of the time, he prays all day long; he humbles himself before French thinking, his prayer is the linguistic control to which he subjects his own spontaneity, a constantly surveyed reading, a laborious accumulation of a vocabulary, the isolation that his refusal of the surrounding Germanness plunges him into. Once again he has an absolute Rule which he wants to define him entirely, to relieve him of facing his own existence, to protect him against other people's requirements. He has dedicated himself to French as the mystic dedicates himself to God; and in relation to his secret French reality (absolute as the mystic's reality for God), his reality as a miserable schoolboy, snubbed and despised, is merely inessential.

At the start, his conversion to French was therefore only a way of regressing to his original masochism. Unable to satisfy others' requirements, unable to be the good little fellow he wanted to be (if someone had called him 'good little fellow' and stroked his head, saying, 'You did that very well, that's just the way everyone should do it', he would have wriggled with delight like the 'good dog' who had been his favourite hero as a child and whom he had wanted to be like), he withdrew from all requirements, isolated himself, imposed upon himself a rule which, alien to the rules around him, permitted him to contest them and, from last, would make him the first. (How surprising he should not have noticed this sooner – his original choice was the 'original masochism' he had just described. Starting here, everything grows clear: his need for an absolute Rule, which might also be called absolute 'value', something by which everything can be measured and by which an absolute hierarchy of things would be established (his anxiety, for instance, during his eleventh year, to know which animal was the strongest, the biggest or the fastest, who was the oldest man, the greatest genius humanity had produced, the greatest composer, writer or explorer, the best athlete, and so on, and no sooner had he found the answer than he set up a cult of this 'greatest', devalued everything that was 'less'); his need for a discipline whose observation would assure him of being good and deserving; his collector's mania (as soon as something seemed good or valuable to him, it was the good, the valuable in itself which he tried to constitute by collecting all its contingent fragments); his confusion when his value was contested by other people's, and his eagerness to convert to their values once they were expounded to him with sufficient serious-ness; his readiness to betray these values for new ones, to change 'loyalties' provided his new master demanded total submission – for he himself had backed no value and, all value being denied him, turned himself inside out to accept other people's, condemning himself to seeing them remain alien to him; his taste for systematization, rationalization – masochistic sub-mission to the Law; and his desire to 'jump out of the window' when he was scolded – a way of making others' reprobation into an absolute and obeying its real demands, that he no longer exist. The same thing was true of his conversion to French. French was the absolute good and value, therefore everything else was rubbish, therefore he would despise everything else and accomplish what the French value required of him; to the degree that he was not French he should no longer exist.)

The first – the first among the last. The conversion to French had the same moral structure as the mystical crisis of three years before. Faced with the French absolute, he was nothing, a little fool struggling in the shadows (who lacked the grace of being French as he had lacked divine grace, and who, during his first trip in French-speaking Switzerland, religiously listened to the railwaymen talking in their singsong Vaudois accent, telling himself, 'I'd give half my life to *possess* French like the stupidest man there'), doomed to contemplate from a distance, respect-fully, the French *lumière*, convinced that such light was not for him, that he was condemned to remain alien to the society of French Men. Absolutely inferior since he was irremediably non-French; but in the very frame of this inferiority, the first among the non-French, since he knew the inferiority the others were unaware of and considered it with horror. How reassuring this religious universe was that he created for himself out of nothing, really, not even the excuse of a catechism class this time. His French theology reveals his original choice in all its nakedness; it reveals that this choice was masochism. How reassuring, in fact, *to be* inferior by birth (for that was what he had chosen to be; if not, why convert to French, which he knew only too well that he could not become?), surrounded on all sides, utterly enclosed within a condition of inferiority for which he is not responsible (it isn't his fault if he wasn't born French) and from which he thinks he can never escape (how could a Viennese-Jewish subman become French?). Inferior, therefore irresponsible, impotent 'in essence' and therefore innocent, he chooses to be the man who can do nothing – save scrupulously and slavishly imitate the masters he gives himself (the French). They are God and His Law for him; he has only to submit to them. The alien Law which he observes as the condition of his mystical accession to being relieves him of the responsibility of coming to grips with existence. All his contradictions are spirited away by this religious postulate: 'When you have made your way into the Law of French, you will become a Man, all your problems will be miraculously resolved.' A Man, an Other. Yet you can never become an Other. He has chosen perpetual servitude. A servitude which (as always) had its 'good side'; to adore French as an absolute good permitted him to feel disgust and hatred for the world around him with a clear conscience. *With a clear conscience*: he was no longer responsible for the hatred and the disgust to which he was spontaneously inclined, he made the divine French stand surety for him; he felt hatred and disgust under protection, by virtue of the absolute superiority of the god he adored. Here he resembled the Moslem or the Nazi who also lets the absolute superiority of his faith and his race stand surety for his resentment; his resentment is legitimate since it is addressed solely against 'infidels' and 'human refuse'.

From his example, I perceive two things: (1) that the victim of the totalitarian ideologies is infected by them to the point where he is spontaneously inclined to transpose them to a different level and to direct them against others who become his own victims (this is the mechanism of anti-Semitism, of caste superiority, of all resentment feelings); (2) that he had assumed (i.e., chosen) his condition of inferiority to such a degree that he spontaneously re-invented it when (for he was rid, now, of the surrounding anti-Semitism) it was tending to modify itself. Accustomed to living with a ceiling over his head (the ceiling of anti-Semitism and parental condemnation, a ceiling which protected him against the dizziness of altitudes, against the anguish of being free to make himself into what he was not, a ceiling which gave him security in his inferiority, persuading him that the world belonged to and was made by superior men essentially different from himself, and that he could do nothing against its course), he reinvented a new ceiling for himself when the old one collapsed. The victim's condition offers at least this moral comfort: The victim counts for nothing in the order oppressing him, he is not responsible for the wrong done him; he cannot, materially, realize his freedom; he can desire it and dream of it without danger. Oppression protects him against responsibility. And I also perceive this from his example: The victim is the accomplice of his condition. That is the best definition one can give of him. The man who feels and believes himself a victim is the man convinced that They are doing him a wrong against which he is helpless. As soon as he opposes oppression by action (by action, not by plaintive rebellion and protests in the name of the Rights of Man), as soon as he refuses it effectively, he ceases to behave as a victim. Rejecting, along with the order which oppresses him, all legality, no longer appealing in the name of the Law, assuming his claims as the basis of a justice which he means to obtain for himself (and not to receive from on high – from whom?), he makes himself the supreme legislator; no longer a victim, but an avenger and therefore already a man. But this transition from the victim's state to that of revolutionary legislative will can only be accomplished by the dialectic of action. And the victim is in fact convinced, by his long servitude, that he can do nothing. To be liberated, he must be flung into action first, in self-defence. If you merely get rid of oppression (that is, if oppression disappears of its own accord) without the victim's being actively apprenticed to freedom, the same thing happens all over again – the victim flings himself into a new slavery. How can he behave as a free man, if he has neither subjectively nor objectively apprenticed himself to such behaviour? Liberated, in his new surroundings, from his racial stigma, he soon invented a new stigma for himself: that of not being French. Accustomed by his infantile situation to conceive of man as essentially Other than himself, he has not, in the shadow of his Swiss mountain, claimed humanity for himself, but projected it upon a France which at the time seemed to him the antithesis of Germany and, by the same token, of himself.

Such, at least, seems to me to be the profound motivation of his conversion to French. The course of events will now enrich that conversion with new significations unforeseen by him, objective significations which he will finally assume and which will lead him to discover supplementary motivations in his choice. This had begun at the time of the fall of France. He had established himself in the war as if it were going to last forever, as if the armed Franco-German opposition expressed an immutable reality. He had converted to a strong France which he believed to be Germany's equal. And now it was collapsing. The Belgian frontier, the Marne, Paris, closing pincers, 'successful retreats', barrage battles of which one heard no mention the next day, 'The Marseillaise' and nasal, bombastic voices that were evidently lying coming out of the radio in the rat-faced Dutch boy's room where he sipped his Dole, the only drinkable Swiss red wine. 'The Marseillaise' meant a speech was coming, military marches, that the speech was late. 'He's giving it to his girl', said Rat-Face. 'No kidding', he said. 'They do that all the time', Rat-Face said. 'It's to calm their nerves.' 'You think so?' he asked. 'Now he's beginning to wash his hands,' said Rat-Face, 'he's pulling on his trousers, his chauffeur is waiting downstairs.'

An eloquent and emotional voice: 'We shall fight to the end, behind the Pyrenees, in Africa', or something like that, and then they knew it was over. The machine keeps running, the gears are grinding, the machine is well oiled, well tuned, Germany is a great machine eating into bucolic, dreamy, cultivated France, the France of poplars, streams, Michèle Morgan, and Giraudoux, Secretary of State for Propaganda, mobilizing his Juliet, her Pacific, and her armadillos against the Nazi tanks. Again the fever, the triumphal marches, the air thickening, time clotting for days on end into a motionless Moment, something stops existing, something crucial begins (as when two hundred thousand Germans on the Austrian frontier wait while Schuschnigg, with his pinched, Jesuitical face, waits for Chamberlain's answer, and it was no, for the answer from Paris, where there is no government, and it was no, while Miklas waits for Schuschnigg to give the order to fire, and it was no, and Miklas resigns, and Schuschnigg resigns, and Globocnik, in his SA uniform, comes out on the balcony overlooking the Ring, *Sieg Heil, wir kehren Heim ins Reich*, Führer command we shall obey, Seyss-Inquart and his murderer's face), the machine triumphs, France falls; it was no. No, man will not win. He understands this suddenly. *Man is defeated.* Man exists only in defeat because the triumph belongs to the machines. And what he has not dared to do before he does now: he begins to hate Germany, its SA men, its language with its knots of silence, murder and mystery, its mystique of machines and motorized power and blood, its arrogant pride to be German. And he understands this too: that Man does not exist, to love French is to love what does not exist, is to affirm nonbeing against being, is to oppose the imaginary to the real. Then his conversion to French suddenly takes on a meaning. He, who does not exist, who is only a nullity rejected by the world and without any possibility save to reject the world in return, suddenly has a brother, and this brother is a whole people, a nation annihilated like himself, existing no more than the dream by which he declares himself against the real machine. France is suddenly a brother in whom he recognizes himself, a nation of bistros and *flâneurs*, of dreamers never at grips with events, men who ask only to live reflectively, composing verses, books, music, and whom he loves because of the drubbing they have received, instead of being angry with them for not being able to defend themselves. He is convinced that the French are like him, that they are his own adventure transposed to the scale of history, men defeated, trampled on, exiled on their own land, atomized into forty million solitudes, each man weeping before his circle of light on a desk of raw wood and secretly re-creating man and France in his imagination, dreaming over a book. To speak, to read, to think in French becomes a means of defying history. In opposition to being, he perpetuates the France which no longer exists, and by the same token creates, in opposition to reality, a world where Man is possible. This possibility (the dream) which I said was the only one accessible to him, in default of a real liberation or conformism, he now found himself swept into by the unforeseen interrelation of facts; it became, after the fact, the objective signification of his conversion to French, he had only to develop it now – a lived signification fitting his personal situation.

## C. 'THE IMPOSSIBLE NULLITY'*

To assimilate, to incorporate French, to create France, to create man from day to day, when neither existed, in opposition to reality – perhaps I'm exaggerating, perhaps he wasn't thinking in terms this extreme; but he must have been living a signification of this kind already when, still alienated in his religious submission, he worshipped defunct Man by worshipping French, resuscitated him at night in masses celebrated to his glory. Masses by which defunct man was temporarily reincarnated by reciting the magic words, murmured prayers by which he himself, who was dead, revived, touched by grace. By speaking the language of man to himself he hoped to become man. He began writing – in a blue notebook, with a mechanical pencil.

---

*Cf. Jean-Paul Sartre, *Saint Genet*.

He did not think of becoming a writer, he was not writing to be someone; for him writing was a way of praying, of borrowing from the language of men the magical means of acceding to that truth which he found neither in himself nor around him. A truth alien in itself, like the believer's God, like Him not to be interiorized, a truth he would have felt presumptuous trying to produce, before which he religiously bowed his head and merely learned his ritual formulae; he made up sentences out of borrowed words and turns of phrase in the hope that true thought would spring from the series of syllables, as true faith was said to spring from prayer.

This was probably why Valéry and his essays on rigour infatuated him so. Here was a man who (in *Variété III*) declared that beauty obeys rigorous laws and that genius, consciously or not, merely chooses the variables of a universal equation (that of aesthetics, which is also that of the universe). What was this equation? To understand it, he took special courses in mathematics; one day, thanks to the universal equation, he too would create beauty and truth. Meanwhile he studied the style of the great authors and imitated Proust in his compositions. Imitated; everything he wrote during the school year 1940–41 was imitation, an attempt to conjure up on paper the thoughts and feelings of French authors, to acquire the technique of this invocation. He did not write what he felt or thought, for he was convinced it was foolish and worthless; he wrote to learn the linguistic substance of other people's truth, in the hope that at the end of this apprenticeship, by speaking as they did, he too would have true thoughts and feelings – theirs. Patiently, with his yellow word book and his blue notebook, he forged himself a soul according to the alien norms he believed absolute and eternal. He wrote to be Other, to get rid of himself. He became true for himself only by transposing himself in writing. Therefore he would never be through writing, forging himself a truth.

It was on this imitation, fabricated day after day, that he built his life. The conversion to French was a desperate escape from the Austro-German/Judaeo-Christian contradiction, petrified by exile. Of course, if he had been twenty-five he might have assumed his contradiction instead of running away from it. There were many possible alternatives: he might have transcended it by a philosophical or historical synthesis; he might have established himself in exile, gone into business or politics, written books, had children, or merely made love and a living as well as he could, feeling lucky to be in Switzerland. Only he wasn't seventeen yet, and, as a *petit-bourgeois* adolescent, he knew nothing of the world; along with his country, his school and his family, the point of view had vanished from which he might have seen the world in perspective, discerned the contours of a future, found his niche. He had never found it because he was too much of a child (the world was the realm of grown-ups) and because he loathed his father's life; he imagined no future because the war's end would have restored nothing he might have hoped to have back (he had had nothing, being only a child). And then (for these same reasons) he didn't imagine the war *could* end; in how many years? He who was nothing couldn't plan years ahead; you must already be something in order to hope for something. He didn't know who he was; he was nothing but a tangle of objective contradictions which came to him from outside and of which he wasn't even clearly aware. On the one hand there was his nullity and on the other, outside, an alien humanity furiously exploding into the incomprehensible quarrels of the grown-ups. He was in the camp of both the victors and the vanquished, and equally rejected by both. He loathed the victors, but for reasons as null as himself. He hoped for their defeat, but there was no one to oppose them; and if there had been someone (which he didn't conceive of) he would have had nothing in common with him. He was a witness of an absurd history which took so long to unravel that its perspectives outstripped his own; he did not know who he would be when the history took a different turn (if it did); he foresaw nothing because his despair was absolute, and his despair was absolute because the world remained alien for him, an absurd world of despair. And he would have to live with that. He had installed himself in despair; and because he refused his individual condition (because he fled the Austro-German–Judaeo-Christian contradiction for the myth of the French absolute), he deprived himself of the means of transcending it. I understood this only much later, six years later. Because I was incapable of thinking my condition, of situating my despair in its historical relativity, of grasping its concrete motivations, I lived it absolutely, as the immutably true vision of an immutably despairing world, as a metaphysical truth against which the historical truth, supposing it even countenanced hope, remained impotent.

I know, most adolescents pass through this metaphysical stage. Because they are no longer children protected against consciousness of themselves and the world by their parents' values and intercession; because (particularly when they are bourgeois) they discover the world (which they still have no means of making or knowing) as an alien reality, made without consulting them, in which they are told to find a place while at the same time they are refused the capacity to take one, they begin a revolt against the world's order and norms which they have no reason to accept, for, not making them, they need not answer for them. Parasites while their parents pay for their education, they hate the benefactor who puts them under obligation and slyly waits for them on the day they receive their diplomas, anxious to teach them that 'you have to grow up' and to bury them alive in a career continuing the old order; pariahs when they must wring their own educations from a society which considers them slugs and which, after having multiplied the difficulties on their road, attempts to win them back by conceding a diploma on condition – 'on condition that you understand it is this society which has allowed you to grow up and that you undertake nothing to disturb the existing order.' Parasites, then, or pariahs, always nonintegrated, oppressed by society or family, they are inclined by their theoretical equipment, having no grasp of reality, to judge the world in the abstract, to contest it by values no society (in essence) realizes (and particularly not theirs), to contest the world by virtue of the infinite number of opportunities of which they dream and in relation to which the finitude of the possible is always, as Bataille puts it, a fall from grace (*déchéance*).

This is the 'despair of youth' (bourgeois youth) – to know it can only decline; to know that the infinity of the possible, of which it can dream precisely because it is nothing as yet, will collapse; to know that its requirements will be necessarily disappointed when it 'becomes something', but *only* this 'something' ('I was like you once, but now I have responsibilities; you can't always do what you want in life'); to know it will end up by accepting the world it now rejects because it has not created it, knows the world will open its sympathetic arms and say paternally, 'What's the use of revolt? We've all gone through it. We're offering you a Splendid Position. You're only hurting yourself by rejecting it.' Then youth accepts the 'splendid position', swearing to keep its soul unsullied. But what good is an unsullied soul when you have a splendid position? Telling yourself you're worth more than what you are, more than the world, distinguishing man from his actions, collaborating with an inhuman society by reading Malraux or *Les Temps Modernes* and hanging reproductions of abstract paintings on the walls.

Feeling this, even if he doesn't think it; about to enter a world which prescribes a role he has not chosen; conscious that the possibility of playing this role is a hereditary privilege guaranteed by and preserving the social order, the (bourgeois) adolescent sees his life already worked out (a fine career) and, because he has not yet lived it, because he still *sees* it as a destiny without glory, he wonders what this world and this life are worth. Not much. And he is right. Only the discovery of this metaphysical truth (the absurdity of the world and of life) remains a sterile one; metaphysical consciousness cannot reach beyond itself toward a morality because it is rootless, an abstract protest, incapable of inserting itself into history by an action for which it does not possess the means. And insofar as he does not create his means, but leaps from the metaphysical adolescence into a ready-made adult career, the bourgeois adolescent continues his despair into man's estate. He is a full-fledged nihilist, a man who 'plays the game' quite cynically and who (remember, my friends?) after a day of honourable work and before returning to a respectable home, trots out, in some bar or other, his agonizingly lucid thoughts.

All this to say that his despair had nothing exceptional about it when he landed in Lausanne in the spring of 1941 and that, like most young bourgeois of eighteen, he wondered why he was on earth – to do what? Nothing. (A discovery which loses none of its truth for having been conditioned by an individually desperate situation. The most fundamental truths are always discovered through individual situations. This does not mean that they are individual. Desperate situations furnish the means of discovering a fundamental absurdity of which they later appear as the contingent confirmation.)

This no longer means anything. I could continue through the years to this minute, but I feel it no longer has any meaning. I am no longer learning anything. It's becoming a routine. Tonight, coming down the Rue Saint-Sulpice (the street of failures; the first time I saw it, that's how it looked to me – over-elaborate, angular, full of antique shops and dark apartments where I imagine those adolescents of the Latin Quarter have ended up, in overstuffed rooms where they outlive the hope of their revolt, becoming bourgeois, pious, and routine-worn), I told myself, 'It no longer means anything, I can go on like this indefinitely, but I'm not learning any more. I have learned nothing, I haven't advanced a step except in theory and in knowledge. But theory remains inoperative. I don't know what to do with my life.' Now (as in the spring of 1941, fifteen years earlier) he comes down the dusty street that smells of failure and wonders, 'What can I do with my life?' and immediately this feeling is reflected in thought, in consciousness of the vanity of the thought of its vanity, then as if he were pulling out a plug at the bottom of this stagnant consciousness, everything flows out, assumes a direction. The consciousness of vanity is polarized by the project of writing about the consciousness of vanity, it is no longer merely the vain and suffering consciousness, it is here in order to bear witness to itself in the form of writing. (As in 1941, during the blackout in the Place Chauderon, looking at the sky, he suddenly realized the immensity of the universe and realized that the Place Chauderon, with its lampposts, its post office, its Vaudois and its blackout turning in the sidereal universe, had no importance whatever, neither it, nor he, nor the war across the border, nor men in general, nor thought – that it had no importance whatever and that it would take a detestable dose of stupidity, pretentiousness, solemnity, yes, abject solemnity, to attribute any importance to what was happening between the Place Chauderon and Warsaw, in some point of the sidereal universe. It was on this thought that he fed himself during the following months, supported by Valéry and Jean Rostand discoursing on frail-humanity-protoplasm's-pathetic-adventure; on this thought, and on its contradiction: that if nothing has any importance, then the consciousness that nothing has any importance has no importance. Yet it had an enormous importance, and he rushed to write this discovery, to write that it had no importance, to write that it had no importance to write it, to write that writing it had no importance to write it had no importance, and, caught in his own maze, to write about the contradiction of writing that writing has no importance.)

Thus, fundamentally I have not changed. Now as then, there is this sense of absurdity and this way of taking it as a literary theme, of making it his object aesthetically by living it in order to write it, and thereby to invent an aesthetic justification for it. I have explained this elsewhere; a consciousness driven to realize its own nothingness, to the vanity of realizing its own nothingness, a consciousness incapable by its situation of living anything but evidence of its own vanity and impotence, confronted with the fullness and unconcern of being, a consciousness which, immured in the universe, is nothing but a cry no one hears – such a consciousness cannot invent any other meaning for itself than itself, cannot find any other purpose than to *be* the cry it *is not*. I mean that such a consciousness, its cry unheard, knowing the vanity of its cry and yet unable to choke it back, having to express its existence as a cry and producing nothing but this deafening silence, such a consciousness finds no other means of manifesting its freedom save to will its cry as it already is; it wills itself to be as it exists (this is all it can be – itself), it doubles its cry, recovers it as the free product of its activity by re-creating it in the form of an object: it begins writing. And what I have written, day after day, was indeed cries, variations on the same theme, ceaselessly begun again, variations trying to shape this silent clamour in language, as if, by creating it in the form of an independent object, I could stop producing it in my own breath and, delivered, could then enjoy its contemplation; everything would be said.

And now the words rustle past, he listens to himself talking. And having talked a good deal (having accomplished his daily task, fixed for seven years now at two pages covered with a tiny handwriting), he can go to bed (or out for a walk), his conscience clear. Suddenly relaxed, he can enjoy everything: breathing the air, looking at people in the street, seeing the city with a painter's eye, as a vari-coloured décor. He allows himself an 'earned' respite; he is at ease with himself. After all, I'm not so bad after all, he tells himself. And if he runs into someone he knows, he begins talking almost lovingly. At least that's how it was for several years. Days that were sometimes terrible, during which he strugged to disentangle confused intentions ('If I can't clear this up, it's because I don't know what I mean'), punctuated by moments of euphoria. Why this euphoria? he wondered, still not forgiving himself for it, reproaching himself for it as a disturbing symptom; did it not bear witness that he was writing less to say something (to do something) than to 'deserve' a moment's respite as he had performed his 'spiritual exercises' at twelve; that writing was a way to get rid of himself, and not an attempt to find himself?

Of course this was true for a long time. And as far as writing is concerned, I could readily busy myself with the same demonstration of a dialectical progression which succeeded so well in the case of prayer and which risks becoming a universal recipe, showing (1) that he began to write to appropriate French thought and to teach himself how to think – this was the period of his stylistic exercises; (2) that in 1941, thanks to the *Pensées d'un Biologiste* (of Jean Rostand) and to the 'Petite Lettre sur les Mythes', the 'Variation sur une Pensée de Pascal' and the 'Soirée avec Mallarmé' (of Valéry, in *Variété II*), followed by *Nausea* (bought

by chance – he had just found *The Imaginary* in a secondhand bookshop; not understanding it, he had bought it and a
month later, in a Genovese bookshop, he had found both *Nausea*
and *The Wall*. 'Well', he had thought, 'a philosopher who
writes fiction. That should be substantial.' And he bought them),
he discovered cosmic (or ontological) despair. First by thought; it
furnished him the intellectual means of realizing that he himself
was living this despair at first conceived in other people's words
as if it were an exterior truth. Or perhaps by trying to reproduce
in himself the despair he found in others, he succeeded so well
that he came to the inspired realization that it was indeed his
own. Tremendous satisfaction: a true experience at last; by
imitating others, he encountered himself. So he too was capable
of truth, or rather truth, a certain truth, was immediately accessible to him! He began writing sub-Valéry and sub-*Nausea*. This
was a religious discipline – to provoke their experiences in
himself, to pour his own experience into the mould of truth (that
is, into theirs) and by doing so to accede to that humanity he
recognized in them and felt himself lacking altogether. He wrote
so that by resembling them he could become a Man: that is,
could escape his individual nullity by transcending it toward the
universal by means of language. (3) That having started out to
become Other (or to interiorize Otherness) and encountering
himself in others, his literary exercise now becomes ambiguous;
he no longer knows what belongs to others and what comes from
himself. He begins speaking of himself in their manner. He
speaks with a guarantee; the orientation of his thought, if not its
concrete content (however little) is furnished him by them,
guaranteed by them. He writes under their scrutiny like a dutiful
student; he lives beneath their scrutiny, since his own experience
interests him only to the degree that it accords with theirs. Thus
his literary activity is alienated and falsified from the start, as
though deflected from its potential authentic signification by the
fundamental religious intention which inspires it. I mean that he
writes in order to dismantle (like a bomb) his own intolerable
experience by transforming it into a pretext for literature and
assigning himself the distant goal (aimed at in doubt and often in

despair) of being a Man like Valéry or Morel. (He calls him Morel because They have corrupted the name J.-P.S. for him, because gossip and public stupidity have seized upon the name of this Man, whom he jealously adored, as an army takes possession of the body of a woman who, though a whore for them, is your beloved and whom you decide to call Kay or L [more pseudonyms], to keep her reality for you separate from her reality for them.)

Here at last is the beginning of a truth. He wrote, he says, in order to shape his cry in language. Yes, doubtless; but this is an *a posteriori* interpretation based on the objective signification of the act of writing. Yet this signification, true in the last analysis, was not dominant at the start. At the point I have reached (supposition 3), I was writing to become the man *par excellence* whom the French author was for me; that is, I was deflecting my lived experience from its original signification in order to transform it into a literary experience. He was deflecting his experiences from their primary meaning, beginning to live them with a view to a second meaning, as 'experiences-for-writing', and the meaning of the activity of writing was to transform his experience on paper into the experience of one of these celebrated others who French authors were for him. He did not write to be an author, but to recover his existence transmuted into literary material, invested with the prestige of literature; he wrote to get rid of his existence, to live its crying absurdity in vain no longer, to produce it as if it flowed from his project of writing.

Therefore, at this stage, he was still writing the way you pray. Literature, for him, was other people's business, and by writing he was trying not to become one of these others (that would have seemed a laughable presumption to him) but to palm off his existence on them surreptitiously, to have it taken over by literature as an emanation of that literature-of-others. And is he doing anything different today? Is he quite sure he is not still writing to transform his existence into a literary work which, joining other people's in the Pantheon of literature, would save him from the contingency of existing (like Antoine Roquentin, dreaming of transforming his existence into something like his favourite song)?

I know; the Pantheon is dead for me, and I no longer believe
in its divinities; literature has lost its prestige. And yet, what am I
doing now? If the evocation of this past disturbs him, if he feels
he is no longer advancing, is still chewing the same cud as fifteen
years before, is falling back into the same rut, it is because he
recognizes himself in this period. Why is he writing? He started
out proudly and enthusiastically, believing that with this autobiography he would forge a new instrument, a new means of
apprehending the world. Now he doesn't know any more. Only
this: if he continues on this road, he will achieve nothing more
than a new attempt at literary lifesaving, or, what comes down to
the same thing, of philosophical lifesaving: a claim to set an
example, to derive from his own case the illustration of a universal
Method; of finding himself included not in the Pantheon of literature but in that of general theories. He must find something else.

More precisely, he must find something to say. His initial
enthusiasm derived from this: he thought he had something to
say, had something he *could* say; he could address himself to
dozens of young men he had run across who, without being half-
castes, lived the contradictions that his own mixed background
had led him to realize (he thinks) and, by speaking of himself,
could help them to understand what makes a man be what he is.
But now he doesn't know any longer. If he had the impression of
a good start, it was because he felt he was speaking to someone.
Since then, by speaking, he came back to the feeling of speaking
in the void. Retiring into a new, imperfect shell; conscious
suddenly that he was existing like these young men yawning on
the Boulevard Saint-Germain who, like him, cover sheets of
paper every night, who write against the world, against their
brothers, who grow furious when someone says what they are
thinking because what is important for them is to say it first –
they write to distinguish themselves, to be the person who
manages to get printed by beating out his friends. Well, he has
nothing to say to such men; they are the fascists of literature.
There remain the others, the ones who are more interested in the
world than in me. It is the world (and someone like me-in-the-
world) that I must tell them about. Yet, at the point I have

reached (1941), there was virtually no world. What I was saying I was saying for nothing, to destroy the thing said, to produce the sideral silence by my self-annihilating words. To reconstitute this experience is to re-create that great silence over the Place Chauderon, far from Voronezh, Kharkov, Smolensk, Bengazi, far from the five thousand booted peasants slaughtered every day on the eastern front; within the reach only of Philippe Henriot, of M. Peyer, the department store's Catholic furniture salesman, who considered that the Army, the defeat and the Maréchal 'formed' youth – 'And you have no lessons to teach us; in your place, my boy, I'd be only too happy they let me stay in Switzerland, and I'd keep my mouth shut'; within the reach of Federal Councillor Pilet-Golaz, crusading against the Bolsheviks in the name of Helvetian culture while the cinemas showed UFA, Swiss (Hurrah for General Guisan and our brave farmer-soldiers!) and Vichy newsreels. To revive this period is to write the solitude, the stupidity, the daily lying, is to speak in order to say nothing (which is one definition of poetry as good as another); it is to do what I was doing then: to write the way you pray, because you're speaking to no one.

There are two ways of writing, as Morel says: for men and for God. Well, when you cannot write for men because you have nothing to tell them, you necessarily write for God. You 'engrave in language a great silent cry'; you create pure literature, beautiful and useless as the pyramids, denying men and their world in favour of their Nothingness. This no longer attracts me. It remains to say how it did attract me for seven years. And it remains to be seen afterward if there is anything else for me to say and do. For, thinking over what I have written, it seems to me that, as usual, the key signification of the project to write was (or is) the one I have not mentioned. Namely, that writing for God, as Morel says, is a claim to establish, as a literary work promised to the Pantheon of bookshops, truth in itself. It is to claim to establish a true relation alone with the absolute. Like the believer praying, it is a claim to recover alone his true reality; it affirms that the latter is on my paper, that I am what I write, that this writing, materialized without the assistance of others, must also be accepted religiously by them as a sacred and incontestable text, since it was produced without their help. And the signification of my writings (imposed, forced year after year on the rare visitors; as soon as they began talking about something, he cut short the discussion and, rummaging in his papers, read them a sacred text, reread it instead of explaining it, referring his visitor to the writing as to a definitive source) has for a long time been this: to establish my being-in-itself-and-for-itself on paper and thereby, deriving it only from myself, to deny all true reality to my being-for-others. Or is it the other way around – since my reality-for-others has no truth for me, to recover on paper my true reality, incommunicable in life for lack of interlocutors? Yes, it's probably the latter proposition that was true at first. But the result was the same. (Or is it the point of departure rather than the result?) For me, other people did not count; they were puppets, shadows encountered every day whom I never bothered to understand. We were not living in the same world, their truth was without effect on mine (and conversely). Yes, probably a point of departure; here is where I started. But a result too; I have so well developed this condition of an exile in a world (Switzerland) without truth – and of an exile from the real world, the beyond-the-Swiss-borders – that nothing I thought brought the Swiss closer to me; I thought against them, and our separation, a point of departure, also became the accepted result of my attitude.

He stops, he admires this regression which has twice brought him to see a point of departure in what he first took for the effect of his choice. For despite all his resolutions, he has a tendency to forget that choice, like scientific discovery, invents only what already exists. I mean that he develops only this or that objective possibility the world offers him in order to feed it on his freedom. Thus with the choice to write – it was produced by a religious attitude toward French literature (a new form of an old religiosity) and also by an intolerable solitude. Objectively null, being nothing but a consciousness of his nothingness confronting a totally alien world, he was immediately offered two possibilities: to annihilate himself, nothing as he was, in a world perfectly unconcerned with him, and this he tried; but since it was impossible without killing himself (and he thought of this constantly), he had to find, once he decided to stay alive, a meaning for his life. It could have only one (this is the second possibility): that of not having any. When you cannot keep from crying out though you know you will not be heard, you may as well decide that this cry which has no meaning has a meaning insofar as it has none – that it is in itself its own absurd meaning. This is where poetry starts. Philosophy too; and, once started, developing a style from the situation itself, it manages to attribute value to this style and to perpetuate this situation.

But what if the situation changes? This is what must be considered. I no longer know what meaning it has to write. I write to find a meaning. But perhaps this meaning, once the situation and I change, is lost. Perhaps reaching the end of this thing, I have 'cured' myself of the project to write. 'Cured' by writing – by writing the cure of a man who is writing his disaffection from what he writes. And who therefore would write the renunciation of his project to write. And who, writing about it, would discover that he has transformed his renunciation of literature into literature. But this is a superficial paradox. He clings to his paper for fear of losing his desire to write, and so that he will have that at least. For fear of leading a commonplace life, of dissolving into anonymity and diversion, of getting to like life's pleasure, of enjoying the life of all these bourgeois whose condition he is beginning to share, of becoming one of them. And – a correlative temptation to which he must not yield – for fear of overvaluing as a heroic achievement his life during the forties.

Molluscs floating in an aquarium: the loquacious and Jesuitical Peyer, who would turn the radio on for the Vichy news when he came into the dining room first; the sugary Violette, turning forty, who discovered the value of her virginity in not having managed to get rid of it; the boorish technician from Aarau who cut up his meat and potatoes as if he were wielding an axe, loaded his fork like a shovel and thrust food into his mouth as if he were feeding a furnace; the two pimply adolescents who dared not lift their pale eyes from their plates; Helen, with her slit of a mouth, her Bourbon nose, her legs like columns, though not without her charm, dreaming of her German aviator, silent, desperately Nazi though she didn't avoid him for that (a little tenderness, even from a half-caste, might have saved her? She ended up in an SS harem, 'proud', she wrote, 'to be chosen to perpetuate the German race. I shall give the Führer an elite citizen') – he stared at them as at molluscs in an aquarium. Stuff yourselves, he thought. He dreamed of walking into this dining room with a revolver and without a word calmly shooting them down one by one, to punish them for stuffing themselves here instead of being in Smolensk, in Tobruk, in London, in Brazzaville, to punish them for the earnestness which permitted no doubt that they must perpetuate their life by eating, to punish them for the presumption that made them think they had the sacred right to live. Men were objects in the sidereal universe, worth no more than the cast-iron lampposts which, in the prescribed blackout, no longer lit up the Place Chauderon. He loathed these useless objects for the assurance which kept them from suffering from their absurdity.

So there was something wrong in his relations with other men (something broken which has not mended, for he stares at them with the same look today – the idlers on the terraces of the Champs-Elysées, the hothouse plants in Saint-Germain-des-Prés, the bonebreakers stuffing themselves with meat, the crimson faces on the Métro stinking of red wine, he hates the flabby efflorescence of human flesh, human meat, the digestive placidity, the burps and sighs); it is as if these relations, based on the affective links with a few really close persons and with a place which might be called 'mine' (geographical as much as social and historical), could only extend to the rest of humanity starting from these links, and, once these were broken, collapsed, deprived of their primordial instrument.

This explanation is valid not only for him. To sympathize with men, to regard them as more than a kind of gratuitous institution, you must doubtless be linked in friendship or love to some among them, you must live in complicity with the surrounding society – a complicity which keeps you from constantly questioning the habits, styles, 'values' of others, a complicity based on the existence of a common experience of humanity, a common surface of contact with the world. A complicity (which is not necessarily complacency) on whose basis alone can an authentic solidarity be constructed.

But nothing linked him to the Vaudois of 1941. (Does anything more link him to the Parisians of 1956? That remains to be seen.) They looked prosperous, with firm flesh, singsong accents, big behinds sticking out under their jackets that seemed to squeeze them under the arms; they dawdled along in their well-scrubbed town with its slow-moving blue trolley buses, walked over the Grand Pont from the Place Saint-François (guarded at each corner by a temple of finance) to the Place Bel-Air in the shadow of its commercial skyscraper. Among their banks, their well-stocked stores, in their thick woollies and their cleanliness, they seemed to be living outside time, with comfortable salaries, a guaranteed future. 'Think Swiss. . . . The Swiss housewife cooks by electricity. . . . Vaudois liberalism. . . .' Federal Councillor Wetter ploughs his field behind a team of three horses; Dr Ruppaner leaves for the eastern front to tend the heroes of the Wehrmacht; Federal Councillor Pilet-Golaz sells Oerlikon guns to the Reich; General Guisan spends a half hour on horseback every morning. 'Switzerland, faithful to its ideal of neutrality . . . unshakably loyal to the values of the Christian West . . . haven of peace and charity in this world at war . . .', Switzerland produces clock movements, butter and potatoes, Switzerland lets the German munitions trains through the Gothard tunnel, fires its ack-ack shells beside the RAF bombers and interns French Army deserters in work camps where they contribute to the landowners' prosperity.

Switzerland does not exist. He took a long time to find this out. Switzerland was watches, gold-stuffed bank vaults, precision machinery, postcard landscapes; it mobilized its worn-out myths, its reform theologians, its brawny peasants to convince itself of its existence, but it did not succeed. Like Austria before 1938, it admired itself in its postcards, its pompous speeches, dug up its dead and chewed over its history, but its attempt at self-

hypnotism bogged down in the placidity of a people sitting on six
years of food and fuel stocks, a people who had nothing to defend
but their comforts, who know that 'neutrality' toward the Reich
and the Allies was a joke, that official Helvetia would always and
inevitably find itself the accomplice of the stronger. I did not
understand that this 'common experience of humanity', this
'common surface of contact with the world' which I lacked was
also lacking in the Swiss of my generation; this country was a no-
man's-land abandoned by the hopes and fears of the rest of the
world; its historical reality was its historical nullity, it exiled its
inhabitants from history and immured them in comfort and
security as in a prison. The situation of Swiss youth, as desperate
as my own (though on another level), offered no toehold in
history, their Swiss-being was the reality of their non-being and
their national reality the reality of their historical exclusion. They
could share only this exclusion and this despair, deride the verb-
iage of the official ideology to commune in contempt and resentment of their nation, and seek beyond its borders, with a determination and a seriousness I have never encountered elsewhere
to the same degree, truths which remained fatally abstract and
alien, for which they conceived nostalgic infatuations, which they
cut into slivers in the course of interminable and sterile discussions.

For Swiss youth too, there was nothing to do. They could not
have genius, they knew that. They were set apart, they watched
history pass by as he used to watch the trains pull out. They were
carried in tow by the exterior world, which did not penetrate
here save in muffled echoes, they envied other nations their
sufferings and their problems, real sufferings, and they could
only trail after the thoughts, the decisions which these foreign
problems provoked. They studiously read their Laforgue,
discovered surrealism and Gide twenty years late; they spent,
like Pierre, twenty laborious years bringing out a study of Dostoevski. Today there are perhaps five hundred of them who read
*L'Observateur* the way other men read the Bible, who have violent
arguments about Yankee colonialism in Latin America, about
African nationalism, about the Chinese revolution, about New

Orleans jazz. They feel that their thoughts have no weight, that they are doomed to be spectators or imitators, to have only an opinion about everything, and that this opinion matters so little; the opinion of the stupidest Frenchman, Russian or American matters more. They too read, think, argue the way you pray: in the presence of the absolute, to summon up the absolute which for them is a historical reality that always belongs to other people, to have something to do, for nothing. And yet, if they wanted to, if they would turn the self-disgust in which they commune to action, what a fascinating undertaking it would be to write a Marxist study of Swiss reality! International capitalism as a whole would be reflected in it, the world-wide influence of big concerns like Nestlé, Ciba, Brown Boveri, Oerlikon. 'Swiss liberalism' would come down from its ideological pedestal and reveal its export industries swollen with foreign capital planted in the four corners of the world. Paternalism, the inertia of bureau-cratized trade unions, the sclerosis of socialist thought, the impotence of Communism and the absence of any revolutionary outlook would be illuminated by the high skills of a manpower working essentially for export, it too alienated in the laws of foreign markets and international finance – a manpower for which it simply has no meaning to claim the ownership of the means of production, since these means of production do not serve to satisfy indigenous needs, since they constitute wealth only when minted by export-import and public relations specialists, since Swiss prosperity rests on investment and loans abroad of capital which has also come from abroad seeking sanctuary in the vaults of Swiss banks. Nationalize all this? First you would have to nationalize Wall Street and the City, start the revolution in France and Italy, constitute the Soviet States of Europe, to which the Swiss would allot four administrative cantons (and not a Federated Republic, for with its value as a refuge it would lose its national reality). A fascinating undertaking, stamped with the same sterility as this tedious country, since it ends up with the demonstration that there is really nothing to do and that, when you are Swiss, you must wait until the world has changed to change something at home; you must wait for salvation from without, impotent, reduced to stirring up thoughts which are only thoughts.

They felt this curse of being Swiss. They had at their disposal the most highly perfected instruments in the world – libraries, famous universities, modern hospitals, engineers, doctors, research facilities and equipment envied by the rest of the world; their borders were open to the intellectual production of every country. And all this abundance shrivelled between their fingers, useless, good for nothing but making money, creamy pastries, comfort for four million lives for whom life had no meaning. Condemned to see humanity from outside, they could encounter it only by invoking an abstract humanitarianism, rejecting the historical density of human reality in the name of a bleating idealism: the Red Cross, Children's Aid, Mother's Day. From the reality of struggle they derived only the ideas it had provoked in others, and their philosophers (staring at the ceiling of the amphitheatre, a toneless voice, a scraggy body) analysed these ideas which had become general and abstract, confronting them, rejecting them one by one in the name of the timeless truths of Plato or Descartes.

The best rebelled, but their rebellion was hopeless. They knew it; either it stopped short or it poured out as literature, and it was with literature that they ended up when they had not drowned their despair in the sour white wine that ruined their livers, or in the routines of their professions. A secret literature, rarely published. A's hermetic poems – A was a navvy's son, sent to the university on a scholarship, who began annihilating the universe with Mallarmé before corroding it with Prévert, then setting it on fire with the Workers' Party, ending up as a professor. B's secret poetry – B was a derided bastard who began with a Vaudois version of Nazism, before turning to Ponge, to Stalin, then to Sartre, ending up as an official writing in a flamboyant style once a month for a bulletin read by some hundreds of solitary amateurs. Poetry of solitude, of impossible love, of despair, of the starry sky for Jean-Marie and for dozens of others who sang their nullity or gravely, in tiny sects, debated utopian socialism and French policy in North Africa. Some went to Germany because they saw in Nazism a great, purifying wind of barbarism which would wrench them from stagnation and permit them to encounter history; and some left at night to join the maquis in Savoy and were ashamed to admit when they came back that they had found nothing or that they had been laughed home; and some smuggled gold for love of danger; there were painters who on rarely sold canvases tried to open windows on the universe or more simply to break the glass of the one that was imprisoning them; and finally there were those who remained in the Workers' Party whose dream of human brotherhood remained without any effect on their condition.

They were all exiles, abstract and contemptuous because their situation offered them no means of communication with either the world outside or the core of the Swiss collectivity that was swathed in lifeless traditions, casting each man back into his solitude within a supercilious conformism.

If he had thought of this then, he might have liked these men, who were somewhat in the same boat as himself. But they were not thinking of this either; the situation they opposed so noisily remained the matter of their consciousness and was not grasped in any clear formulation. He did not know he might have transcended his own misery by sympathizing with that of others and by explaining the latter's causes to them. He was too full of his own woes, chewing them over and over, making everyone he met responsible for them.

'Date of entry into Switzerland? Proof of resources? Validity of passport? Military status? Purpose of visit?' He stared timidly at the bald, grey-eyed immigration official who repeated the same questions every three months, then disappeared with his dossier into the chief's office. Verdict? 'We'll let you know.' Three months more. Three months' reprieve. Behind the chief's padded door was a god who would apply his rubber stamp – 'Granted' or 'Refused'. And above the cantonal chief of police came the Federal Chief of Police, and above him, at the top, the Chief of the Federal Department of Justice and Police. Justice and Police – you had to be Swiss to think up an association like that. He watched the official's grey eyes, and he felt guilty. The eyes were indecipherable, perhaps a trifle ironic, and he thought he could read in them what Peyer had told him over and over: 'Play it soft, my boy. You're being tolerated here. As long as your German passport is renewed you'll be kept on; you're under the Reich's protection. But we know how far we can depend on the Reich's protection in your case. You're half Jewish, aren't you? You can't study in Germany. So you came to hide here. Nice that Switzerland exists. But you don't like us. Well, we don't like you either. There are millions of guys like you. They say they'd like to come here for three months, but all they can think of is how to stay. And you think we can keep them all? You think we'll keep you when the Reich tells you to go back? And they *will* call you back — you too. For the moment you're in the Ersatz Reserve Three n.z.v. N.z.v. — that means politically suspect. So you won't want to go back when they call you. I can see it all — one of these days you'll ask for right of asylum. Only that won't work, for you. You're not a Jew, are you? Your parents are still in Germany, aren't they? You've been granted a passport? Then you're not a refugee. We're keeping an eye on you. I suppose you'll hide and then come and find us after the passport expires — a *fait accompli.* But we weren't born yesterday. You won't get away with it. We'll come and get you some night, two cops and a car, and bang, the frontier. Alien passbook. Temporary visit.' He looked into the grey eyes, the grey eyes looked at him. Behind the padded door, the chief sent out signals. Green light. Red light. White light. Go sit down, sir, you'll be called. Silence. The usher's shoes creak. Identity card? Your appointment notice? Without an appointment notice, I can't do a thing for you, sir. The grey old man glances around him; no one comes to his support. Every man for himself here. Under the usher's impassive eyes, they shrink down in their seats. Guilty. A perfumed lady comes in with a dog, whispers in the usher's ear. White light. green light. Please come with me, madame. The shoes creak, the padded door opens on pale-blue smoke. The chief receives the lady and the dog. Impassive stare of the usher wandering slowly up and down the row of aliens. 'Try and make a fuss', the eyes seem to say. 'No. You're afraid to. Good.' Then down to his register again. There is a law for each of you; you will be judged according to your file. You will not know what's in the file. Nor the law. You will be pleading all the same.

'Origin?'

He pleads, 'Austria'.

'You mean Germany.'

Badly pleaded. The grey eyes examine him. 'Austria has no juridical existence. Do you intend to return to Germany?'

He squirms. If only he knew what was in the dossier. He tries to reason it out quickly. If I say no, I admit I want to stay; they'll deport me. If I say yes, I'm declaring myself a Nazi. They'll suspect me, but will they deport me?

'Yes', he says.

'When?'

'After the autumn exams. In October.'

Something is written on the form. What? 'Three months extension.' The form is hidden beneath the ringed hand. You will be judged according to the file. First the chief; then the Department of Justice and Police. Plead. There is a law for each of you. For perfumed women with dogs, and for the others. The law is without appeal. Yes, there is an appeal in the marble bank: ten brown thousand-franc notes. Leave ten brown thousand-franc notes and the Helvetian Confederation will take you under its protection. Justice and Police. Rich communes and poor communes. The Swiss law says the poor are to be maintained by their commune. An indigent alien must not fall to the maintenance of his commune. The indigent remains an alien. Ten thousand-franc notes will soften the communes' hearts. The rich alien will be a peaceful citizen. Look for a poor commune; five thousand francs are enough to soften its heart. Provided you spend ten years there. If you're not expelled the day before the tenth year is up.

Two days a week a policeman follows him. It is forbidden to travel without authorization. The German consul looks at him banteringly and salutes, his hand raised. '*Heil* Hitler! Three months' reprieve. We don't know if we can renew your passport after that. Why don't you go back to Germany? Studies? Study, my boy. We understand each other.'

The Germans have their police and their friendly informers too. 'The enemy is listening', the signs said. That was it. The enemy was everywhere, he was surrounded by enemies, he was being watched, he was under suspicion, he turned around in the street to see if he was being followed. Do those eyes belong to the policeman who will put handcuffs on him and take him to the border? Undesirable. Under suspicion, undesirable, supernumerary, useless mouth; pursued like an escaped criminal, guilty in the eyes of all the police of the world; starting when someone whispers behind him in class, feeling the back of his neck shrink, avoiding all contacts for more than a year, regarding with resentment, envy and abject self-pity the groups that formed at the university, the couples flirting during class, telling himself, 'They have a right to. They're where they belong, safe, with a future. You're eating their bread, they don't want anything to do with you. Dirty foreigner, *boche*, *Jude*, why should they want you around?' And, repeating this, feeling his old and ignominious desire to cry rising in his throat, the desire of the boy beaten up by his schoolmate, the lost puppy, the child scolded by his mother. He knew he was exaggerating; no one here dreamed of persecuting him, these people paid no attention to the Nuremberg laws or whether he ate their bread; anyone else in his place (his mother, for instance) would have tried to 'make connections', but as a matter of fact this situation fitted him like a glove – only too happy to be able to tell himself he was persecuted, suspected by all these police, despised and rejected by the whole world, merely a hole in the hostile universe.

This lasted more than a year. Not a single person to talk to. Dreams of persecution; supposed executioners imagined everywhere; the desire to become the victim he imagined himself. The hunger he inflicted on himself to save 140 of the 340 francs a month sent from Vienna (for how much longer?). The sleep he refused in order to read Gide, Ruyer, Broglie, psychoanalysts, characterologists (to be done with the human, to put each man in a characterological and typological pigeonhole, to pin him down like a dead butterfly, since he could not knock him down, to rid himself of these persecuting stares by reducing them to biochemical reactions, to escape the human realm into the sidereal universe). The disciplines of the engineers' school (chemistry division) where he was officially registered because it was the only diploma recognized abroad (neither literature nor medicine were) but also because he could exploit this practical consideration to mortify himself – until he no longer knew if he had chosen chemistry because They refused him the right to do anything else, or to do the opposite of what he liked, or to feel guilty for hating studies for which first his parents and later a philanthropic couple sent him an allowance soon reduced to 200 francs a month (out of which he had to save sixty for tuition and laboratory fees). An objective situation immediately exploited to victimize himself, the constant thought of suicide, and for several months bottles of chloroform stolen from the lab with which he sometimes anaesthetized himself in the evening, supposedly to fall asleep, actually hoping he might not wake up again, or that he might catch pneumonia or cardiac syncope.

He had reached this point by '42 when, moving out of the family pension into a little room without meals, he turned rationing and poverty into another means of mortification, imposing a regime of one Maggi cube and oatmeal at noon (plus a carrot or a tomato), a pint of milk, 225 grams of black bread and forty grams of cheese at night, giving away his meat and fat coupons (or trading them for bread), and glorying in the fact that he could feed himself for less than sixty francs a month, that he weighed only 117 pounds, his face looking rather impressive, he thought, emaciated and sombre. He meshed in so well with his objective situation that he no longer distinguished what corresponded to practical necessities in his behaviour from what resulted from his taste for mortification; what he refused because of lack of money from what he refused 'because you're no good and good things are not for you'; to what degree the world was the totality of what was refused him and to what degree it was the totality of what he refused himself, a knife he turned voluptuously in his own flesh, an objective exclusion he interiorized in order to exclude himself. There was a real objective malediction, but instead of developing it, interiorizing it, choosing himself as cursed and excluded by humanity, he could, like C (a Berlin half-caste whose mother was in America), have grown a little moustache, worn striped bow ties, assumed a knowing look and prepared himself for a career as an industrial chemist ('Think how valuable they'll be after the war!'), or, like D, an Italo-Turkish Jew, have dissolved the world into odours, thrusting his huge, voluptuous nose into the necks of bottles, deciding that Switzerland was a big stupid cow for him to milk, a matter of passing the time until, having sniffed and made love all he wanted, he could become a great perfume tycoon, sending great aphrodisiac gusts around the world and using his millions to ride in an Alfa-Romeo, to promote some explosive enterprise (dynamite for anarchists, subversive publications or Communist night school, he hadn't yet decided).

D, C – they intended, in their way, to appropriate the world, to be smarter than other people, to prove they couldn't be kept down; they regarded their exile as a joke, a temporary condition, they adapted themselves to a situation in which he regressed to his infantile masochism in order to conform to complacently magnified prohibitions. Of the same social origin, what was so different about them? This in particular: they were spoiled children, persuaded since infancy by the adoration their mothers showed upon them that they had rights (this was obvious from the way E, grasping his fork, speared his food with authority, triturated the lumps of sugar in his coffee cup, and – away, useless object! – set noisily down his cup in his saucer when he finished), that the world was there for them to make use of, while he had been convinced by his mother that whatever anyone gave him was the result of an undeserved generosity ('. . . all I've done for you, and that's the way you thank me') and that he had a debt to others which he could never repay, a guilt from which nothing could redeem him.

This, at least, is what those first years of solitude and mortification were good for: to provide him with occasions to push his complexes to their limit, to descend as deep as he could into the

consciousness of his guilt and his nullity, permitting him to grasp
not the origin of his attitude in his complexes but, in the empirical situation of which they have made him aware, certain fundamental aspects of the human condition, such as:

– that each consciousness is alone with itself;

– that *what is* is the site of an infinity of possible meanings, all
equally unjustifiable and gratuitous, and has no meaning in itself
save that of not having one;

– that this truth (that being has no meaning which is not
gratuitous and that every vision of the world is both unjustifiable
and true) has no special privilege, since it, too, is one truth
among others, stamped with relativity and guilt.

From these primary truths, one can derive an infinite number
of consequences. The one he derived is significant of his basic
attitude and of his situation at the time:

– Each consciousness is a nothing colliding with the plenitude
of being; logically, it should annihilate itself in its own nothingness in order to permit being to be. Yet it cannot annihilate itself,
for even its efforts to be the nothing which it is perpetuate it as
consciousness, oppose it to being with a dramatic intensity,
widening its separation from being. Consequence: Existence is
contradiction, and to become conscious of this contradiction in
no way permits its resolution, but reveals consciousness to itself
as a 'metaphysical fault' in the plenitude of being.

Moral: One must crucify oneself upon this fault with no hope
of expiating it save by death.

– Each consciousness has its own truth, but insofar as its truth
is necessarily exclusive of all other truths – that is, individual and
finite – it is also a fault. Total consciousness would include all
truths and yield to none. Yet such consciousness, far from
surmounting the guilt of its finitude, would raise it to its zenith,
for each consciousness claims to raise its truth to the absolute,
and total consciousness, relativizing all truths and preferring
none, rejects them all. In so doing, it raises to the absolute its
particular truth (namely, that no truth is preferable in itself to
any other). The latter must therefore return to the circle,
renounce itself in its turn as a truth like any other. It can do so

only by cancelling itself out. Yet in cancelling itself out it would also cancel out its original affirmation as to the equal truth and error of all truths and would leave intact the infinite diversity of individual truths, each tending toward the absolute. This total consciousness which would identify itself with total indifference (or with its own annihilation), is therefore both necessary and impossible. Its necessity is the foundation of philosophy. Its impossibility condemns philosophy to failure.

Moral: The only valid philosophy is the one which demonstrates its own impossibility and abolishes itself in silence. It is to this demonstration, in the form of an essay and a novel, that he had harnessed himself since 1942, dreaming of demolishing everything in order to demolish, finally, this demolition itself, so that once everything is said, nothing would really have been said at all.

There are two kinds of commentary to make on this procedure, the one affecting its motivations, the other its reality (which will occasion new motivations in its turn).

## Motivations

It will be fiendishly difficult to find a thread running through the overlapping 'subjective' and 'objective' motivations. However, here is one immediate impression: This crucified nihilism which delights in turning around in the circles of its own contradictions reveals a situated consciousness but it reveals it in such a way that only the consciousness, not its situation, becomes immediately apparent. In other words, this nihilism claims to be timeless truth, and that already means two things:

1. Its thought has an ontological quality. It is interested in what is fundamental and irreducible: in essence. There is a historical reason for this. This man's reality had fallen to pieces, he was divided against himself because the world was divided, and he could make no camp's truth his own – neither Judaic nor Christian, neither German nor Allied (in whose eyes, as neither victim nor enemy, he quite simply did not exist) nor Swiss.

Ignored by history, he felt he was the world's victim, and this historical exclusion reminded him of his prehistoric situation as a child persecuted and threatened with abandonment. This is why he does not refer his nullity, his guilt and his exclusion to transitory historical events, but experiences them as a permanent and fundamental condition. He does not dream of protesting against this condition nor of changing it. He interiorizes it. It furnishes the themes of his thought. But this thought has an immediate signification: to destroy the unacceptable truths which oppose each other by seeking beneath their historicity a fundamental truth. By adhering to this truth he can (a) decide against all those who decide against him – in fact, against everyone, (b) decide in favour of himself against everyone by converting his own error into the only truth, (c) join the rest of humanity by displaying what, in man, is irreducible. As a matter of fact:

a. If you are wrong in the eyes of every constituted group, you are excluded by humanity, and to decide against humanity is no use at all. It is merely a stylistic exercise, your demonstration of the universal will be listened to by no one, you will be speaking in the void. More precisely, your words, assured of being heard by no one, addressing no one, are a religious invocation, an invocation of a suprareal absolute in whose eyes my absolute wrong would become right, would assume a meaning. It is a way of praying because no one can willingly suffer and be wrong for nothing, because the purely absurd (his absurd existence within eight square yards of walls, his feeling of being immured by a motionless eternity where nothing ever happens, where nothing can ever be changed, a prisoner of life, so that the most reasonable thing to do would be to lie down on the floor and wait for death) is intolerable, and because there must be someone to dedicate this suffering to, to give it a meaning and make it of some use. It is this someone whom philosophical reflection (in the same way as prayer) conjures up; it addresses itself to 'God', it calls God 'total consciousness'. It is for this consciousness, on behalf of this consciousness, that philosophical reflection speaks, and speaking (writing, the only way of giving the unheard word a trace of objectivity) is the very act of conjuring up this absolute to

which one dedicates oneself. To conjure up this absent presence
is a way of short-circuiting all humanity, of speaking over its
head, in its absence, and of absenting oneself (abstracting
oneself) from it in a language alienated from humanity by being
violently ground up until it has clots of nonmeaning and silence
within it – in short, by making language serve the annihilation of
the very humanity which it manifests. Which is to say that such
language is poetic. Claiming to communicate nothing save the
impossibility of communication, knowing itself to be useless, it is
(even if it takes the form of the digression and the antinovel – that
is, an appearance of prose) a trap laid for the world; apparently
reasonable, this speech begins by seizing human reality in its
snares in order to talk about them, but its discourse ultimately
collapses into silence, nothing has been said. Thus the world is
reborn from the annihilation of thought as unthinkable and
unusable. In one sense, everything has been destroyed, and in
another sense nothing has happened except nothing. The
thinker has produced the verbal monument of destruction; he
has recreated his own drama on paper; all he can do now is
begin again.

b. By raising his wrong to the rank of the only truth, he took
his revenge on all (everyone, in fact) who doomed him to silence
and nullity. But this truth is not practical, it is poetic. It declares
that wrong is universal and that he himself, in proclaiming it, in
no way escapes it. It manifests the error of all truth and the
failure or vanity of every undertaking – the unhappiness of
consciousness. The historically unhappy consciousness deepens
its historical unhappiness by perceiving in it the sign of
consciousness's ontological unhappiness. It glories in this unhappiness, assumes consciousness of it as the sign of its greater
lucidity; takes credit for it and contemptuously goes out to do
battle with the complacent fools who conceal the consciousness
of their unhappiness. Thus, thanks to the discovery of the essential unhappiness of consciousness, historical unhappiness
becomes, for the concretely unhappy consciousness, the instrument and sign of its election; because it is the most unhappy, it is
the most conscious. Despairing of conquering its unhappiness, it

*chooses* it, attributes value to it. This is why it must fail and suffer even in its demonstration of universal unhappiness and error; this demonstration must not succeed, otherwise consciousness would emerge from its unhappiness and nullity by having accomplished at least that much which was 'positive' to lodge in. It will therefore demolish this demonstration by showing its vanity, by accusing itself of pride, and by proclaiming that the truth it has just expressed is itself impure; that this self-accusation also participates in the pride it denounces; that philosophy, truth and authenticity are impossible and unhappiness not to be escaped.

c. In so doing, the unhappy consciousness has the satisfaction of affirming something which seems valid to it, which prevents anyone else from speaking, wrings cries of admiration from some, and permits him to incarnate consciousness, once admitted to the sanctuary of libraries, in its abstract universal essence, consciousness made book and man, soaring above individual concrete consciousness and proposing itself as an appeal to their essential vocation – that is, as value. But this is a task which is not at all easy. This excluded and ignored consciousness can encounter humanity – that is, a form of universality – only by continually reducing itself to a  kind of 'final simplicity', by raising itself above its contingency (above the form and the concrete causes of its unhappiness), by eliminating what might be individual in its experience and its discourse in order to present itself as consciousness-in-general, impersonal and disincarnated. It will take advantage of its concrete nullity to make itself absolutely null, to be no one and nothing and, thanks to its extreme poverty, to gain extreme wealth; insofar as it is indeterminate, it will be both the negation and the abstract possibility of all determinations; insofar as it is no man in particular, it claims to contain the possibility of becoming all men and of subsuming, in the form of possibilities in suspension, all that is human.

Yet this attempt is doomed to failure: for it knows that the 'last simplicity' cannot be 'given' but must be constantly *performed*, without ever being achieved, by the refusal to be anything at all, by the indefinite contestation of all possible determinations, and

that this refusal and this contestation are attitudes determined by
contingent motivations – preferred attitudes which exclude all
other possible attitudes and constitute the particularity of this
consciousness. It must therefore interrogate and contest even its
attitude of contestation and interrogation; in its project toward
final nullity, this consciousness collides with its own existence as
that which separates it from its universal essence. It can indicate
universal essence only as the unrealizable value which shimmers
on the horizon of its self-denunciations, which becomes the
cipher of its failure and in the face of which attempt is failure. But
it claims this failure as man's final truth and, in proclaiming it for
itself, tries to drag all men down in its wreck.

   2. The exile's isolation and nullity, reinforced by infantile
masochism, the attitude of persecution he returns to on this occasion as to an old habit, pushing the experience of his condition to
a metaphysical extreme – this radical despair, if you like, is the
meaning his empirical condition assumes in the light of his
original choice, and his despair, in a sense, is comfortable; the
vanquished, the impotent victim are safe 'at the bottom of the
pit', nothing can happen to them, nothing more is asked of them,
they have nothing to do. To love failure (and it is clear that he
loved it) does not mean one does not suffer from it. And suffering
talks drivel; it is the consciousness of nothingness (consciousness
that what you feel and want is an objective nothing colliding with
the massiveness of being, rejected and rendered impossible by it,
and with no reality logically) which spontaneously tends (lacking
any object in which to love itself, to actualize itself, to realize
itself) to produce itself as an object; it cries, dreams, and, by
choice, writes; it creates literary objects in which it substitutes its
own nothingness, raised to the status of being, for the reality
which it destroys by this narcissistic promotion.

   Yet, the activity of writing, initially a solution of despair, has
its own unexpected weight (for after all it is an activity, and to
recreate your own nothingness is, without your having desired it,
to *create*; I'll come back to this shortly); and the systematization
of a counteruniverse of despair in literary digression is one way of
engaging yourself in the world. This way will provoke new moti-

vations; it discovers literature as a weapon and a power, the power to dismiss reality and to prefer oneself to it absolutely. It writes against the world in order to destroy it; it elaborates the means to hate the world and discovers its resentment against it at the same time that it makes it real.

You despise me? I cross you out with a stroke of my pen. Language is a weapon. Through it, I appropriate the body of all thought, and I take you prisoner; if I manage to incarnate in it thoughts which owe you nothing and which stand of themselves, I have won. I escape your laws, I oppose my own to them, my own law which is their opposite and their subversion.

You hold me captive in your universe? I *assume* this captivity and fling it in your face; it suffices that I desire this exile you claim to impose upon me, that I enjoy the sufferings you inflict upon me. You claim to possess me by your contempt, but if I *want* you to despise me, I escape you; you do my will instead of imposing yours upon me. I transform my situation without changing anything in it, by deciding, after the fact, that it is the result of my will and glorying in it. I interiorize the law imposed upon me and, without producing anything save an inoperative will, a mere 'movement of the soul', I set myself up as legislator of an already given order, which I permit to remain intact, whose canons I adopt. The power is yours, the interior freedom is mine.

This attitude of arrogant and touchy defiance can be encountered historically among oppressed minority groups when, incapable of overcoming oppression and considering it as virtually immutable, they become aware of the fact that for and in relation to their oppressors, they are different: Negroes assuming their Negroness, Jews their Jewishness, children their infantilism, reinforce the difference imposed on them as an exclusion from the society of men and reverse it as a weapon against the latter. I am a Negro and it is by this Negroness that I escape you; you claim to dominate me by it; but now I invest myself with it, and this difference that you claim to impose upon me, for the moment that I assume it, you become impotent to destroy – it marks the limit of your power; you have excluded me, but if I *desire* this exclusion as the place to which I am entitled, I repre-

sent it to you as your impotence to integrate me. The Otherness
you have conferred upon me I wrest from you; you claim I
belong to you because of it? I teach you that, because of it I no
longer belong to you.

Thus the victim wrests the initiative of his exclusion from his
oppressor and transfers it into the movement of his freedom, but
of an 'interior' freedom residing only in the consciousness of his
nothingness, enjoying itself without risk since it is dependent on
the order that rejects it and impotent against that order. Strange
freedom, accomplice of what destroys it and at its peak in failure.
In one sense, it is nothing; in another, it is a sovereign operation
by which nothingness happens. For this slothful freedom, though
it produces nothing, nevertheless functions, it is utterly occupied
acting out – like a role whose rules it has invented – what it is
forced to be. This imposed being which it receives from without
and in which it cannot recognize itself as its product, which it
cannot produce because it is already there as the negation of
itself by another, it begins to produce as value, that is, as an
obligation-to-be. Its functioning consists of wanting what is –
that is, of putting the world in parentheses in order to pretend to
re-create it, starting from nothing; it makes itself the nonsite of
the world, the hole through which being is engulfed, evaporates
into appearance.

The bad faith of this attitude is patent. I loathe its touchy,
vulnerable pride, the intense, aggressive expression of Jews or
Negroes flaunting their Jewishness or Negroness as it has been
defined by others; their stiff ostentation whose *voulue* arrogance
reveals the inferiority they pretend not to suffer from. These men
are failures; so they have been made, so they choose themselves,
but because they cannot *live* their role, establish its value, settle
into it comfortably, they force themselves to *act it out.* They create
a defiant façade, concealing their need for humanity in
order not to have to suffer from the impossibility of satisfying it.

And yet this attitude is something like the dawn of a morality.
Because they do not have the material means to make themselves
free, yet will not be enslaved to their objective image as fabricated
by others, they claim the only material freedom left to them: to

be what they are. They ostentatiously alienate themselves in their objectivity because that is the only way they can declare themselves to be subjects. But since they have not invented the norms to which they submit, since the objective image with which they invest themselves remains inevitably exterior to them and can be neither recognized nor experienced by them as their human reality, these men are ascetics. Intense, concentrated, self-centred, censoring their sensibility in order to admit only whatever conforms to the social canons, they undertake an exhausting reflective labour to make themselves into something they cannot experience or even properly create (but only try to conjure up in other people's consciousness). This immense labour upon the self leads nowhere, produces no action by which one can establish oneself, and aims, ultimately, only at defeating the self. Yet in its very nonproductivity it produces something: itself. Not much; just this: a kind of detachment, an absence – that is, the consciousness of the self as a nonsite of being. Since I cannot be this role I am playing, I am nothing – save for this indefinite power of acting a part and assuming appearances.

When a man begins acting a part, even the part objectively assigned him by society, and this part, since it does not affect his original situation, remains unlivable for him, furnishes in the most favourable eventualities only a discipline and in the least favourable only a mask beneath which his contradictions increase, then this man exposes himself to the discovery that his reality is not what he does and seems to be, but an activity aiming at making him seem something which he is not, at producing appearances. He exposes himself to the discovery that his authentic reality is his acting; and this discovery will all the · more probably be made as the gap widens between the part he plays (whether he is required to play it by society or whether he assumes it *faute de mieux*) and the original situation he lives – all the more probably in that this part does not permit him to assume his effective relation with the world and its contradictions. Conversely, there are men who have no objective possibility of assuming their original relation to the world by coherent behaviour: unfitted for everything, bastards, half-castes,

men torn between the contradictory systems of behaviour
imposed upon them by a divided world, a divided family, an
empirical reality having no common measure with their
primordial engagement in the world. They will inevitably feel
they are acting. No socially consecrated behaviour engages the
totality of their being or transcends their contradictions, all
behaviour seems to be fake; they constantly feel they are acting
and that everyone else is acting – cheating.

For the Southern Negro or the Jew in a racist society, this
discovery is not immediately accessible. The part he is playing
with dignity or pride is the only one he can play; the part his
oppressors play is sedimented in formidably efficient order.
These actors are kept from consciousness of the ludic character
of their freedom by the rigour of the social decorum and by an
existing order arranged to impose their role to the exclusion of all
others. Their role, defined by social praxis, is as difficult to
modify as the praxis itself, impossible to question without interrogating the entire social order. The impossibility of modifying
my role, or of modifying it without losing my place or my human
dignity at the heart of the social order, impedes the consciousness of its inauthenticity and its ludic character. This is why such
consciousness is generally achieved by men who are incapable,
because of their history and their individual contradictions, of
'playing the game' and who therefore have nothing to lose by
denouncing an order which excludes them in any case.

But in whose name will they conduct this indictment? If only
they were Negroes, oppressed for racial stigmas, or Jews, persecuted by a society unable to realize its cohesion in other ways!
Then their exclusion would have a social and economic substra-
tum, a historical dimension; their alienation would be social and
they could denounce this society in which they were born, this
world which they produce as well as the citizens with rights, in
the name of their own ideal right to recognition and social integration, in the name of their legitimate grievance against this
society which refuses to be theirs. They would have a problem,
this problem would be social, its particularity would connect
with the universal, for their indictment of this society would be

conducted in the name of a society to be constructed whose agents they would already be – in the name of the possibility of this society's becoming really universal (that is, just) – and in whose preparation they would be united with all the other exploited men for whom man is still to be created. They would have, if you like, a 'cause' and a hope. They could create an ideology for themselves; their struggle would determine man's value.

Lucky devils, he would have thought if he had thought at this period, to be a Negro in South Carolina, a Jew in Poland, a citizen of an occupied country, to be able to touch oppression with your hands and point to its mechanism and its causes, to know that they want your head and that by wanting your Jewish, Negro or Polish head they assume an absolute wrong whose punishment can be demanded of history. But he was neither Jew, Negro nor Pole, a member of no nation or class, oppressed by no particular society, excluded from no community in which he might have claimed membership. The roles were assigned, there was none for him. (Requests for employment sent to each of the Swiss chemical works were returned with 'appreciation and regret'. 'Influence' was brought to bear on a manufacturer to accept him as an unpaid apprentice ['And don't forget to say thank you'] but the manufacturer retracted his offer after having said yes to the 'influence'. Lessons given at cut rates and clandestinely, articles written for half rates and unsigned.) The world created itself without him, he was excluded for no tangible reason, except that his mother had set him down in Switzerland in 1939 after the scuttling of Austria (where he could no longer even claim the integration anti-Semitism had refused him), that the Reich had defrauded him of his nationality as insubordinate, that Switzerland had no reason to recognize him as her son – a kind of lost object, fallen from someone's pocket by accident, whom no one mistreated, whom no one wanted to take responsibility for because the owner was perhaps still in the vicinity and because no one could see what it would be good for anyway. Then whom could he revolt against (if not the Reich; but in the eyes of the Allies, he had no existence whatever, and they were so

far away)? And with what cause? No individual or general wrong
had been done him; on one side they had let him escape; on the
other he was tolerated; on the third, they were unaware of his
existence. No role was assigned him, not even that of pariah. And
if, with Switzerland for horizon, he had gradually discovered a
human order in which everyone acts, deceives and steals, in
whose name would he have conducted the indictment of that
order? It is scarcely correct to say that he was excluded from it;
he had no right to integration, even ideally, having no affinity
with this community and no part in its construction. No one
defrauded him of anything. He had no historical or social grievance, no individual 'cause' that might connect with the universal.
His grievance could only be absolute, and his problem, and the
solution to his problem. Absolute – that is, metaphysical.
Because he had nothing to gain from any constituted group, had
been neither excluded nor defrauded by any of them, could be
integrated into no society, even the best in the world, had a share
in no historical struggle, there was nothing in whose name he
could question the order that surrounded him. He had nothing
to reproach it for, save its existence.

Yes, here is where the final explanation lies. Since the wrong
done by Switzerland's hypocritical social order (as by Germany
and France) was absolute, the criticism he could make of it was
necessarily absolute, therefore destructive. No community could
repair this wrong by a contribution of justice; the defect of all
communities was their very particularity and their historicity,
whatever they were; the fact that every existing society is not a
willed creation of the mind but the development and the transformation of a body of experience made up of innumerable
products of past undertakings – a great flabby body which you
can animate only from inside, a body which you either have or
haven't, flesh which you never tear yourself out of if you came
into the world inside it, and which you never incarnate yourself
in if you were born outside it. The defect of all societies, as of any
undertaking, is to be incarnated, to have its own style, themes
and instruments that cannot be deduced by reason, and which
therefore cannot be assumed by reason. Everything is always

done 'like this', 'like that', permeated by the smell of wine, vodka
or beer, by historical and literary reminiscences, mannerisms,
local mythologies. Every human action, if you prefer – and for
him this was its absolute defect, what separated him from it absolutely – was contingent, could not be referred to an idea or to a
distinct will and promoted only particular, fragmentary truths
caught in the lime of historical density and unjustifiable a priori.
Every truth was permeated by errors, comedies, lies and chance,
and unless you were its accomplice by birth you could not share
it. Everything that was, for him, was Other, the substance of the
world was Evil.

You understand his nihilism now? It was the image of his situation. For him concrete, historical reality was always the absolute
obstacle separating him from the others. He could join no group
in its always particular and concrete tasks, for he had inherited
the patrimony of no group. His situation resembled no other. He
was not even persecuted and excluded by all communities and
undertakings, for no one had bothered to exclude him, he had
not even been granted a traitor's reality. Ignored, merely a dark,
dry body floating in a closed world, with neither past nor place
nor future, he was, in his utter nakedness, an abstract individual
– his particularity was to have none. His particularity was his
absence of particularity, his not belonging to the world of other
people. Neither Jew nor German, nor Austrian, nor Swiss, nor
French, nor refugee, nor friend, nor enemy, nor exploiter, nor
exploited, he was nothing of all he had to define himself by. And
being nothing of all this, he had to contest all this, to contest the
Jewishness which rejected him among Aryans, the Aryans who
rejected him among the Jews, the Germans who had suppressed
his country and destroyed France, the Austrians who had
committed national suicide, the French who despised him for
being Germanic ('*Autrichien – autre chien*'), decadent and suspicious, the Swiss who regarded him as the potential germ-bearer
of a distant epidemic, to contest himself, finally, insofar as by his
incapacity to be anything at all he was the obstacle which
separated him from others and, by his perpetual contestation of
others' particularity, the very source of this distance between

himself and them. Yes, he had to contest everything, including his own contestation – the particularities because they are, in their contingency, the source of separation and division; and the contestation of the particularities because, in a world where everyone has a particularity, not to have one (to lay claim to the abstract universal) is to particularize oneself too.

Then what was it he wanted? He was not sure himself. He contested every particularity, not in order to obtain reparation or assert his rights – that is, not in the name of a particular, positive and historical purpose – but in the name of an absolute or abstract purity. He condemned banal and inauthentic existence ('All these people living because they've been born, shaped like jelly in the mould of their environment'), its rancid loyalties, its pride, its complacent needs and habits, and, by showing its contingency and absurdity, assumed an absolute superiority of contempt over it. He condemned concrete man in the name of an unrealizable abstract, conscious moreover that he himself fell within the scope of his condemnation. Everything that was himself was hateful. Here he joined all those other solitary and uprooted intellectuals, poets, theoreticians of the apocalypse – Aron, Sperber, Caillois, Abelio, Éliade, Malraux, Monnerot – who, incapable of participating in the struggles of their time, alien to its hopes, exiled from its history, either because they are bourgeois or because they belong nowhere, consider it from the sidereal viewpoint as an object and, being unable to pursue any objective with mankind, claim to raise themselves above it by prophesying the apocalypse; they want to terrify. Thereby they take revenge on this crawling humanity with which they cannot live (neither with the bourgeois, too stupid, nor with the Marxists, who do not offer glorious roles in a period of revolutionary stagnation) and to which, by reason of their particular situation, nothing affectively links them save their resentment. *Déclassé* exiles, they take their revenge by doing their best to frighten the bourgeois, to whom they arrogantly announce their deserved catastrophes, and the Marxists, to whom they promise the guillotine or Siberia, or else by annihilating humanity in the name of Carnot's principle, by some mythological analysis or apocalyptic

exegesis. All conduct their prosecution in the name of a trans-
historical and transhuman absolute. Prophets or poets, their
language describes the uselessness of the world. They are soli-
taries without hope.

For him, the transhuman absolute assumed the figure of 'total
consciousness' (something like Hegel's 'immutable'), and it was
in the name of this consciousness – essence, relieved of the
contingency of existing and of the 'metaphysical fault' of finitude,
that he contested every particularity. I have showed he was
doomed to this contestation by his factual situation. But he was
not compelled to accord it value. Now, like the Negro flaunting
his Negroness, he paraded his exile, wanted it to be absolute,
claimed to derive it only from himself; instead of enduring it, he
developed it on his own account as an unconditioned choice. He
wanted himself to be the refusal of all particularities. He arrogantly refused everything that, in any way, was refused him
(friendship, nations, society, history, the lives he would never
live, expensive food, even food within his means), and by this
proud and inoperative refusal he expected everything to be
restored to him as an unused possibility – or, rather, as an ideal
right; by this refusal of every luxury, every possibility, he
declared an ideal right to them which he would not have deigned
to take advantage of. He who was nothing and could be nothing
turned his nakedness into wealth, his nullity into omnitude, his
universal inferiority into an absolutely superior being.

This was one of the meanings which his fated contestation
offered him. He had slowly discovered and developed his objective signification. It had first been indicated to him by others, by
the anxiety and fear his questioning and destructive mind
provoked in them (not understanding, at first, that he might
inspire respect, that he who felt inferior to everyone might be
considered superior to everyone, he finally was emboldened to
act the unexpected and Mephistophelian role that had been
foisted on him), but it had not been original. The first meaning of
his contestation, which the anxious admiration of an unexpected
public enriched with an unforeseen signification, was that of an
*ascesis*; to create a means of access toward others and pierce the

barriers by which other people's particularities isolated him, he
had to appeal to what was universal and authentic in them. But
what was it? The question was vital; he decided that life was not
worth living, unless he could answer it. But at the same time the
answer seemed one that no man could give, for the universal
could only be the negation of the particular; yet man exists as an
individual, the mere fact of existing is a fall from grace, a separation and a fault in the universal. In consequence, existence was
a fall, and man, like Plotinus' hypostases, 'fell' from the One,
and all attempts to reverse the fall were doomed.

He might have said with Kierkegaard, had he known his work,
that 'before God we are always guilty'. But he had a horror of all
religious terminology, which he considered an instrument for
producing guilt, a war machine of moralism. He atheism was
limited to declaring that God, the universal, the immutable, did
not exist, and that consequently the effort to achieve them was
sterile. There was a moral to be drawn from this declaration, that
guilt is not, as the mystic believes, a fault against an (abstract and
nonexistent) universal, but that *mysticism itself*, in its contempt for
finitude, and therefore for concrete men, *is a fault against the others
who are really existing*. The exclusive love of God (or of the abstract
universal) is guilty *par excellence*, since it renders itself guilty
toward everyone by its contempt for human reality.

He had drawn this conclusion, but only to live it in laceration
and without being able to renounce an ascetic morality. For if he
favoured a positive morality that would regard the universal as so
much wind, he was no more than an individual among individuals toward whom he was absolutely in the wrong since he did not
resemble them and could not join them at any point; a bundle of
flesh battered about in the universe, he might as well sit down
here and let himself die. If, on the contrary, he favoured an ascetic
morality, he found himself in the same boat with the rest, he was,
like them, an unhappy consciousness fallen from the universal;
but if he was then just as incapable of joining them, at least he
gave himself the sterile satisfaction of knowing his unhappiness,
of declaring it and, in declaring it, of drawing others with him in
a common and irremediable dereliction.

I should like to be able to say that he experienced the agony of being torn between these two moralities. I should like to be sure he unceasingly burned both ends of this candle, hating men in their inauthenticity and unable to forgive himself for this hatred, immediately blaming himself for it, mortifying himself in order to punish himself for it. But I cannot say this. He had, I think, no such high intention, and if in fact he burned both ends of the candle, if he did not definitely favour an ascetic morality, and sainthood, if in fact he was willing to be torn by the antagonism between these two moralities, it was for contingent reasons – for instance, because he had not the strength to despise everyone, to claim the consciousness of his unhappiness as the sign of his election, and to declare himself prophetically in the right against everyone else; because, by virtue of his early masochist background, he still needed to conform to some order, to be persecuted, victimized and guilty. I think that was what kept him from taking his *ascesis* seriously, made him realize that his pursuit of the universal was necessarily a procedure accomplished in a particular and contingent way, that his arrogant contempt for others was, in its earnestness, at least as hateful as they were to him. I must therefore turn to psychology, must recognize that it was for contingent reasons – by virtue of a contingent choice reaching back into the marshes of childhood – that he could not embark upon an arrogant and mystical quest for the universal but saw in the contestation which he conducted against others another role he could merely act, which, in its contingent reality, he would still have to contest, because he who claims to be right against all other men is in the wrong toward them insofar as he has contempt for them and wrong *with* them insofar as he remains, like them, a finite and contingent existence.

Arrogant insistence on exile, indefinite contestation of the truths which remained alien to him, pursuit of the immutable which would afford him an absolute viewpoint over those truths, guilt for not being able to join the others on their own concrete grounds – it was by virtue of such heterogeneous motivations and not of an originally philosophical intention that he discovered a contradiction which was finally fruitful. A

contradiction which originally, perhaps, was merely the 'psychological' conflict between the obligation to contest everything and
the nostalgia for an order which he could obey and which would
unite him to other men within the truth – but which, experienced and reflected interminably, made him aware of the philosophical problem of the universal and the particular, the general
contradiction of consciousness on the one hand being given as a
fact and on the other wanting to derive only from itself. The
philosophical project did not break like a storm in the blue sky,
but as an attempt to subsume an individual contradiction by a
fundamental contradiction and to justify his division-within-
himself as a universally relevant insight into the human condition.

That, for him, was what the activity of writing was (writing
anything at all, provided that an abstract thought was born
under his pen and that the lived experience daily incarnated itself
in ordinary words) – to manifest the world, in its contingency, as
that which is desperately in excess; to question the inauthenticity
of those (that is, of everyone) who act out the comedy of hope and
deceive themselves about themselves by believing in some immediate redemption; then, having contested everything, to contest
himself. A process starting with the concrete, dissolving it into
abstractions, then turning back on itself in order to negate itself
in its turn. The universal toward which it tended was, in the
image of the very mass of the universe that crushed it, undifferen-
tiated nothingness – nothing at all, not even itself. A dream of
making itself a bomb annihilating everything by its explosion,
including itself. A universal power of negation incarnated insofar
as it refuses all incarnation; in sophisms, poetic contradiction,
little prose poems which capsize meaning into nonsense, a
speech into silence. And there was this too: he, who could be
nothing and whose objective reality was always the reality of his
exclusion and his solitude (Jew? yes-no; Austrian? yes-no;
chemist? yes-no; and so on), he assumed his nullity as a refuge.
To be nothing, invisible and indefinable, offering no surface to
attack, taking refuge in the pure interiority of the negative;
nothing but the faculty of pronouncing 'the nonsite of every site'.

An ironist, really. His written thought constantly tried to bite its own tail, to step back from itself or to produce by interior monologue (a technique carefully studied and always disappointing) the image of the absence of all thought, the rustle of words evoking silence. A concerted enterprise of annihilation, tinged with self-punishment. To write was for him what flagellation is for the mystic: a way of raising himself above his particular existence by incarnating it in language, a vehicle of the universal, and then, because a spoken existence remains no less an existence, destroying again what has just been said. An interminable labour whose purpose is nothing, the immediate product always disappointing, but which, despite his intention, has a positive reality: a man starting out to be nothing and to say nothing learns to say many things not altogether commonplace, discovers that he can make himself understood and that thought, even when it tries to be the negation of everything, is a means of access to the universal, is universal itself provided it is coherent. It was in 1945, freed from the tedious chemistry courses by obtaining his diploma, that he began writing a treatise, already begun several times, in which he would make a systematic interrogation of every human attitude – re-creating and dismantling them, revealing their bad faith, then throwing them aside.

## Reality

The goal, inevitably, was missed, but by pursuing it he discovered this astonishing thing: *I exist.* That is, he was more than whatever he did and could do, even more than his being-for-others, since he could indefinitely undo what he did, act what he was not, deceive as to what he was.

He thought he was a nothing, that nothing he could do would be of any consequence (not even suicide, since he would not be there to experience it), that he was condemned to endure until death the tedium of life-on-earth-for-nothing, and that the best he could do was to annihilate his absurdity day after day by decanting himself into literature. Yet insofar as a man works, even without hoping for results, he exposes himself to surprises. Even when he thinks he is doing nothing but the 'nothingness he is', by the mere fact of making his nullity objective, of creating precisely what he is as an aesthetic work, he learns two things: (1) he apprehends himself in the eyes of others as a determinate power possessing a certain efficacy; (2) he apprehends himself in his own eyes as a free creative activity, free even toward his work. His discovers himself as a 'negativity in general'.

'Reduced to the supreme poverty of a power without object', as Valéry says, he feels capable of no matter what, he is the absolute void. Everything seems possible for him at the same time and for that reason indifferent; his possibilities are always 'no matter which', with one double limitation: everything is possible for him except that one thing should be possible for him to the exclusion of all others; or (the second aspect) he cares for nothing save that indifference which refuses to care for anything. Nothing, save the nothing which he is and which constantly tries to coincide with itself in rejecting all determination – leaving it to the others as a slough from which he has withdrawn himself.

In this indifference (his room reduced to its minimum volume by black hangings; minimum utensils – one spoon, one knife, one bowl, one chair, one table, one secondhand bed; minimum of food; minimum of gestures, actions, acquaintances) there is also the least repose. It is an *ascesis* – continuous activity. It is (or wants to be) constantly regained over all 'temptations' – continuous creation, enormous energy expending itself for nothing, in order to produce nothing. This is the opposite of ataraxia. This man doomed to inaction, for whom the world is an impregnable fortress and whose impotence reduces him to the pure insipidity of being there, invests his pride and his freedom in the creation of nonbeing. An object discarded by history, stamped with every prohibition except the prohibition to live, remaining, like a plant, at the spot where he has fallen, his situation and even his life can be only endured. But since man defines himself by what he does, he sees his vocation in the activity of undoing, of destroying this inert thing that he is. Vocation is perhaps too much to say; destruction, love of nothingness is the objective meaning proposed to him by the logic of his situation. He verifies this law of existence: If you deprive a man of any possibility of declaring his freedom by actions, his freedom – since you cannot prevent him from being free – will manifest itself negatively. For it is impossible for him not to be free, and yet impossible to be free effectively. A futile contestation of a situation with no way out, his freedom is reduced to being the sterile negation of a facticity that cannot be transcended in any direction (that I am here, that the world is precisely such as it is). And since this negation cannot be inscribed in the real, cannot impose its stamp upon it by trans- forming it and by realizing itself in its action, it transcends itself as pure loss – it passes into the realm of the imaginary. It produces itself as sterile opposition to being, unable to be a fruit- ful opposition. It characterizes existence as a dichotomy in which being – the absolute obstacle (that is, Evil) – is everything which keeps freedom from declaring itself and in which freedom, pure nothingness of all being, is identified with love of nonbeing, with the affirmation of that which is not.*

He might have adopted Mallarmé's remarks on 'the dreadful sensation of eternity', on the 'vain forms of matter'; might have declared like Mallarmé, 'I am perfectly dead'; or again, 'In my eyes, the only occupation for a self-respecting man is to stare at the blue sky (*l'azur*) while starving to death.' Too bad he never bothered to study Mallarmé; he would certainly have taken him apart – and himself, by the same token. He would have grasped concretely what he already knew in the abstract: the poet, a nihilist in the full sense of the word, cheats contemptibly. He tells for others the horror of the world, his own wretchedness and solitude. But he *likes* the world to be corrupted by Evil, he loves to describe the Evil that corrupts himself. He establishes himself in his defeat and converts it into his glory. He proclaims that

---

*This is Mallarmé's 'admirable lie': 'Therefore I can deny all that exists in order to affirm what does not. Admirable lie . . . I want to give to myself the spectacle of matter, conscious of its being and, nevertheless, desperately hurling itself into that Dream which it *knows is not* and proclaiming before the Nothing which is Truth these *glorious lies.*'

man is great only by his failures. He wants to fail admirably. He wants people to say of him, 'He suffered martyrdom and died because he was too pure, too intransigent for his time.'

This sad cheat constantly crucifies himself for the public. He wants to recoup his real, historical, relative suffering by raising it to the absolute, for all to see, in poems which bear witness to the Impossibility of Man. He speaks from beyond the grave – *d'outre-tombe.* He wants to be the fixed stare, laden with silent reproach, of all the martyrs who were defeated by history yet whose unrealized ideals persist (when anyone remembers them) like the presence, beyond being and yet petrified by it, of the eternal Subject Value.*

But what I most reproach this traitor for is that even while loudly proclaiming absolute Evil, he claims to make use of Evil. The whole world is Evil for him, because he has nothing to do with it; he therefore decides that the world will be useful to him, precisely insofar as it is useless, an absolute obstacle. He behaves like the saint who blesses his executioners and thanks God for his tortures; he *wants* the world to be the instrument of his failure and his martyrdom. The meaning of the universe in his eyes is to crush him so that he can utter his admirable groans. The world of Evil becomes the means of 'glorious defeat'. Then everything is suddenly saved; Evil will have served to bring the value of man to fruition as a stubborn nothingness in the midst of being; the universe will be saved in all its horror for having produced the poet. Established in the imaginary, contemplating himself through the eyes of a posterity which will curse his epoch, he re-creates this inacceptable life as his absolute purpose, sets out to desire it with a literary intent.

A facile, slothful solution which leaves everything as it was but which can nevertheless lead to a real way out if the writer gets detached from himself and his literary prestige, accepts himself as the creative consciousness which he is in fact becoming, makes use of the dialectical resources he creates to search methodically for a path – not for complacent descriptions of his unhappiness.

---

*See in this regard *Saint Genet*, pp. 178–83.

Methodical search for a path – he was far from thinking of that when, one winter day, he began writing in a torn notebook the first pages of 'The Essay', determined that this time he would put everything into it, that he wouldn't go back to that novel of his, 'Dead Life' (a description of despair and the vanity of life which he wanted to make monumental), before having shown that it is impossible to assume one's condition without cheating and that this demonstration itself was a kind of cheating.

He didn't have the remotest intention to 'search methodically for a path', since he was convinced that none existed; 'The Essay' was merely an attempt at coherent thought. Yet to think coherently, even and particularly if you want to dismantle and demolish the absurdity and the failure of everything, you must be interested in everything, even out of hatred for everything; you must first understand the world you want to assassinate – and it is this passionate interest, passionate loathing for everything, which the essay of an 'Essay' will have achieved for him. When a man macerates for years in his masturbatory and metaphysico-ascetic juice, it hardly matters whether he is interested in the world for 'good' or for 'bad' reasons; to be interested in it at all, even interested in cursing it, is already a first thread linking him to reality, and this thread, if he doesn't let it go, if he doesn't give up his demolition work, will perhaps become the path he was not even looking for but on which he will find himself travelling. Until the day when, discovering himself on a path in the world (though this day may never come and there is no certainty he will discover himself on the path if it does), he will consent to revise the motivations that led him there despite himself, so that finally – 'Look! a path that I can take' – he can advance along it intentionally. But to advance along it intentionally he must revoke the very choice which led him onto it despite himself.

He was ready neither to discover himself on a path nor to revoke his choice of despair. There were eighteen months to come before the first dawn of discovery, eighteen months which seemed an eternity to him because nothing indicated that he would ever emerge from them. He seemed, in fact, to be interminably sinking. Despair, moments of the terrible beauty of

despair – like that December evening after spending the whole
afternoon splitting logical hairs, dealing with the 'illusions of the
will', when he reached a point of such complication in his exposition, and yet of such vivid intensity of proof, that the verbal wall
he was erecting suddenly collapsed and he saw himself, as if
pierced by a bolt of lightning, chained to that illusory labour of
abstraction and self-refusal; then he stood up, convinced of his
capital discovery and that he would never manage to express that
discovery and, in silent, self-coinciding anguish as he stood in
front of the window, staring at the prostitutes' dolls in the
window opposite, he smoked a cigarette butt that scorched his
lungs. Like that Christmas Eve, in the soup of grey snow, watching all these people who had somewhere to go and who had
money, the city, the world, the future, the law on their side,
suddenly inventing the desire to do something he would remember and going into a bookstore full of people, carefully choosing,
among the rare books, the two thickest and rarest volumes, and –
feeling himself weak with fear, merely a scandalous object seized
by the collar and handed over to the police, yet, in perfect opposition to this object, entirely the absolute subject residing in the
complete negation of what he seemed to be – calmly putting first
one book under his arm, then the other, walking across the shop,
passing the cashier's counter and then behind it, slipping the
volumes in his briefcase, and then, his briefcase stuffed with loot
worth three hundred francs, leaving the store to sell his plunder
down the street at a third of its value a few moments later.
Moments in which he believed he was living – as if gathered up
into an engrossing drama which lasted the space of several
seconds without anything happening – the essential drama of
consciousness. Like that summer night in his attic room in the
Old Town, when he had leaned out the window before going to
bed, suddenly seeing the deserted town, a heap of stones abandoned by a defunct humanity, and, on the pavement twenty yards
below, the tangible possibility of his death, the attraction of this
possibility, while he had held his life in suspense, hesitating
whether he should hold on or let go of the hand rail. A moment
in which he dissolved himself into anguish, convinced that this

alone was authenticity, this instantaneous flash when everything was in question including the question itself suspended on the brink of suicide, that the rest of the time we only act out the comedy.

He called this the 'neutral ethic of total refusal' ('neutral' for the impossibility of choosing anything effectively, and 'total refusal' for the contestation of all choices, refused by virtue of their equal contingency), and it was an ethic of Being: Nothingness, yet Nothingness aware of itself as a proud failure indifferent to everything, glittering like a black diamond – what consciousness would be if it coincided with itself as pure unqualified self-consciousness, omitting, rejecting all being in its inessentiality.

Reality: the reality of this attitude was its hatred of everything that determines man, and the poetic love of everything which is the negation of that determination; the hatred of daily existence, particular and inauthentic, and the love of the secret unhappiness by which (in the nostalgia for impossible elsewheres, dissatisfaction, suffering) every man contests his particularity and reveals himself, within his positive and objective reality, as a core of nonbeing, a pure, solitary and unhappy subject, escaping all attempts at realization – as failure. He began to probe for this essential and concealed unhappiness in everyone he met as their share of authentic universality, by which alone he could communicate with them, assuming in their eyes the disturbing figure of the kind of man who, seeing through you, knows more about you than you know yourself, who – doctor, psychoanalyst or chiromancer – possesses your truth that shines in his eyes, fascinating but unrealizable. He began to hunt for unhappy souls; he gave the girls an understanding look and, incapable of offering them the fun they were looking for, applied himself instead to acting as midwife to their unhappiness. This was a role that suited him perfectly. And when he discovered a soul in pain and conscious of that pain, he felt a warm delight; when he fell in love, it was with unhappiness, the longing for the impossible.

With the boys he knew, it was the same thing. He had no friends, because he frightened people, but his passion for other people's miseries, his passion to understand others in order to put his finger on their unhappy consciousness won him many confidences. Boys came to him as to a kind of confessor when they had problems, and he listened to them, explained their source and origin. For instance, that they were necessarily obsessed with the impossible because they were Swiss, that they were doomed to revolt, to literature or philosophy, because of their unacceptable condition, but that revolt feeds on what it is vainly and quite safely revolting against; that their great romantic loves would not batter down the walls of exile, solitude and mediocrity their Swiss reality had raised, but would merely offer a poetic evasion (an escape outside this society, in a locked room where they annihilated the social and historical order by making love *against it* with the pastor's daughter); that virtually nothing but literature or philosophy could open a window on the universal, but that this window was imaginary because thought would not batter down walls but nourished itself instead on its collisions against obstacles. Only this remained, to make unhappiness conscious of itself, to resist the temptations of mediocre facility, and, by this gratuitous resistance, which, for the moment, had apparently no other purpose than itself, to maintain within this worm-eaten order – subsisting only by inertia and having lost faith in its ideological justifications – an entirely subjective demand for change which, on condition that it were there at first, would not let the objective occasion be lost when it presented itself.

This was a great deal of lucidity for a very little hope, and as his Swiss acquaintances grew older and found work (teaching, law and medicine) they began to accuse him of demolishing everything and offering nothing in return.

'I can't offer what our situation does not offer', he answered.

And Franck: 'You stink of intelligence the way some people stink from under their arms.'

And L: 'You've found your way – you write. That means you don't have to live. For you, everything is a pretext for intellectual speculation. Deep down inside, you don't give a damn.'

Deep down inside, he didn't give a damn. It was easy enough for him to advise against complacency in the given state of affairs, for, even had he wanted to, he couldn't have been satisfied here, alien as he was to this Swiss reality. He enjoyed the role of alien witness – other people's bad conscience. But as other people changed and integrated themselves, growing older, they stopped being as receptive to his lucidity and refused to share in his exile. They attributed to his psychological circumstances the vision of the world they had once agreed was objectively founded, that is, true, and which they now decided should be regarded from the perspective of psychological relativism. And there was a deeper misunderstanding: for these young bourgeois in the process of integration, the universal was *given*, they bathed in it as in the objective spirit of their society, and in order to join it all they had to do was surrender themselves to the promptings of the surrounding conformism; for them the universal threatened engulfment in anonymity, and what was *not* given, what they could or had to conquer, was their singularity. It was by individ-ualizing themselves, by making themselves distinct, that they conceived their freedom. For him, on the contrary, it was his singularity that was given; he was imprisoned by it as if by a certain impossibility of joining the others, as if by the others' propensity to consider him as 'a case'; the universal was refused him, and it was by conquering it against his isolation, by tran-scending his particular problems, that he affirmed himself freely as transcendent. For him it was a matter of personal salvation to demolish psychological relativism and to establish an absolute hierarchy of attitudes – to erect a complete system in whose various echelons all values found their place. He had to reinvent everything human to justify not his own particular preferences but his refusal of this rotten and alien world, and the side he would take – after finishing this inventory of all values and received ideas – with full knowledge of the case, by virtue of universally valid criteria.

Such at least was the signification his work began to assume for him as he advanced upon it, advanced backwards, recognizing the empty and artificial quality of his theoretical demonstrations and classifications, recognizing the sterility of an attempt consist-ing of the uniform denunciation of attitudes arbitrarily grouped and which refused to fit into the original frame. And the recognition of the theoretical inadequacy of his framework, and of the fact that writing might become a road leading to other men, was doubtless furthered by three events occurring in the course of twelve crucial months: his meeting Morel; his breakup with L and, less decisively, with other people he was beginning to annoy; and his discovery of reality through journalism.

# *You* *

It happened early in June 1946. Morel had come to Switzerland
for a lecture tour; and while waiting for 'existentialism's pope',
Swiss reviewers published various bitter-sweet opinions on the
hopelessness of atheist existentialism and the depraving influence
of this man Morel, who wallowed in nothingness, in the mud
and the immorality of an 'unrestricted liberty'. The Swiss had
filled the great hall of the Capitol movie house to overflowing at
five o'clock in the afternoon in order to examine him, they had
applauded French thought and the still fresh memory of the
resistance, and that evening they had invited him to the 'Friends
of Art' (or something of that sort). And they invited me there too,
because they wanted to show Morel that there were men right
here in Switzerland who had read everything he had written. I
suppose I was, in fact, the only one who had read everything. By
the end of 1943 Morel had dethroned all the preceding divinities
(Gide, Ruyer, Dostoevski, Valéry), I had steeped myself in *Being
and Nothingness*, at first without understanding much of it, fascinated by the novelty and the complexity of its thought, then, by
dint of persevering in my reading of this great object, infecting
myself with it, adopting its terminology, raising it to the dignity
of an encyclopaedia which, since it treated everything, must have

*Gorz uses the familiar 'toi' [Tr.].

213

an answer to everything, and at last living in a universe having *Being and Nothingness* for its frontiers. Any experienced or observed reality was at once referred to such and such a page, where it was dealt with; Morel assumed the proportions of a demiurge; I imagined he had an answer for everything, since he announced that he had further answers in store, and I resented his keeping to himself the remainder of his thought, perhaps out of malice, to keep me on tenterhooks, or merely because he didn't care one way or the other; for I had the impression that he had thought of everything long before beginning to write a line, since in the first piece he had ever published ('The Transcendence of the Ego', 1936) he had already suggested the subjects he was still reserving, in *Being and Nothingness*, for a forthcoming work – pure reflection, authenticity, the 'ethics of reconciliation and salvation'. In short, Morel was not a man at all, but God. (It was lucky, I tell myself now, I hadn't come across Hegel first! The German would have satisfied my craving for systematization and, conscientious as I was, I would have found an answer for everything in Hegel, would have shut myself up for years on end in the raving universe of his *Logic* with little chance of ever getting out, since first of all it took me three years before I escaped from the universe of failure constructed with the materials of *Being and Nothingness*, and second, Hegel was not the kind of man to jeopardize his whole system by questioning it or even admitting doubts, and third, I should never have been able, encountering Hegel, to realize he was a man and not God Himself.) Yet Morel was a man. This was a confusing discovery. He had turned up at the 'Friends of Art' – short, heavy-set, looking somewhat disgusted by all these pundits who surrounded him and asked him academic questions about Heidegger and about subjects explained many times over in *Being and Nothingness*; he was the only man in the room who didn't look like a mummy, he gestured as if to get some air, to dispel the intellectual fumes that concealed the floor at his feet, knocking cigarette ashes on the professor's vest and spilling wine on the judge's sleeve. He had a robust and oddly concrete look, this Morel, occupying all the space around him with his voluminous gestures (when he took a draw on his cigarette, he lifted his entire arm to the height of his shoulder, so that it was dangerous to come near him if you didn't want to get an elbow in your neck) and hemming in the world as if he were weaving it by his tireless gesticulation. Then, when he was sitting down, I leaped for the chair next to him and there, for two or three hours, I asked him questions, monopolizing Morel, more moved by his quality of happy vitality (the life which he communicated to everything he said or touched and which assumed a kind of evidence and truth), by the real cigarette and the real glass of wine in his hands, than by the familiar subjects we discussed. The evidence of all this, which only Morel's person could communicate, was that this man 'loved life' – that is, loved work, resistance overcome, things and people – that he had a horror of abstract ideas, that for him philosophy had to correspond to a search, a personal need, in order to contain an ounce of truth, and that it was this search by which a man tries to create a path for himself that interested him, and not the fact that a man wrote or thought skilfully.

He discovered in Morel, for the first time in his life, the value of generosity (or rather, generosity as a value): a way of wanting to make men and things exist ('the passion to understand men', as he was to write later in *Saint Genet*), to discover at the heart of a man's attitude a certain freedom at work, and to bring that freedom to birth (or to help it be born) by discovering it. 'And now, tell me something about yourself' – a typical phrase with which Morel received him eight days later in a Geneva bistro, granting him half an hour of his attention and leaving him, despite a mutual incomprehension, the memory of the only true dialogue of his life, because everything, had there been time for it, could have been said and because the interlocutor's passionately comprehensive interest conferred for the first time on his own philosophical problems, and therefore on his person as well, a complete reality.

'All the same,' Morel had said (and this was the point where they had ceased to understand each other), 'you take up a certain amount of room on the earth's surface. What happens here

concerns you too, doesn't it? You may think as you do in
Switzerland, but if you had been in France, certainly you would
have had to take part, to make a choice?'

'Gladly', I had said. 'Which doesn't keep any choice made
from being unjustifiable, so there's always a possibility of
wondering, Why me in particular, here in particular, this in
particular? And when you really wonder about that, you can't
carry on.'

'But you exist none the less, and you necessarily make a
choice, even in refusing to make a choice – even by abstention.'

'I know,' I said, 'but that's not an argument. Because abstention is unjustifiable doesn't justify its contrary.'

'You don't mean, though, that you'd advocate abstention?'

'No. But since any choice is unjustifiable, how can I stick to
one, knowing that?'

Morel thought for a moment. 'I think you rather despise the
concrete.'

'Yes, I do', I answered.

'You seem to be somewhat essentialist', he added.

I said yes again. And we stopped there. A man with a big
black dog came in and Morel wanted to leave five francs tip.
They told him not to. I was somewhat essentialist and I despised
the concrete. I wrote Morel a long letter which I did not send but
in which I explained for the first time this scorn of the concrete: I
was a man from nowhere for whom here or anywhere, this thing
or that, made no difference, all meant the same, because no place
was a 'here' but only a 'there or anywhere', because no work was
actually his own but some task or other to which nothing necessarily bound him. Of course, *if* I had been French, I would have
made a choice. I would have been forced to. Only I was neither
French nor anything else, and I was forced to do nothing. All the
commitments others had to make within relativity I had to make
by an unconditioned option, without any necessity capable of
masking their contingency for me. I was not situated in relation
to other people's undertakings. In the name of what would I
commit myself? That was it, that was my problem. It admitted of
no solution. I was a man in suspension, or sitting on a turntable

with a circle of rails radiating out around me, which for others led somewhere, but not for me, I had no seat on any train. And so forth.

After which he left for Brussels to look for a job as engineer in the Belgian Congo. This was an attempt to commit suicide, but it failed. They wouldn't even give him an appointment at the Upper Katanga mines. At La Forminière they did. It was 103 degrees in the shade in Brussels, an attic room with a dormer window cost fifty francs, and down below, in the Place du Midi, there was a fair and a honeyed voice that sang '*Un oiseau chante dans mon coeur*' from morning to night. The day before his appointment at La Forminière he had bought *Being and Nothingness* for L, because she was now his only link with the world, and he had written in it: 'For L, what will have been truest for me, whatever I may say about it later.'

He imagined the Congo as a uranium hot bath; he wanted to go there because it was unhealthy, in order to cut his chances of longevity by half and, after five years, to have made enough money to write for ten. And after five years of the Congo, he told himself, perhaps people would have forgotten that Austria was beaten and guilty and perhaps the ushers of the French Consulate would no longer slam the door in his face. At the offices of La Forminière, there were photographs of the Congo; a child sick with yaws was sitting on his mother's arm; she was staring at him with bestial tenderness; half the child's face was eaten away by a canker, and in the background a palm tree was writhing in the heat; beneath it was a group of people – frozen, eternal. He would everlastingly have to wait for M. Merquell, and when M. Merquell came he would have to give him a letter from M. Tostet. M. Merquell opened the letter. His fat, beringed hand hid itself beneath a pile of papers. When it reappeared, M. Merquell launched into an embarrassed little speech. 'You understand,' he said, 'your case is extremely complicated. In the Congo, we take only Americans now.'

He made a telephone call. He had white hair, a red face, his nose had been broken and a bone removed from it. 'Personally,' M. Merquell said, 'I hate the Germans, you know. A race of barbarians. They should all be killed. All except the children, at least not the ones who can't speak yet. Are you Jewish?'

'My father is.'

'Then you're Jewish. There's no reason for you to conceal it. I'm pro-Semitic, myself.'

M. Merquell was sorry not to be able to do anything more for me than write a letter of recommendation to M. Jentgen; and M. Jentgen was sorry not to do anything more than write a letter to M. Berlage. M. Berlage was inclined to be optimistic and wrote a letter to M. van der Straaten. M. van der Straaten was on an indefinite leave of absence. Which was where the Congo venture ended. I returned to Lausanne, determined to 'despise the concrete' no longer and to stop being 'somewhat essentialist'. Passing through Paris (twelve hours' authorized stopover) I bought *The Phenomenology of Mind*.

The second half of 1946 was the great period. De Beauvoir brought out *The Ethics of Ambiguity*, Sartre *What Is Literature?*, Merleau-Ponty *The Phenomenology of Perception* and *The Yogi and the Proletarian* (alias *Humanism and Terror*), Jeanson *Sartre's Thought and the Moral Problem*, and Domarchi a Marxist article on money (in the *Revue Internationale*). Everything seemed possible, and because people felt they were making a new start, after seven years during which the old forms had burst open and theoretical intellectual activity had lost all sense of an object, thinking assumed a terribly important status. One could begin again as if at the zero point in practical affairs, and therefore in theory too; one could believe that theory would impose its imprint on practice provided it outstripped action, or that a theory of money or a demonstration of the superiority of socialism would affect the course of history. Therefore one thought with zest, joyfully began the examination and redefinition of the most standard notions and controversies (for example, liberalism versus control; what is democracy? what is socialism?), asked questions which, normally, congealed or deliquescent societies prudently left alone, since in any case they can reach no effective conclusions (for instance, what is justice? law? morality? the meaning of life?). One could say everything, and there was everything to say, and there was a public for every question because the facts had not decided any of them. (Five years later there would be neither public nor questions.)

Therefore, provided he managed to say something, writing – a gratuitous exercise of crucifixion – could become an action, and theoretical intelligence an element of reality instead of its sterile negation. Historical conjuncture accorded intellectual speculation an objective meaning, after having denied it any consequence for six years; it suddenly had an important quality, whatever one might say, and the stupidest writers all at once felt themselves called upon to be intelligent, to have something to say.

Historical conjuncture investing his plan to write, no matter how poetico-religious it still was, with an objective meaning, it was the possibility of this meaning (to clarify the notions everyone was juggling, to prepare certain norms and criteria that might facilitate the choice of young men like himself, assailed by a multitude of possibilities, and permit them to orient themselves among opposing moralities) that he progressively discovered, thanks to the five works mentioned, thanks particularly to *What Is Literature?* and to Merleau-Ponty, whose rather empirical descriptions overturned his well-ordered universe by introducing into it their contingent nuances.

He felt himself spurred on by all these intellectual heavyweights, fearful lest before long everything would be said by them that he would like to have said himself, waking up at eleven in the morning obsessed by the image of Morel, who began to haunt his dreams, stocky and bustling, drawing on his cigarette, lifting his elbow, his round handwriting by this hour having already covered a pile of graph paper (in *Being and Nothingness* there was a mention somewhere of the 'fresh vivacity of morning work'; and he had stolen from the publisher for whom he translated third-rate American novels a sheet from the second draft of *The Victors*), whereas, he himself hesitated listlessly on the threshold of a day which he must spend alone between four walls, squeezing out his two daily pages of dubious value after

three in the afternoon, convinced others would have long since
settled all the questions he tackled.

He wanted to enter literature as if it were a convent, to become
not the peer (he did not feel worthy) but the honourable second of
the protagonists of French thought, which for him represented
universality and was comparable to nothing else except the
Church because it expressed for him the Truth of the Present,
dominated the historical controversy in the course of sacred
conclaves, and because, in a general way, the intellectuals of
French-speaking Switzerland lived with their eyes fixed on Paris
as the Catholics did on Rome. Consigned to the sterility of
provincialism, these intellectuals considered Paris the capital of
the mind and followed its disputes, even the most Byzantine,
with the same respect as that with which the French Communist
officials, made sterile and provincial by the force of events,
followed the sinister Zhdanovist controversy.

He was living focused on Paris and felt diminished by not
being there, writing as if he were and despising everything that
did not originate there. But this was nothing new.

The new element appeared one day in November 1946. He
discovered that you could not live as if you did not exist, being
both pure mind and a man at the same time. And that it was
perhaps worth more to be a man, but that this was the most difficult thing in the world. It was especially difficult because a man
can realize his own humanity only if a woman realizes hers (a
woman and the rest of the human beings around him, but
particularly a woman), because it is only for her that he can be a
man totally.

I suppose I should set forth here a theory of the couple and of
the alienation of the couple in capitalist society, but this is precisely
what, among other things, I was doing at the time, thereby
becoming an extremely irritating kind of man, a moralizer. The
couple cannot be a complete success, I used to say to L,
unless each member desires the other's freedom more than
anything else, but each member cannot desire it concretely
unless, through this individual freedom, he desires a universal
freedom – that is, if this freedom has, in its singularity, a univer-

sal content, if we can collaborate in view of a goal toward which
each person transcends his cherished ego; our respective freedoms cannot will themselves concretely, cannot encounter and
acknowledge each other except outside, in the midst of the
world, through an object that serves them as an emblem. Now,
what have we, what can we do in common?

'You've found something', L said. 'You write. What could I do
to help with that?'

They saw each other on weekends, from Saturday afternoon to
Sunday evening. She made an hour's train trip to be with him,
which made a fair hole in her budget (thirteen francs fifty per
weekend, out of a monthly salary of two hundred and fifty francs,
then three hundred, and then three hundred and fifty) and on
the Saturday afternoon, after having looked into each other's
eyes for five minutes, quite happy, and after having said 'You',
then 'Are you all right?', then 'What's new?', they had nothing
else to tell each other. Then he said that their freedom must have
a content, and she 'What a pain you are.' He would have liked
her to do some writing, because her letters were often peculiarly
good; she had tried and decided it wouldn't work. For a while
she had thought of becoming an interior decorator, because she
had a feeling for materials, for shapes and colours, but he told
her that these were 'small matters', aesthetic questions
unaffected by morality, that the interior decorator was the
accomplice of the bourgeoisie and in league with this class, since
to have taste you had to have cash, and that it was unworthy to
sell one's taste to wealthy people just because they had none
themselves and thought you could buy anything.

'So, what do you want me to do?' L asked.

He answered that women were alienated by men and by
androcratic society, and that she must free herself. How? He
didn't have the least idea. ('Do something . . .') And besides,
each human being must find his own way, and if he found hers
for her, then it wouldn't be hers any more, since she would be
doing something in order to please him.

After an hour of this sort of discussion, he felt he was wasting
his time, and L curled up in a corner of the bed and no longer

said anything, looking vague and wretched, staring at him as if he were a picture whose evanescent meaning she was trying to discover, tasting the horrible solitude into which he was rejecting her once again. And he, confronted with this distant, mournful accusing glance: 'You don't look very pleased.'

Then she grew angry because with him one was always looking pleased or displeased, and she was sick of hearing all the time about how she was looking.

In the evening they went to the movies, and on Sunday they played chess, and when they separated for the week they felt defeated and melancholy.

It was on such an evening, when they were killing time in a café, that she asked him if he would be annoyed with her if she went to bed with another man. It was merely an idea, an experiment – just to see – which wouldn't come to anything, but she wanted to ask him first, all the same.

He told her that of course she was free, that it was only normal to want to experiment, that he wouldn't be angry with her, that in order to fulfil her womanhood she would doubtless have to sleep with any number of men. And he would be interested in hearing her impressions. He felt quite remote and rather generous, like a big brother, he had been very bored that day, but at the moment he felt a great abstract affection for her. As if that had been something he could still give her.

This leads me to believe that he had a possessive generosity. He spoke continually of other people's freedom (and liked to be asked to give advice) but on condition that others received their freedom from him. He would have liked to make them into his creatures, to produce them free and so that they derived, in their freedom, only from him. What he wrote of the adventurer could be applied to him: that, being unable to find himself in any concrete undertaking, contesting each on behalf of its share of failure, but nevertheless pursuing freedom, he tries to incarnate this abstract freedom transcendentally projected as a pure value and a subjective requirement, to define it with superb indifference to all its possible concrete countenances, as though these were the appearances which it assumes but which he refuses to take seriously. The truth of this playful declension (namely, that freedom remains transcendent to its appearances, as the capacity to accord them to itself), he can make real only in others' eyes, and that is why the adventurer ends up as a writer – in order to realize what action leaves unrealized. He needs a public.

His personal concern was Existence and Freedom. He wanted to show other people how existence and freedom developed in their contingent aspect, were merely the verification of his general theory. He kept himself above them like essence above existence, the law above jurisprudence, and the state above the citizen. And he classified them. 'You're an aesthete', he said to L, and to Franck, 'You're a rebel.' And he would explain to them the rank they occupied in the absolute hierarchy of attitudes. His relation to them was that of God to his creatures: a unilateral relation, in which he did not engage himself (he believed), making himself the witness of this relation as if he were not involved, analysing the dialogue as it was spoken and construct-ing its theory. He acknowledged in others just enough freedom to admit the well-foundedness of his opinions, but not enough to contest them, for if they argued against him they were putting themselves in the wrong and he promptly demonstrated to them their bad faith or their resentment. ('How can you love someone when you know he is of bad faith?' Franck had asked.) But he immediately forgave them their rebellion or, worse still, sincerely affirmed that he had nothing to forgive, first (and this he actually said), because he didn't judge, understanding them too well for that, and because they did not delude him but themselves, and second (and this he did not say), because he was incapable of being angry with anyone, was too steeped in his own guilt and too conscious of the gift others made him by listening to him, to draw attention to *their* guilt.

I say 'worse still' because his negation of others' defections toward him conferred a great nobility upon him in their eyes; they saw a generous forgiveness where in reality there was only indifference (it was not him they were offending, but only his ideas, and he, entrenched behind a wall of ideas, made himself actually absent from the terrain as an individual), and they felt

unworthy confronted with such greatness of spirit. (Kay, reacting
to the inhuman indifference of this negation of her own faults,
cried, 'You can't just say it's nothing and act as if nothing had
happened. Reproach me, blame me, get mad, at least show that
it touches you.' He drove her to despair by his way of reducing
their personal conflicts to an aspect of Conflict – 'We're not talking about ideas, we're talking about you and me!' – and of being
all the more detached and calm as she became more emotional;
or of withholding from Kay a forgiveness she explicitly asked him
for.

    'Tell me you forgive me.'

    'But there's nothing to forgive.'

    'Yes there is. I was unfair.'

    'Well, it's over.'

    'Say you forgive me.'

    'Who am I to forgive you?')

    Out of reach. Taking refuge in the realm of ideas, where all
things are only their transparent reflection for the theoretical
intellect, contingent illustrations of a general idea. I know that
this is the most widespread philosophical attitude ('Philosophers
have done nothing but interpret the world . . .'), the last development of aestheticism. In fact, the aesthete claims to justify the
real by acting as if it were there only in order to annihilate itself
(be annihilated) in beauty (in order to give birth to a poem, to a
picture, to contemplative pleasure). And when the aesthetic
'finalization' of the given can no longer be lived, or when the
given does not lend itself to a livable aesthetic finalization, adapting itself to its object (or enlarging itself in order to absorb new
regions), the aesthete substitutes the finalizing thought for the
feeling and claims to make the world into a garden planted for
and by the mind. He gives himself the satisfaction of deriving the
real from general ideas as a confirmation of the latter. He
explains what is by virtue of ideal abstractions which, in fact,
have for their condition the existence of what is. Thus the philosopher by interpretation, as the aesthete by art, justifies what is
and shows himself fundamentally a quietist – that is, a conservative; by interpreting what is, he demonstrates its 'necessity'

and permits himself the illusion of re-creating the world out of his ideas, whereas in reality he is only producing ideas which leave the world intact. Like the aesthete, he is a deserter from the real, to which he prefers the imaginary essence. His demonstrations are in fact always a posteriori (he lives, like Hegel, facing the past, establishing history's balance sheet and advancing backward) and retrospective (or retroactive), the only prospective philosophy, Marxism, offering itself as a denunciation of the philosophical attitude (and calling for perhaps still another philosophical clarification of its basis). Philosophy remains today the substitute for action of impotent thinkers (that is, thinkers incapable of effective action) who try to construct the world by means of thought, lacking the power to do so by action. It remains an aesthetic and religious project.*)

---

*In one sense, it will always remain aesthetic: it is the moment of reflection by which the man of praxis, the historical man, 're-enters himself' and tries to grasp the significance of action. And this grasp is to all intents and purposes always idealistic; it presents the subject as the unconditioned creator of significations and as the subject of history, whereas in fact he is always the object of history as well, inserted within it as in an objective development whose meaning transcends his original intentions and whose significations, before having been created by him, were proposed to him by facts. Nevertheless, what chance is there of humanizing the world and of inflecting its meaning, as far as possible, toward the 'emancipation' of man, unless we reflect history by thought as if it were our conscious work and unless we unreservedly ascribe it to freedom, in order to measure thereby the discrepancy which subsists between the real and the ideal – the degree of alienation? Marx himself did not fear this ascription, it was in fact the very basis of his critique: the world and the activity which produce it are and must be ascribable to man, and wherever this ascription does not correspond to a deliberate project, wherever it is possible only as an affirmation of right over fact, it brings to light (1) the alienation of freedom from its product; (2) an intention of alienation which exists as such in fact only by deceiving itself as to its own nature, and which its exposure contests and criticizes, for an intention that cannot will itself *as it is in reality* exposes itself in becoming conscious, and that is precisely why it is important to make it conscious, to present it to itself as subject, to call upon it to answer for its reality.

Philosophical reflection will therefore keep all its rights in a Marxist society. But it will be only a moment of action in that society, integrated into action as a function of its constant criticism and readjustment. In capitalist society philosophical reflection cannot assume this function. If it criticizes the class of oppression, it is on condition that it cut itself off from or break with that class, for, unlike the revolutionary class, the class of oppression is not consciously

Last development of aestheticism, the attitude of pure contemplation and disincarnated criticism drifting over his own relation with L. Above the battle, out of reach, until the day when L came in one November Saturday and, looking disturbed and overly playful, said 'It's done now.'

'What's done?'

'You know – I've slept with him.'

There had been something else in his detachment and his possessive, abstract generosity. His attitude of pure contemplation was also a horror of asking anything for himself and he

---

engaged in the enterprise of building a human world. The criticism of this class will therefore be entirely negative, a summons to resign, since this class does not bear within itself the desire for its own emancipation but has produced this desire objectively only as its exterior negation, in the proletariat. Ineffectual, the criticism of a class which cannot be led by that criticism to renounce its own existence as a class is therefore perpetually tempted to take itself, in its ineffectuality, for its own goal, and to enjoy this state of affairs which it denounces; in fact, the latter offers to criticism the artistic possibility of laying claim to clairvoyance and the spirit of justice, of incarnating alone the humanist values in their ideal purity, and of harvesting from the very society it denounces the professorial functions and honours suitable to a distinguished mind. As for criticizing the action of the revolutionary class, in the hope of inflecting it in the 'right direction', I hold that the philosopher would be unfitted to do so in a capitalist society and in a period of 'class struggle', because (1) the revolutionary class is not yet sovereign, its action is still dominated by objective necessity much more than by a project of premeditated construction, and it is senseless to criticize an action dictated by objective conditions which cannot be ascribed to it but to the opposing class; (2) as long as the criticism comes from outside – that is, from the philosopher (who is bourgeois in any case and whose public is necessarily and particularly bourgeois) – it necessarily assumes the aspect of a class criticism weakening the cohesion, the discipline, the policy of the revolutionary party and will consequently be denounced by it; (3) since it is made from outside, this criticism is here again ineffectual, purely negative, and tempted to enjoy the superb solitude of the 'spirit of justice', for it can in no way hope to influence the revolutionary party insofar as it remains outside it and thereby possesses neither its audience nor its confidence. If, on the other hand, the philosopher joins the Communist Party, he will realize at once both the political inopportunity of his criticism and its necessity but will not necessarily be better situated to render it effective, for (1) as a member of the party he will be committed to its discipline, and (2) as a bourgeois philosopher he will be the object of an understandable suspicion, which he will be able to dissipate only by giving pledges of discipline greater than other members', greater than will appear desirable to him for the efficacy of his constructive criticism.

arranged matters so that he would never have to ask for anything. Originally this behaviour was doubtless founded in his guilt complex. In his relations with others, he made himself into a self-effacing cipher (foreseeing the supposed requirements), for who was he to ask anyone else for something? Neither protected by any order nor integrated, he was incapable of taking any of his desires seriously (of insisting on anything at all); confronted by someone else's desire, he yielded to it, it seemed natural to him to do so, since the other person was sure of what she wanted – and also because to yield to someone else's taste was for him the

---

His situation, whether outside or within the party, therefore remains unhappy and manifests the objective fact that there is no place, in a class society, for a philosophy that is both good and effective. If he is unwilling to renounce either consciousness or efficacy, the philosopher can transcend the contradictions of his situation only by addressing himself to that thin fringe of the bourgeoisie which is more or less Marxist (but how many are there in France, where Hegel has only begun to be studied in the last fifteen years and where ignorance of Hegel makes most minds refractory to Marxism – also unknown in its philosophical basis, for of Marx's most important texts, which are, I believe, also the most important texts of contemporary philosophy, no more than four thousand copies have been printed to this day), whose active sympathy is objectively necessary to the progress of the Communist Party. Therefore, bearing upon the party by means of the bourgeois Marxist fringe and on the other hand deepening within the latter the influence of Marxism and of pro-Communist sympathy seems to me for the moment a possible procedure for the philosopher. But the effectiveness of this double and simultaneous contestation supposes a condition that is also double: (1) that there is an opportunity, even a remote one, for revolution – that is, that the revolutionary forces are objectively expanding – since this condition is necessary in order that (2) the Communist Party judges it important to preserve or to increase the progressivist fringe of the bourgeoisie, instead of retiring within itself and developing an ideological sclerosis, as it inevitably does in a period of stagnation or retreat of the revolutionary forces. Now, the first of these conditions has hitherto not appeared to be fulfilled (even if the objective presuppositions happen to be brought together, in fact) if the second condition is not also fulfilled at the right moment. There will not be an open, vital Communist Party without revolutionary opportunities, but the revolutionary opportunities will not become actual rather than potential if there is not a vital and open Communist Party.

That this procedure of a double and simultaneous contestation, whose concern for efficacity, moreover, contests the philosophic concern and vice versa, is not easy (not easy to know if and when and to what degree one does not attach enough or attaches too much importance to efficacity or to moral norms; if one puts too much confidence in the objective likelihood of a correction of

only way of conforming (to an alien order). So by his attentive, self-effacing tolerance he appeared spineless and shifty, and indifferent too, since he never asked anyone for anything and let others be, pleasant enough when he was approached but never making the first step, never approaching anyone else. The objective consequence of this attitude was that he did not expose himself, always letting other people expose themselves more, in the solitude of demands without reciprocity. He had received L, had let himself be attracted by her, without ever giving more than she asked, without the spontaneous impulse that might have made her feel he really wanted her. Did he want her? He

---

errors and if one is therefore wrong to denounce the latter insufficiently, or if the contrary applies) the events of June 1956 make quite clear. The negative and complacent critiques of both the party and the bourgeoisie, the 'just' and the 'leftist intellectuals', made a great show of triumphantly reproaching the other progressive intellectuals for not denouncing the Stalinist errors sooner and sufficiently; these 'just' men believed that the Khrushchev report justified their having remained intransigent judges and entitled them now to be the only ones who had a right to speak, because they were the only ones who had always 'seen what was going on' and unflaggingly criticized. Only, if this anti-Communist left had indeed criticized throughout, it was without any concern for effectiveness, but merely in order to feel justified and to be in the right against history. So if history (the autocriticism of the Communist Party) today confirms in part the criticism made by the intellectuals, it is in fact despite them and without their having any credit for it. For they are not interested in changing the course of history, but in incarnating against it certain eternal values. This is why, instead of rejoicing in the Communist Party's autocriticism and coming to its assistance, making themselves the mediators between the party and the revolutionary fringe of the bourgeoisie, they claim to see in the Communist autocriticism an additional reason for throwing discredit on the Communists 'who were wrong all along' and to claim the monopoly of criticism. This is because in reality these distinguished minds feel their monopoly of 'just' criticism threatened; if the Communist Party begins to denounce its own errors, what have they left to say? If their own previous criticisms are in part taken over by history, how can they still claim to uphold the cause of the true and the just *against* history? The only way for them to confirm the excellence of their pious intentions would be to help in their 'historicization' now. But in order to do this they would have to give up wanting to be 'just', and because they prefer the fine role of thinkers-above-the-battle to the efficacity of their thought and do not wish to give up this role, they apply themselves to demonstrating now (following *The Rebel*) that history is always bad and must always be opposed.

As for the progressive intellectuals who, out of their concern for efficacity,

didn't have the slightest idea, and that was what drove her to despair. She had exhausted herself for more than three months to obtain the slightest manifestation of reciprocity from him.

'Am I essential to you?' she had asked.

'Nothing is ever essential', he had said.

'Of course. But I think that for me . . . I think you're essential to me.'

'You mean,' he had philosophized, 'you need to be essential to me.'

'While you, obviously, are content with yourself.'

(And it had been the same thing afterwards with Kay. For weeks on end, after she had been turned out because of him and

---

have hitherto toned down their criticisms, it is true that today they would have more influence over the fringe of the potential bourgeois sympathizers if they had criticized the party sooner and more openly. Yet had they done so, they would have been cut off from the party and their criticisms would have remained without effect. It is of no use having retrospectively been right against history by oneself and too soon, for the important thing is not to be right in the absolute and before God, but to inflect history in the direction you want it to take. And in this regard, it can be more effective to say too little about it and to compromise oneself than to speak a great deal without result.

I shall have to return to this parenthesis later on, I believe. I interrupt it at the very point where interpretation should yield to the sketch of a plan of action, and that is why it still participates in the aestheticism mentioned above. It participates in it (1) by its interpretation of the intellectual's situation, by the justification it affords of his double contestation (which is perhaps not, after all, the best possible way out − that remains to be seen) and of the idealism and aestheticism of his position; (2) by the procedure of double contestation which I have just proposed and which, even if it be the best possible procedure objectively (and this too remains to be seen) tends to justify whatever taste and need I have for contestation. I am well aware that men capable of fulfilling the function which a given conjuncture proposes and requires (whether it be the case of a Quisling or that of a contester) are those who are subjectively prepared by a taste for this kind of function (by their 'character', so to speak; Quisling surely dreamed of being Quisling long before history gave him an opportunity to do so, and that is why it was precisely he who discovered and seized this necessity − it corresponded to an a priori personal vocation in himself). But it is this a priori taste, too, which renders their affirmation of objective necessity suspect; they are too pleased that this necessity exists not to be under suspicion of having forced the interpretation of the facts and wantonly invented a necessity which was perhaps not so evident after all, and which they continue to proclaim when it has in fact disappeared. That is why the validity of the envisaged conduct remains to be seen.

they had been living together in one room half-filled by an
enormous table, he came and went without saying a word,
spending days over his papers and answering her in impatient
monosyllables, while Kay, sick and knowing no one, not speaking a word of French, begged for a little of his time.

'You're self-contained', she said. 'I'm no use to you at all. I
waste your time.'

He protested feebly. It was true that there was no room for
anyone in particular in his life. No one in particular to whom he
wanted to devote his life, because he did not count as an individual and therefore could not be concerned whether someone
should grow attached to him as an individual. If he could hope to
count, it was only by ideas that transcended his individuality;
and if he could interest anyone, it was only so long as his ideas
were at stake. To Kay, who would have let herself be cut into
ribbons for him and who, one way or another (taking poison,
marrying an old man, or becoming a nurse) would have
destroyed herself if he had let her go, he had sent, in response to
her questions, a dissertation on love and marriage: 'You cannot
give more than the other person is ready to receive. . . . You
cannot commit yourself to someone for your whole life, except by
a purely formal and meaningless ceremony − because you
cannot know in advance the circumstances which, in five, ten, or
twenty years, will modify the meaning of your commitment and
make it null and void. A commitment is valid only if you are free
to confirm or revoke it. Contracting it for life is a formal and
abstract gesture. That's what marriage is. Besides, could you
swear that in twenty years you will still want to live with me?'

He must have grown remarkably thick-skinned to make use of
such pretentious arguments at such a moment. She was trying to
save their life together, he his philosophical point of honour. But
she knew what she wanted, and he, although he accused her of
living by false principles, knew only what he must want on
principle. That is why, after long discussions, obliged to choose
between Kay and principles, he discovered that the principles at
stake were after all, from the moment that he was the only one to
defend them, not so important, since they were now identified

with his will as an individual quarrelling with another will. He chose Kay over the principles, but ill-naturedly and without even realizing that she accepted for him – and without complaint – hunger and poverty.)

He stared at L over a plate of saveloy vinaigrette, tried to 'realize' she had been to bed with another man, and – as on every occasion when something happened to him which concerned him and which he could not keep himself from experiencing to the full, without the help of ideas and abstract principles, something that demanded of him some action or attitude that would affect the future – he escaped by means of aestheticism. He began to analyse what he was feeling or was going to feel ('You're going to behave like an ass and start suffering now'), what L must be feeling, and to compose a scene; to tell himself the present as if it had already occurred, to re-create it in his imagination, to recover himself as its author (imaginary too, of course) in order to escape the intolerable intensity of actual experience. He was in fact living the scene, the most perfect of all, in *Man's Fate*, where Kyo finds May again after she has been to bed with a doctor from the hospital. ('He wanted to so badly', she said.)

But he is not going to write a novel now. Yet the temptation of making use of just this story in a novel, the complacency with which I tell it, the attraction it holds for me do not derive only from the fact that it is one of the few real episodes I have experienced, but doubtless from the fact that I find gathered within it, as in an archetypal situation, all the affective themes of my life. I was totally concerned by it because totally challenged.

– Dismissed (but not right away); that is, excluded from the community of men which was now confined to L. Yet he couldn't complain of this exclusion. He had wanted it (abstractly, without conviction) as he had always wanted, for years now, to rid himself of everything that kept him in reality and forced him to exist instead of merely thinking existence.

– Annulled, but by himself still more than by L. Because there now was something irreparable between them, she became for him, by that part of herself which now had its truth in Someone

Else, an independent freedom, Someone Else herself whom he began to value desperately.

Of course, it was ordinary enough: You live for months or years with a woman whom you take for granted more or less and who, by virtue of a situation that seems quite settled, becomes a familiar and rather tedious object. And the day this woman leaves you or 'deceives' you, you discover you don't 'know' her, or, rather, you rediscover her autonomous existence, as during those first days together, and what is called her 'mystery' – you realize that there is a part of herself not adequate to her exterior as you know it, that her look has a subjective underside, that for her the world and you yourself exist with a taste and singular values you do not comprehend.

But if he had merely rediscovered L's autonomy and subjectivity, he would perhaps have been excusable. Yet he was not. He knew that if she came back to him as before she would bore him as before, and that the value she now had for him derived from the fact that 'before' had become the impossible. He loved the impossible for its own sake (as he had once loved A), he wanted to retain L's old reality for him because that reality, transcended and denied by her, was no longer anything but unreality, a being which she had been for him and which, objectively, was now nothing but nonbeing, the error which he insisted on maintaining against the evidence and for love of which he thrust himself deeper into nonbeing: a love of the impossible, a longing for nonbeing, perseverance in error, hours spent torturing himself by imagining her with someone else in order to realize (but this was impossible, and such impossibility comprised the irritating evanescence of suffering) the nonbeing of what she was for him and what he himself, as love of this nonbeing which he was henceforth alone to maintain in being, was – pure nothingness, existence of error.

To liquidate L would have been to liquidate his own aestheticism, his love of failure and suffering, his poetical attitude, his masochism, his choice of nullity, all suddenly reactivated, in which he fell back as into an old rut and in which nothing, this time, justified his falling back, for he himself had desired and provoked the occasion of his backsliding, persuaded that it would be quite easy for him to do without L, but when the opportunity presented itself he had not been able to resist the temptation, he had insisted on experiencing it as his failure and on thrusting himself voluptuously within it. Not right away, moreover. He had let the trap be set at some length, offering L his friendship (sincerely), accepting hers, constructing with her, starting from their enhanced independence, a more authentic dialogue.

Had they really set out to liquidate what was false between them and to build, starting from their unsettled love (and a love made impossible by their mutual fault – L's because she had adored him as a god, setting him too high to receive anything real from him and offering him no opportunity to give anything but the spectacle of his divinity; his own because he had not been able – even though he was bored up there – to get down from his pedestal and offer L an example of humanity instead of speeches), a relation of reciprocity? It was doubtful. If they had set out in this direction, they had in any case not succeeded in travelling far. He was dreaming of constructing a new love through friendship, and this time a true one – a utopia. To succeed he would have had to liquidate what was religious in L's love for him, and to manage that he would have had to be able to offer her more than anyone else on the human and physical level. Yet, despite several efforts to transform himself from a god and an idea into a real man, his metamorphosis had not taken place. It came too late. He was behaving like the discredited regime which, when the revolution is on the point of breaking out, suddenly offers all the reforms previously refused and, on the basis of these reforms, demands a reprieve – even more, demands to be considered as the incarnation of the revolutionary reforms conceived outside it. This regime that has not kept up with history will either be swept away or else, if granted a measure of confidence, will subsequently fall back into its former errors; what it has done under the pressure of events it will not be able to continue if the rebels lay down their arms.

Perhaps L felt this, but (just as the rebels cannot forget the former aspect of the *ancien régime* from one day to the next) she could not believe in the reality of such a change. For her he remained the remote divinity to whom sacrifices were offered on certain days, while more profane satisfactions were pursued elsewhere. She kept him like a precious relic in her jewel case.

'You, you're different', L said. 'Even if I go to bed with other men, I consider you above all the rest.'

It was an unbearable remark. By it she, the only anchorage of his individual humanity, refused him the character of a man in order to maintain him in the capacity of a god or an idea at the very moment when he would have liked to descend among men – and the worst was that he had not stolen this exile among the divinities.

(It is only today that I understand the distress implied in this sincere and 'unbearable' remark. Incapable of living only with an 'unlivable' man (myself), whose tenderness was so furtive, who even in his way of making love seemed to ask forgiveness for his own existence; attracted on the other hand by a man difficult to reach (the other man), who in trying to dominate her revealed to her the 'prey' aspect of her femininity and would have liked to despise her, she was unwilling to forgo either one. She had to hold on to the friendship and the esteem of the first in order not to feel herself disgraced; she needed the other's desire in order not to feel buried alive. In remorse and guilt she was living out the contradiction between her femininity and her humanity – between her social role of woman-as-prey and her unsatisfied need to accede to the universal as human transcendence. She did not see by what synthesis she could surmount this contradiction and tried to maintain both terms together by belonging sometimes to one, sometimes to the other. Her situation was typical of woman's condition in bourgeois society, which is, in immediate terms, hopeless. It left her only the aesthetic satisfaction of playing her role as desirable object for the other man, of enjoying the new appearance she was assuming, or, rather, of enjoying her capacity to assume an appearance, and, in this *make-believe*, to catch the other man in the snare of his male pride, agreeing to be the object he wanted her to be in order to slip between his fingers – an object simultaneously offered and out of reach, which transforms itself the moment you think you can possess it, ceaselessly offers you unexpected aspects, exasperates the male's desire for possession, satisfies it only in order to disappoint it at the last moment, thus sending the male back to his own subjectivity and seizing itself in his ferreting gaze as freedom object, that is as a traitorous object, a magic object, a disconcerting object. This is the game of seduction, and it is because woman finds, in the structure of her feminine alienation, no other immediate possibility of manifesting herself as freedom, and because the freedom object is perhaps the highest of the values offered by the situation, that her project of liberation, failing the actual transformation of the situation itself, rarely gets beyond that aestheticism which consists of play-acting beneath the master's eyes and of deceiving in complete security his desire for possession. A subordinate role, since she remains the inessential; if the master is to be trapped he must still desire to possess you; your freedom exists only as the object limit of his own, and since it is he who establishes your objectivity you depend on him. You deceive him, subjectively, but objectively he possesses you even in your deception. And then all he needs to do is turn his eyes away from you for your stratagem to dissolve into what it really is: false appearances which you assume, by the playful creation of which you escape him; but you do not escape him in your substance. You know the solitude of being for yourself the reverse or the denial of what you are for others, and of being for others a false being which denies yourself. And it is perhaps because your situation, in its contradictions and its solitude, resembles my own; because it consigns you to the contestation of the male universe at the same time as to that of your own particularity; because this ineffectual contestation is tempted to take itself for an objective goal (what can you do, how can you realize your subjective freedom in the given state of affairs?); because your situation conditions you to a vocation as victim in revolt and as poet; because you rejoin the world of men only by making them forget who you are and who they think they are in relation to you, that I have sometimes thought I fraternally recognized myself in your unhappiness and discovered only one way out of it: to write.)

So he denounced her bad faith and the vanity of her aestheticism. He condemned her in order not to feel condemned
himself. He said, 'You don't mean anything to me any more.'
And she answered at first, 'The flowers were withering in their
vase.' She felt all sad and empty, all that nothing she was. And
later: 'Go back to your books and your nothingness.' She too
needed him to be in the wrong. But neither she nor he was ever
convinced that all the wrongs were only on the other side.

Out of all this there remained the conviction that a living man
is worth more than a dead philosopher. And that it made little
sense to torture another person for the love of an idea (and in
particular an idea of love). That a life was not built out of fiats
handed down a priori, and that in practice the intransigent fidel-
ity to a priori thinking is the refusal of real existence. What use is
it to have universal ideas in the abstract if these ideas prevent you
from being a man, even if only in the eyes of a single person, and
if in their name you refuse yourself and to another person what
can make life livable? Is this an apology for compromise and
resignation? I do not think so; and I think that we are all in this
position. We glimpse a morality beyond the disintegration of our
society, but because this disintegration has not yet reached its
term this morality is not yet one we can practice. We know what
the relations between a man and a woman (and other men)
should be, but neither the man nor the woman of this
relationship exists yet universally. Is this a reason to reject someone who comes to you, to send him away to die in solitude? (A
question which I asked myself along with these others: Is the
man who disapproves of the black market entitled to starve
himself and his family? Is the man who denies the system of
capitalist profit justified in letting himself die of cold and hunger
in order not to compromise with the system by buying food from
the shopkeeper around the corner? He will die; the shopkeeper
remains. Refusal has a meaning only if it is collective, since its
negation is then incarnated, assumes a positive aspect, becomes
effective. As a solitary act, refusal is only an egotism, a way of
preferring one's self in all its 'purity' to the universe.)

'If we are together only for a moment,' Kay said, 'I prefer

leaving now and taking with me the memory of our love intact.'

He had equivocated for a long time. Then, that night, he had the revelation that if he let Kay go, if he had to remember all his life that she was dragging about somewhere between Rome and Bucharest, seeking refuge in her devotion to the sick or her duty towards a family, he could no longer look at himself in a mirror. If as a 'philosopher' he refused to 'compromise', as a man he would be a traitor and a coward. And then, if he was not certain he would be able to live with her, he was sure he did not want to lose her. He pressed Kay close to him and said with a sort of deliverance, 'If you leave, I'll follow you. I couldn't bear to have let you go.'

And after a moment he added, 'Ever.'

They knew it would not be easy. She because she would have to fight for her place against abstractions, be only a part of his life whereas for her he was her whole life. He because their life together virtually incarnated the contradiction between morality and life, between the philosopher and the man, the first not managing to raise the second to his own level, and the second failing to incarnate the first, each guilty in the other's eyes, tempted to sacrifice him or to sacrifice himself to him, to reproach him his existence as a defection (the man's defection against an ideal morality, the philosopher's against the reality of the man, of all other men). And the reproaches he could make to himself that he was neither sufficiently a man nor sufficiently a philosopher, but the living contradiction of the two, it had been inevitable that Kay should make them to him ('I feel you could do without me so easily') and to herself ('Your life would be so much easier if it weren't for me'). And since they knew that this contradiction reflected the general contradiction of the world they lived in and would probably not be resolved in their lifetime (she believing she could never integrate herself in a socialist society, even if she theoretically approved of it; he that he must try to, if the occasion presented itself), a sort of division of labour was established between them: he represented for her her moral justification, she standing for the justification of his life as a man (wage earning submitted to, material pleasures accessible after three years of common wretchedness), his place and his mediator with the world that opened to her as if by magic. The episode with L had taught him this at least: that you do not transform men (or yourself) according to your a priori idea of their relationships, and that there is, between the evidence of what these relations should be and their effective possibility, the whole thickness of a world to be changed. That it is easy to gain acceptance intellectually for the value of ideal relations, but that intellectual acceptance is of no consequence when it does not find at hand the instruments of its accomplishment. That it was perhaps a praiseworthy enterprise to question oneself as to the ideal nature of human relations, but that it was neither up to me nor to anyone to reform humanity. That a priori moral requirements are only rootless notions which have opportunities to become effective only in the finite sector in which each person has a chance to act, but that as far as I was concerned this sector was neither the Negro problem in the United States nor the world revolution nor the emancipation of women nor universal peace; for no one, except the philosopher, proceeds from the universal to the particular; one must proceed concretely to attain the universal, from one's individual sector; otherwise one will have produced only an abstract idea incapable of taking any concrete form. It was during this first half of 1947 that I produced almost all the ideas subsequently developed (of which a good half remain to be developed). As for knowing what my sector is, this is not so simple to decide, and it is doubtless one of the objects of my present interrogation.

The spring day in 1948 when I said 'Ever' to Kay, I did so in the conviction that she was my sector; not all of it, but at least the only tangible element of a sector all of whose other dimensions remained to be defined. For her, I was a man and I was responsible for my countenance as a man and for the course that her life would take; if I followed her I would perhaps succeed in the only concrete undertaking I could bring off: to make life livable for one person and, who knows, perhaps for myself too at the same time, even if, for that, I would have to take a job and for the most part lead an 'ordinary' life.

Today I know that Kay was one of the moments of the contradiction there is for a man who cannot accept the world as it is (either because the world is crushing him or because he remains a stranger to it), to accept it and even profit from it in details while refusing it as a whole. To accept it not in a spirit of compromise but 'because there is nothing better to do', because the little that can be done is, in details, livable even when the entirety is not, and because the acceptance of detail permits some action in the direction of the transformation of the whole – but not enough, nevertheless, to be justified.

Yet I maintain that we must all live this contradiction, because we cannot (without staging an arrogant, ineffectual and complacent revolt) refuse altogether or transform at one stroke this world so inacceptable as a whole. There is no means of avoiding this contradiction, there are only opposing ways of facing it. The first, which is to content oneself with the little one believes one can do while giving up doing everything – with the livable details of the corrupt whole, by concluding that things are not so bad after all; the second, more tempting, is to refuse the present, that is existence – and the temptation of finding it livable after all, because it is human – by taking refuge in the totalitarian ideological refusal of this world and its possibilities, by affirming against reality the purity of a future in which the contradiction will be resolved and by fanatically rejecting in the name of this future (albeit mythical and desiccating for lack of a relation with the present) all the world's 'impure temptations'. Implicit in our situation is the double temptation of the cowardly man who, because he would like to live well, would like to find things not so bad after all, and of the militant fanatic who, as long as the revolution has not been brought to pass, considers life itself a sin, a vice to which only the decadent bourgeoisie consents, and whose attitude leads him to imagine the condition of the most wretched as strictly unlivable, forgetting that their revolt has a meaning only because it implies the need for humanity which the fanatic censures in himself as a dangerous weakness. (And is it not evident in fact that I was speaking of Kay as if of a weakness and in an apologetic tone of excuse, as if one had to apologize for living?)

Hailed by the British Navy off the coast of Palestine, the *Exodus*, with a cargo of Jews rescued from concentration camps, was forced to turn back. It berthed in Port Bou in the spring of '47 and remained in quarantine there until ordered to return to Hamburg. The five hundred Jews on board declared a hunger strike.

A leftist weekly happened to ask him for an article about the incident; after which he began to write other such pieces. It was because the weekly wanted his articles, and because he had no other source of income, that he began to interest himself in current realities and discovered, at the same time, that he was qualified to speak of nothing to anyone, that he had no sector, no point of view that was really his. Unless it was the outlook of abstract reason, which consisted in demonstrating the absurdity of all politics (absurdity of the plans for the dismemberment of Germany, absurdity of the war in Indonesia and Indochina, absurdity of the belief in the continuing reality of the American monopoly of atomic power), and the viewpoint of the persecuted, the oppressed and the rebellious (Jews, Malagasy, Indochinese, American Negroes, Greek Communists, South African Negroes). This led to an abstract condemnation, in the name of high principles, of the established powers, to the demonstration that man is crushed by an inhuman history, that the world is bad and that the cause of its inhumanity could be summed up thus: The determining reasons of human actions (capitalist profit with its struggle for markets and national prestige) cannot answer for and control their objective results; to obtain what they desire, men do what they do not desire.

But rather than set forth here certain thoughts on the capitalist regime, which I conceived (not having bothered to read Marx) from the contact with empirical reality, it would be better to try to understand these thoughts in the light of my relation to the apparent truth of this society: money.

For him, as far back as he can remember, money was something you received, stole or took but did not 'earn', the fact of receiving it or taking it where it could be had being comparable to theft. Something that floats about in the human world like manna, is always appropriated by 'those who have it' ('They have money', his mother used to say. 'I don't have any more money. Can you give me some money?' 'Where do you think I'm going to get it?' his father would say. 'Oh,' she said, 'how I wish I had money the way they do!') and cannot be acquired except by taking it away from them. And to this end there are various ways (service, sale, borrowing, beggary) which all come down to inducing the possessor, by ruse or deception, to give you some of it, the sum he gives you having no immediately intelligible relation to what (if the situation arises) you offer him in exchange, but only to his own estimation of your needs, the need he has of you, the degree of sympathy he feels toward you.

(The newspaper paid him thirty to forty francs for an article three or four pages long and paid others up to sixty francs. 'I can't pay that man less', the editor said. Another weekly paid twenty-five francs maximum.

Conversation with the editor of a Parisian daily:

'How much do you make?'

'About sixty thousand.'

'But that's pretty good!'

'It's not enough for the work I do.'

'For a boy your age, after a year in the firm, I think that's doing very well!'

'You've just hired X, who doesn't do anything in particular, and you pay him eighty. And Y, who doesn't do half the work I do, makes seventy.'

'I can't go into such considerations.'

'But you can't keep me from making comparisons.'

'Look here, my dear G . . ., you know I'm very fond of you. But you're a boy without any particular needs. You don't have a car, you don't have mistresses, you don't have debts, you don't have a way of life to maintain. Now X needs a lot of money. . . .')

So a vast sector of society is organized in order to make money from those who have it. (And since the latter get hold of it by depriving those who don't have any, they participate in a double exploitation – first they make people work to deprive them of a share of the market value of their product, then they make others work in order to be able to spend a part of the profit realized on the first. So it is the first group, farmers and labourers, who support at their own expense the workers of the luxury industries from which they can't afford to buy anything.)

The only way to get hold of money – that is, to take it from those who had it – was therefore to satisfy a need the latter thought they had: to rent or sell oneself to them. And the only means of being freed from this prostitution was 'to have money', by inheritance, by theft, or by lottery; then you could afford the luxury of doing as you chose. There were therefore those who 'earned every penny they had' by selling themselves, and those who paid for everything by buying themselves. And, between the two, the great floating mass of the middle classes who buy and sell themselves at either end, ignobly servile toward the possessors and ignobly scornful of the nonpossessors.

He, as it turned out, was one of those for whom everything was to be bought, except that he couldn't pay, a *petit bourgeois* without money. There could be no question of earning money; he had nothing to sell that anyone might have wanted to buy from him. Banished from the social machinery by being forbidden to work, he was well placed to observe this machinery in which each man is to the others what he is in relation to money, in which each man has money by having the money of other men. That was what a city was (insofar as a city is a market) – a human concentration which, by its extent and its density, appears to each man as a swarm of men objects. For each man, the city is the city of the others and he himself is the will to exempt himself from the common fate by profiting from the others without letting them profit from him. The city is born as the collective involuntary product of each man's particular will. Because the others pass through it or happen to be there, men have come there to profit from their presence, they have constructed houses and stores there, each man for himself, without a concerted plan, without perceiving that they were thus becoming for each of the others a part of those others and were producing despite them a collective work, not knowing it was collective, and a common fate which for each man, wishing only to profit from the others, consisted of exposing himself as one of the others to each individual's will to profit.

Urban society: a strange body whose reality is produced by each man's attempt to influence this reality and to exempt himself from its law. A human landscape which, by its density, overturns nature; where nature (the uncreated given) is for each man this quantitative humanity; where the exploitation of nature by man becomes the exploitation by man of the human collectivity considered as an external fact. Each man regards as natural laws the molecular laws of the urban collectivity, without realizing that he himself is a part of this collectivity, promotes its laws, and falls beneath their sway *by his very efforts to influence them*; the attempts to profit by the statistical laws (market, exchange) in reality establish these laws, verify them and perpetuate them without ever increasing the total number of opportunities. Man profits from men as if they were alien things (has nothing to ask of them or offer to them save money), without realizing that he thereby makes himself the promoter of a reifying order in which he himself figures only as an alien thing (demanding or dispensing money). It is because no one feels himself responsible for this alienating order that it continues to function – thanks to the myth, to which each man clings, that a man can succeed by himself in evading the logic of the system, that one can (and should) be the only subject exploiting a collectivity of insects not deserving the name of men. The crematory ovens are within the logic of the system. And dictatorship too, of course, and this for two reasons:

First, because the truth of bourgeois society remains exterior to it as an involuntary consequence. When this consequence, by the activity of each individual, becomes detrimental to all, appeal is made to the providential saviour who rescues each individual from the consequences of his own acts, but rescues him *from outside*, by external intervention, without asking individual sacrifice of him.

Second, because the public interest, in a bourgeois regime, is the interest of no one, is incarnated in no group whose activity would be consciously to the interest of all. There is not, concretely, a public interest common to both large and small landowners, to consumers and dealers, to white-collar workers, farmers and factory labourers.

The abstract and formal public interest common to these antagonistic groups exists only to prevent each of the other groups from making its particular interest prevail – by endowing the state with an extremely relative independence as arbiter: by demanding its intervention against this or that particular interest which is too powerful – without each man's lessening his attempt, nevertheless, to make his own private interest prevail if he can.

The completely formal and negative public interest of each group therefore exists to prevent the victory of any concrete interest – but if it succeeds in this intention it must renounce in its turn any hope of victory.

This is why the private interests which confront one another at the heart of bourgeois society struggle against all the other private interests and *at the same time* against the state's power of arbitration, which each man tries to confiscate as the instrument of his private power.

Hence what is wrongly construed as the expression of the public interest (the power and the independence of the nation, the independence of the organs of administration and justice, of instruction and information, civil liberties, etc.) and as the 'values' of this society is in reality only the consequence of antagonistic interests neutralizing each other and each one trying, out of fear of the others' triumph, to perpetuate the conditions of their antagonism. A result of a balance of forces that is in essence precarious, the 'values' and 'liberties' of bourgeois society are also permanently threatened by each of the private interests in the struggle – for each of the latter is ready, as soon as it has the power to do so, to suppress the 'regime of liberty' for the profit of its own domination.

The bourgeois liberties are in essence fragile, for they are not willed by any social group, except perhaps by a minority of professional liberals who have become the beneficiaries of a regime that has created them.

He began thinking about this apropos of the black market in France and of Gaullism in 1947. Particularly in regard to the invincible black market, by which each man thought he could exempt himself from the common fate (until the common fate no longer existed except as a fiction against which one took precautions), to the point where a people was composed in the majority of men who considered themselves specially privileged, and where exceptional privileges became in fact the rule: the struggle of each against all, hoarding, speculation, inflation, generalized selfishness and the mystification of every need as a need for money. Money was the only universal value because universally desired, but an abstract universal, as if animated by a magical life, melting away between your fingers, which each man desired to own privately.

There would be material for a long dissertation in this contradiction of individually coveting what is a universal substance, since this contradiction, as it is activated in relation to money, sums up the fundamental contradiction of capitalist society (the individual considering freedom as his private affair and his universality as what he possesses by depriving others of it)*; and perhaps I shall someday return to this dissertation begun during the winter of 1947–48 as if (while Kay wretchedly dragged herself about, eating nothing but oatmeal and boiled barley which they had Walter pay for by taking him *en pension*, for one franc per meal, around the huge, cluttered table on which they made a little room for three glass bowls instead of plates) as if he had finally found a means other than nihilism of pronouncing the annihilation of the world.

A dissertation, pugnacious little articles (and later venomous ones, each containing a discreet dose of poison, the materials of an indictment omitted so that the facts could speak for themselves): this was not an annihilation that he had in hand, nor a revolution, but a matter of getting paid by the bourgeoisie for assembling a dossier that would overwhelm it, to lodge himself in

---

*See Marx, 'The Jewish Question', *Philosophical Works*, vol. I, pp. 192–201, Costes edition.

the capitalist world like a poisonous spider in the middle of its
web, decoding the vibrations and rejoicing when things were
going badly. To be the lucid witness and the judge of the world's
absurdity. It was a taste for this attitude that found him, a year
later, writing propaganda for the World Citizens, a movement he
had at first rejected as a *petit bourgeois* manifestation, demanding
the abstract union of equally abstract men of good will; presenting himself to strange audiences (Protestant youth movements,
parish reunions, Quakers, etc.) as a decrier of Western politics;
conducting before these naïve minds the implicit prosecution of
bourgeois states; taking towards the world the viewpoint of a
judge, the outlook of Sirius.

   Nothing new, all in all, in this role that boiled down to saying
'I am not one of you, I see you from a point where you cannot see
me'; World Citizen – that is, a man from nowhere (and not from
everywhere) contesting real particularities in the name of an
abstract and unreal universality. A way of dissolving the
concrete, while simulating an interest for it, in the abstract, and
of denouncing it afterward in the name of his opposition to the
latter. This said, it would be surprising if despite his dissertations
on the fetishism of money, he had not been fascinated by its
abstraction; money was the annihilation of the concrete in the
abstract, the metamorphosis of real products into currency, of
the thing into its imaginary possibility, the triumph of the
imaginary (of the belief in the power of a piece of paper, founded
on the belief of each man in the belief of all the rest) over the real,
the denial of diversity, the suppression as well as the preservation
(*Aufhebung*) of duration (duration of work preserved as savings
after having been negated by its payment; duration of life and
inactivity possessed by the assurance of having 'something to live
on' for a few weeks or years), the annihilation of concrete doing
and being in a perfectly impersonal having that, since it is the
only payment asked of you, permits you to pass unnoticed and
silences all questions as to your passage. He who pays has no
accounting to give, has no need to pay with his own person.

   No need to look much further. I think that this time I have put
my finger on the 'original complex' to which all his attitudes

toward other people refer (the silences, the horror of assuming any identity or role in the eyes of others – that is, timidity – the avoidance of concrete relationships by theorizing about these relationships or by psychoanalysing the interlocutor, the preference for relationships in which all that is asked of him is a theoretical intelligence, the refusal to pay with his own person in order to substitute ideas and to identify himself with them, the refusal to speak a common language and to say common things, the absence of spontaneity, the taste for self-annihilation) and from which other attitudes (masochism, effacement, what I have called 'treason', opposition and contestation) flow as an empirical consequence. It will perhaps take quite some time to explain this, but I shall try, without falling into psychologism and still allowing historical dialectic its share.

# I

*What consciousness does in isolation is,*
*furthermore, without the slightest interest*
*– KARL MARX, The German Ideology*

I must turn back to the place where I first touched on the original complex which I should now like to clarify further for myself. I have referred to the norm which regulates all our behaviour and whose lack of realization causes the individual to feel not so much guilty as in danger of loss, in danger of losing its identity, its value, its orientation, its place in the world. This is what the psychoanalysts call the ego; this ego does not exist; it is an ideal image of the self (an ideal 'I'), thematized, often rationalized, drawn from a swarm of possibilities and temptations. It is the image according to which the individual attempts to identify itself. To identify itself with what? With itself as Other. The ego is an Other.

It is not an accident that I have spoken of myself throughout in the third person. I had intended to give a theoretical justification for this at the end, but what follows will probably dull my taste for such elaboration. This is because, aside from all theoretical considerations, he has a horror of 'I'. More simply, he has no ego – no character, no declared taste save that of effacing himself, none of that comfort of a man easy in his own skin, no spontaneity, no personality. For other people, he emerges from a mysterious silence only to manifest himself as a theoretical intelligence or, gaining confidence, to play with his instruments of communication: to play with language by puns, to play with his voice by making animal sounds – sheep, pig and duck – to play with his body by a grotesque gait or gesticulation. These games have an ironic quality: he destroys the very communication he sets up and negates the means of communication by the way he uses them. All in all, he emerges from silence only to create silence by self-destructive communication (or remains plunged in it by the impersonality of his theoretical discourse). It is not enough to speak of 'a horror of the ego'; he has a *terror of identification*: a terror of being identified by other people with an ego that is an Other, a terror of saying more than he means or something different from what he means, consequently a terror of saying anything at all. Hence his voice is low, indistinct, monotonous, and it easily goes unnoticed. And there has always been this terror, as far back as his conscious memory extends, back to the age when he was beginning to speak; it is the meaning which communication with others by means of language immediately assumed for him; it has always paralysed the act of speech. It is the most original and fundamental of his complexes.

I should have suspected this when I was describing his strabismus, his lisp and his childish stuttering. These are signs – signs (as is the child's anxiety to know whether it is himself or only her son his mother loves) that the discovery of his existence for other people (that is, the discovery of his ego) has been a traumatism; that there has always been an intolerable discrepancy between what he was for himself and his being-for-others; that his singularity, discovered simultaneously with speech (he asked, emerging from the darkness behind the heavy red velvet curtain, how it was that an *eye* could *see* and a *head* could *think*, dizzied at the age of four by the mystery of an exterior object – eye and head – doubled by the interiority of seeing and thinking, the scandal of an interiority having the object's exteriority as its unrealizable reverse), consisted in never having adhered, like most other men, to his ego, his speech, his being-for-others as to the norm of an ideal and successful identity with himself.

They corrected his strabismus with glasses, his lisp with a metal loop, his stammer by mechanical exercises, and he spoke perfectly, but with a voice so low and so fast that his mother was forever complaining, 'What are you saying? Talk louder! What are you mumbling about now?' and they nicknamed him Mumbler (*Nuschler*); even hearing the dreadful word kept him from wanting to speak. So he learned to bray, to low, to whinny, bleat and grunt, because these animal sounds, impossible to be mistaken, meant what they meant, their meaning was identified with the determined vocal possibilities of the animal – 'natural' sounds without mystery, all intention inseparable from this simple-minded act of speech, since for the animal no other was possible.

With language the situation was entirely different; and language, for man, begins with the body. Previously immersed in his body as in the matter of his nonthematic experience, he discovered one day that this body which he identified with himself signified something for other people and that this signification escaped him. The lived meaning of his behaviour was stolen from him by a hedge of faces leaning over him which suddenly burst out laughing or delivered weighty commentaries (explosions of merriment which his first stammering provoked; childish witticisms repeated dozens of times by his delighted mother, who exhibited him to strangers as if he were a trained dog, making him repeat his pearls whose meaning escaped him), having received a mysterious message from his body. This body itself was stolen from him, it spoke to others in a language he did not know; he *was spoken* by his body. Unrealizable significations, intentions he was certain he did not have because he did not understand them, came to inhabit him from outside, establishing themselves within him like parasites that eat away the flesh or, worse still, the consciousness, without his being able to turn around and see them. He became for others an Odd Little Person of whom they spoke in his presence in the third person, a strange object (playing with the little wheels on the bars of the kind of cage they put him in at the age of two, he felt their eyes, their silence upon him; 'I suppose he'll be an engineer', his mother said in her encouraging voice; for them, he beat on the wheels wildly; something was expected of him, what was an 'engineer'?) before whom grown-up men got down on all fours and made faces and ladies went into high-pitched ecstasies. They saw something on him he was ignorant of, he 'told' them something he did not know, they expected him to play a role. He did not understand them, he did not understand his role. They terrorized him. He hated them.

His entire childhood was spent under this tyranny of identification, for he was always required to identify himself with the role, with the ego his mother wanted him to play and necessarily imputed to him because that was how she wanted to see him. She saw him as she would have liked him to be, she showed him his imaginary ego as if in a mirror, and this ego was an Other, a lie, unless it was the other way around – unless it was *he* who was an Other, a lie. Yes, it probably *was* the other way around, his mother couldn't be wrong, she was sure to see him as he really was – so he was a lie, an Other, and guilty of not feeling the way she saw him. He was an Other, other than his ego, and being unable to identify himself with his ego condemned him to being rejected – as a lie, a ghost, a consciousness ashamed of disappointing and deceiving – into the outer darkness.

I suppose this is what is meant by 'moral consciousness' (or the superego), this image of yourself which is always shown to you as what you are, and which, since in fact you are nothing else, you should be from now on, lest you lose yourself in the shadows of being nothing. You interiorize the requirement to identify yourself and, in order to conform to the ego presented to you, you apply yourself to producing it by 'censoring' what contradicts it – that is, by thematizing only those elements in your intentions and behaviour that confirm it – the rest, like the dark side of the moon, remaining unknown (but not unconscious) for you.

There would doubtless be a difference depending on whether your ego is a real objectivation of yourself, originally corresponding to your real possibilities, or a false image presented to you by systematically misinterpreting your real possibilities, and which, not corresponding to them, can only be achieved by wanting to deceive, to play a false role. In fact, your objectivation is never immediately true; you are presented (this is education) an unreal image of yourself in order that it will suggest possibilities of achieving it by your behaviour. It remains to discover how you can adapt yourself and if, in the way you do so, the possibilities suggested (by interpreting you, decoding you, by *speaking* you, in the transitive sense of the verb 'to speak') can be adopted and developed (because they already correspond to a rough draft of behaviour) or if they remain alien either because you are simply being lied to about yourself or – it comes down to the same thing – because you are being tyrannized (by being made to feel that your ego does not belong to you but to others, and that in order to come into possession of it you must deserve it, pay for it with obedience as if it were something you had pawned, thereby contracting a debt which must be paid). It remains to be seen, in other words, whether the language which you are, in fact, for other people is revealed to you as your power over them or as their power over you, as your possibility of manifesting yourself in the intersubjective universe of speech, or as your fall into the *other people's* universe of discourse.

I know, it is never one *or* the other; but there is always one aspect or the other which is dominant, and for him it was clearly the second. Language (like the whole world, moreover) was the exclusive property of his mother. She ruled over words in order to rule over men by cascades of talk, holding her disconcerted interlocutors paralysed, as if in a glue. Language was her kingdom, and to speak was to enter this realm and immediately fall under her jurisdiction. Speaking necessarily meant serving her in her own language (since she confiscated it) and providing significations over which she expected to rule incontestably. Speaking (and keeping still) always meant saying what *she* meant, and the flood of words that responded to his murmur (or his silence) made him say what *she* thought or wanted to hear. He was a prisoner in the kingdom of maternal discourse, fettered to the fabulations by which she identified him, and, unable to free

himself from her verbal ascendancy, could escape only by a stubborn silence. (An impression renewed after eight years of
wartime separation: her welcoming words in the station were like
an attack, a spider web she was spinning around him, binding
his limbs, insistently reducing him to the appearance she wanted
to find, assailing him with questions, exclamations and
commentaries to which there was no possible personal response.
'Let me look at you! My poor little boy! How thin you are! Did
you have a good trip? Could you sleep on the train? Was it
crowded? Oh, your hair! We will go to the barber tomorrow.
You can't go out with a thatch like that. People will turn around
and look at you in the street. Don't you go to the barber
regularly? But you must be dead tired! You certainly haven't
grown any more talkative in all these years! You look at me and
tell yourself, "She doesn't even give me time to breathe!" Ah,
these mothers! Come on, we'll get a taxi. You can take a bath
when you get home. You can tell me everything then. But tell me
. . .' Then he began staring at her with incredulous amusement,
trying to guess how long she could go on talking by herself, and
how many subjects she would rush through once she got started.
And then he fell into the trap of her questions again; answering
even one meant seeing that answer immediately crippled,
maimed, swept into a verbal vortex from which emerged judgments, and a portrait of himself and further questions and
demands that he deal with problems as she saw them. They
began to quarrel, then he adopted the tactic of brief ironic
replies, then stopped talking altogether because she was invincible, the verbal wall behind which she took cover was not to be
pierced, not even by someone whose voice was loud and whose
breath long, because she wouldn't have the patience to listen to
him. Then as some twenty years earlier he fell silent – the way
his sister had fallen silent, emerging from her mutism only by
defeatist sallies, verbal provocations uttered in a victim's accusing
tone because she felt beaten in advance and sought nothing more
than the proof of her defeat.)

To escape the kingdom of his mother's discourse, to elude her
constraints, her eloquence, her judgments, her terrifying insist-

ence on seemliness (to which the rediscovered photographs of his childhood bore witness: the year-old baby swathed in lace, wearing white gloves and a cap down to his ears; later in a beach robe by the Adriatic, or in pajamas, to prove that he had plenty of clothes; and then leaving this beach in midsummer, dressed in an overcoat and wearing gloves because that was how 'one' travelled, wearing an overcoat whatever the temperature. An object of display, a symbol of respectability and wealth, clothes made the man, like the well-mannered formulas she taught him to recite) — that was probably why he had thrown himself early into the simultaneous refusal of language and clothes as if into a self-punishing *ascesis*. There was nothing else he could do. His mother expected a role of him which could only be played (she had spent her own life happily acting out such roles); but at the same time she discouraged his childish play-acting by demanding sincerity. He could not act the role of the well-brought-up, well-dressed, 'cute' little boy to satisfy her ambition and at the same time feel in accord both with his mother's requirements and with himself. He was not in accord. Either he was acting and then he was lying, or else he was not lying and then he was disappointing her. He was disappointing her by what he really was, and realizing that he did not come up to what was expected of him made him lose confidence in his capacity as an actor. The expected role did not correspond to his own possibilities, language was a dreadful trap, no ego was presented to him that he could adopt and develop on his own. He had to apply himself, force himself, make himself an Other in order to prove at all equal to the part. He was living in the constant terror of What have I said now? What have I done now?, transfixed at seeing his own spontaneous behaviour petrified into criminal acts supposedly premeditated, haphazard words construed as deliberate offences or even as clever jokes; feeling himself exiled in the other people's universe of discourse and incapable of finding a suitable expression, the consecrated formula which would satisfy their expectation; incapable too of making them accept as innocent (and forgive or even understand) the silly intentions which had made him act and which, falling into the cunning universe of grown-ups, assumed significations of an incalculable effect and Evil. So the union between what he was for himself and what he was for others was not accomplished; he had not achieved that outspokenness, that ease, that amiable and talkative spontaneity of the 'normal' man – that is, of the spoken speaker who has managed to assert himself as the subject of his speech or, rather, by alienating himself in it, by releasing himself confidently in his own commonplaces, feels himself able to act out the expected ego, feels in league with those who expect this comedy of him, knows, in fact, nothing but this comedy and desires nothing better than to be identified with this ego They have chosen for him, thereby protecting it (and protecting himself) against his solitude as a subject.

I know, of course, that the distrust of language, the constant fear of being misunderstood, of being credited with intentions that were not his but which others discovered in him as faults – I know that this complex lies deep within each of us, like the inevitable failure of communication, like our irremediable solitude. But I also know that we are not alone and that any authentic dialogue is based on the recognition of its own failure, on the recognition of the fact that we have never said everything and that everything still remains to be said. And authentic dialogue is impossible precisely when one of the two speakers refuses to recognize this failure and assumes something like an armour of impersonal language, an eloquence being spoken through him.

Yet his whole life was constructed on the belief that others were not in isolation, that they coincided with their impressive roles and were therefore not trying to understand him, but were expecting only a role determined in advance and which he could not fulfil. It is because he was convinced from the outset of his essential inadequacy to other people's expectations, convinced of the immutability of the rift between himself and who he should have been, that this rift was never closed. It was because of his guilt for not being an Other like the others, that he had immediately accepted Jewishness as the confirmation of an exclusion he bore within himself. Who knows, perhaps he even provoked the stigmatization of his Jewishness by his timidity, his odd and deferential behaviour, and perhaps his schoolmates would never have thrown it up to him had he not already designated himself as a victim. And because he was convinced he had betrayed the ego he should have been he did everything, objectively, to make this conviction a matter of fact. Lying in wait anxiously, timidly, for demands to identify himself, asking only to satisfy them, and certain in advance that he would be unable to; accepting exclusion as normal, as almost foreseen; trying without conviction to play a role among the others and forever feeling alien to this role whose nature he left it up to others to define; then choosing this role, resigned in advance to its extraneousness and therefore contesting it even before having begun to act it; dreaming of a world where he would be judged only on the objective efficiency of his acts, where he could therefore acquit himself of his social role by the performance of a task exterior to his person, rigorously determined beforehand, in order to be his own master the rest of the time; attempting to acquit himself of this role with a payment of words and immediately pulling back into his shell; dreaming of a world without men, or of a conventional isolation, or of money, so that, once rid of his debt or far from any eyes, he would be happy being only what he would be for himself. . . .

Many other mysteries are clarified in the light of this fundamental complex: his insistence, for instance, on changing languages (speaking a German dialect slang before converting to French) in order to get rid of his mother tongue, a term whose meaning now explodes with all its force; his predilection for foreign languages, which, in a foreign country, permitted him to offer other people words that clearly did not belong to him and were therefore nothing but a currency that did not engage his person; similarly his taste for abstraction, also a foreign language since: (1) it is not legal tender in normal interpersonal relations, and (2) when employed nevertheless, it excludes them. And his tendency toward opposition, also a refusal of ordinary speech, a negative attitude in which the subject, rejecting all identification as false, claims to derive only from himself; a tendency toward 'irony' and 'treason' in which the subject, confounding all attempts at identification, refers the interlocutors to the silence flickering behind the mask, presented as such, of his speech.

A horror of the serious and the conventional in every form, a repulsion for all the disguises (including dances, uniforms and feminine preparations) assumed ready-made, and particularly for the woman alienated to the prestige of her femininity and for the man who has identified with the prestige of his function, for both of them expect of the masculine interlocutor that he identify himself with a certain image of virility which was precisely the one his mother expected of him (the chivalric, strong protector, energetic, self-confident and imbued with the sense of justice and honour). A sympathy, on the other hand (almost a sense of brotherhood, in fact) for anyone in revolt against the requirements of identification – for Negroes, for colonized peoples, for women who, because they were unwilling to be a floral object, fragile, affectionate and desired, no longer expect anything from the 'virile' male and are themselves no longer 'someone' in the bourgeois society, which has not yet allowed them to constitute a new ego in place of the one they take exception to, the ego that is Other.

A taste for writing, last of all, for to write is to speak in the absence of others and to refuse them speech, it is to claim *Selbständigkeit* for my words, to forbid another person to make me say what he means (to 'speak me'), constantly obliging him to ask *himself* if he understands the meaning of the text, the writer's intention removed from his influence. To write, in sum, is to create a nocturnal reality hidden from other people's eyes, a reality they will never see, hearing only this speech rising out of the darkness and falling silent when day breaks; the writer is an anonymous and invisible subject. This is probably why I hate talking about what I write and assume all kinds of pseudonyms, a way of declaring that the ego I must be is merely a disguise I disavow, and that I intend to recognize myself only in the nocturnal and nonidentifiable voice of my solitary speeches.

*And here we come full circle. Because this reflection upon myself has been made in writing and intended its completion in the form of the text, it necessarily reflected and confirmed my fundamental choice to write out of my terror of identification. This text could therefore not hope to affect that choice; it participated in it.*

The goal of this work must therefore be revised. Instead of writing to disidentify myself, to liquidate what I am (using the third person, addressing myself to no one, speaking in the void, creating for myself, under the eyes of an anonymous and silent public, an ego which, under analysis, I should have created for an analyst: the witness of 'I as an Other' waiting for the intellectual detachment of my descriptions to be admired), I should write in order to define what I can be. But to do this, one must be two; to know what I can be I must know to whom I can speak, for whom I can be whoever it is that I can be.

This text has therefore not escaped what analysts call transference: it sums up perfectly the meaning and the nature of my relationship with others. It should now become an instrument for transforming this relationship. To begin with, it must from now on be written in the first person; and I have acquired at least the possibility of doing this, since at last the knowledge I have gained of myself meets my own experience.

That choice: indeed it is a choice that is in question, since what was originally a terror of identification (an identification always made, treacherously, by other people, like a theft and a violation) was subsequently developed and thematized as a choice of nonidentification, a choice to contest all alienations, even the objectivity of the act by which the silent subject, residing only in his lived experience, falls into the world of objects and is there handed over to the exterior determinations applied to him by other people. And to motivate this choice, the infantile complex does not, obviously, suffice. It simply permits the explanation of certain terrors which survive in me, muted, like faint memories whose texture has been forgotten. It does not even permit me to explain *why* these terrors have survived until now. Fundamentally, it explains nothing (or everything, which comes down to the same thing); and so I return to what I was saying at the start: that this original complex has survived only because it has confirmed and enriched itself during the course of my history

with significations that were not there at first; only because it has
been instrumental in disclosing a reality which urged it to
develop itself, which confirmed it as a true grasp (that is, a grasp
based on facts) of my real situation, and not only of my particular
situation – of the human condition. This complex has not been a
fit of insanity, nor the psychological residue of an infantile drama
irrationally surviving the circumstances that occasioned it. It has
become the contingent rooting of a choice which has developed
from this point as the continual renewal of objective significations and dimensions in events until it became a sufficiently
coherent vision of the world to be able, in certain respects, to
furnish its own theoretical justification.

The dialectical process of the choice therefore seems to me as
follows: originally there was a complex, an irrational attitude
assumed in childhood to avoid a situation the child had no
means of dealing with rationally. This original and dated
complex could in no case survive as such into adult life; if it
survived as such in all its childishness, it would be like the foreign
body in a patient's stomach, a meaningless accident to be dealt
with by surgery. If the original complex survives instead of falling
into oblivion with the rest of our childish attitudes, it can do so
only to the degree that it has become much more than the
original complex it was at the start. It is not the *attitude* of the
child's original nonidentification in relation to his mother which
is perpetuating itself, but a *project* of nonidentification which
discovers in events forever new reasons for development, forever
new possibilities for refusing identification, and forever new
significations for this refusal. In other words, this original attitude
is invested, during the subject's history, with unforeseen and
unintended objective significations which either confirm or deny
it. To continue my recent image, the attitude 'is spoken' by the
empirical event. The latter slips new words into the vocabulary of
its primitive 'sentence', words which the subject has never
spoken, which are or are not susceptible of being integrated into
his sentence, and which, when they are susceptible, *can* be
integrated there or, in the opposite case, be discarded as 'freak
words', devoid of sense, which I am supposed to say but which I

take exception to. The dialectical development of the complex into a choice is the activity of the subject assuming on his own account the words which events slip into his rudimentary sentence in order to enlarge the signification and the effect of this sentence. The latter can become still more complex and, at the same time, free, since the assumption of the 'freak words' proposed by events is optional and since the place, the signification and the value I assign them in my sentence depends on me alone. The sentence which I happen to be saying at thirty is therefore quite a different thing from the childish stammer it started from. The latter is scattered through it like the words '*un coup de dés jamais n'abolira le hasard*' in Mallarmé's poem or like the fundamental theme in a fugal variation which can no more be reduced to its theme than it can be deduced from it. And just as the fugal variation, having reached a certain stage of its development, can properly transfigure its theme within certain limits and make one of its variations into the dominant theme, in the same way the choice that has been developed out of a complex can, within certain limits, return upon the latter and 'transvalue' it. This at least in theory.

In practice, I still do not see where this discovery can lead or, rather, what I can make of it, for I see the indefensible contradictions of my choice, and I also see its productiveness. Finding it productive, I should like to follow it some of the way; observing the failures it is susceptible of, I should like to revise it somewhat. But how proceed at the heart of a personal choice in which everything necessarily relates to everything else? How renounce one's unproductive contradictions in order to preserve only the productive ones? How profit from a complex to the degree that it can be revealing of the human condition, while at the same time liquidating it as a 'complex'? How assert its consequences while at the same time liquidating its premises, resolutely perpetuating it in certain aspects and dissociating myself from it in others? No longer rooted in prehistory, voided of its status as a complex, would not my choice be deprived of its emotional resilience (which inclines me – spontaneously, irrationally – to argument, reflection, the detection of contradictions) and become a fragile rationalism which perhaps could not withstand contrary inducements?

I know what the answer should be: you have just shown how much every man cherishes his complexes; you prefer to rely on the internal logic of a complex you yourself admit to be irrational and emotional in its resilience, in order to persevere in an attitude which you consider productive, rather than rely on your freedom to persevere in the same attitude without the aid of a complex. Fundamentally you are afraid of your freedom, afraid of losing your complex because you might become 'ordinary', like 'everyone else', instead of preserving your precious and incommunicable singularity. You love yourself and you mistrust yourself. Your complex is a crutch without which you are afraid to walk, and yet are there not enough contradictions in your situation for you to go on thinking and arguing without needing a complex?

And the answer should also be: if the complex, to the degree that it is irrational, can protect me against contrary inducements, this is only because it is a structure of conduct heterogeneous to empirical reality, an element of the sentence that cannot fit in with certain propositions of the mundane context. The complex is a permanent factor of disadaptation; it is here, precisely, that it is irrational. Yet if it forearms me against a complacent adaptation to the empirical state of things, the complex also forearms me against *any* adaptation, against *any* effective action. By maintaining a permanent discord between what I am and what is offered to me, the complex quite conceals the dimensions of the real and its opportunities, and it inclines me in certain respects to a sterilizing vision of the world. What I must now look for, then, is to what degree there are, in my empirical situation, real dimensions somehow passed over in silence by the interpretation which my original commitment imprints upon what should ultimately be my total discourse, to what degree these dimensions, insufficiently assumed or even misconstrued, are perhaps those which would permit me to initiate the transfiguration of my choice, provided I centre my sentence upon them.

What strikes me now is the time it took me to grasp my original project in its truly original sense. I have always had all the elements within my grasp. I have never strayed far from the point in my interpretations, and yet, while I was speaking of my 'nullity complex', my 'treason', my 'masochism', I was not dealing with that 'evidence' which the term 'nonidentification' affords me. There is no doubt that I proceeded too quickly to interpretation by objective meanings. I was incapable of deriving every possible advantage from it subjectively; for, as long as I had not clearly grasped my original project (or complex), it was impossible for me to decide what, in a dated attitude, was the objective signification of the situation in fact and what was, as a personal formulation of this situation, imputable only to me, subjectively.*

In attempting to grasp the signification of the nihilist *ascesis* upon whose contradictions I was crucifying myself I should doubtless have mentioned the Austro-German/Judaeo-Christian contradiction, as well as the nullity that exile imposes. But this contradiction had always existed, and the exile has lasted much longer than the nihilism. Complacency in the one as in the other, writings that were no better than silence, could be understood only in the light of my nonidentification project, which found a marvellous opportunity for flowering in the empirical situation.

I knew this and even spoke of it, but without understanding it completely. Without understanding that I had created my total solitude because I had always dreamed of not existing for others. Without understanding that I was exaggerating my exclusion, my persecution, the precariousness of my situation, because I wanted to have an objective being totally exterior to myself, imposed by violence, injustice and incomprehension; for only such an objective being could be totally impugned by me ('I am not the way they see me'); *for only so total an alienation could guarantee the integrity of an existence which wanted to be totally interior*, residing only in its consciousness of itself, deriving only from itself,

---

*Which confirms the fact that the subjective interpretation must come first. It is only if I single out my original choice that I can understand my history as a progress toward its meaning, as a signifying and gratuitous formulation of an empirical reality which extends, as I will know at that moment, far beyond what I have grasped of it.

never objectivizing itself. It was in order to reside entirely within myself, to offer no exterior hold upon myself, to remain non-objectivizable and nonidentifiable, in order to be nothing ('null', as I was saying) that I adopted the contradictory and untenable position of the nihilist *ascesis* which resembles a form of sainthood. And so forth. . . .

I no longer believe, as at the outset of this work, that a man can change radically, can liquidate his original choice. But I am now convinced that by a careful analysis of his empirical situation, he can discover in his choice potential objective significations that permit him to reach positive conclusions. This is the whole question. You are never asked to change yourself altogether, but to learn to employ your resources, with full knowledge of the case, in view of a positive action (if you prefer, to learn to make use of what you are in order to transcend yourself). This is the point I have reached. The 'complex of nonidentification', since I have recognized it, has drained like an abscess. Instead of keeping the world at a distance like an enemy who must not be allowed to get a grip on me, I am learning to yield to it; to see it, to begin with, to taste its density, my presence within it, to listen to a man talking in the depths of his speech (instead of listening only to the surface of what he says). Not to feel quite so ill at ease in my own skin; to say what I think with the conviction that I am at least as sure of the rightness of my remarks as my interlocutor is of his; to be able to enjoy the passing moment, a light, an aroma, a look, a sound; to hold on to life, to want it to be full of all there is to be lived, including contradictions and risks that cannot be escaped – I am learning. I would not let anyone live it in my place. This is a task which belongs to me and in which only I can succeed. And if I do succeed, it is not I alone who will profit from it. Rather the inverse: to make a success of your life is to make a success of something that goes beyond it, that speaks and acts beyond it, externally, for all men. Which men? Not all. For I shall surely never be understood by those who say, 'Listen, mister, you can talk about the Arabs all you want, but I *know* them!'; who say, 'You don't know what you're talking about! I've *seen* Russians!'; who say, 'When wages fall back to normal we can breathe again!'; who say 'Sartre's ultra-Bolshevism'; who say, 'You have a revolutionist fixation!'; who say, 'The treason of the intellectuals, the Communist Party is in Moscow', 'You always bite the hands that feed you.' This much is certain: that I am on one side (the side of those who do not have enough and are not numerous enough to know they are a side), that I have no possibility of changing sides, that I will not change even if they try to buy me for the other side because it is 'really' my own, and that the other side will always be the *other* side (that of men who suspect you, spy on you, watch for imperceptible impulses of subversion, pay some because of their position and others only for work that can be demanded 'because it's paid for'). I am on the side of those who have neither constituted Law nor Strength in their behalf, but only their own strength, which consists of ruse, bluff and the capacity to take advantage of its own weaknesses.

This is still not a profession of faith; these are merely facts. A fact that when a man is evicted, imprisoned for his opinions, censored, deported, boycotted, gagged, starved, it is I who am the target. A fact that the people who aim at me are the ones who surround me where I am and not the ones invoked by the exploiters of this part of the world as an alibi for their own violences. For me, for us, the violences of the socialist societies or of those societies attempting to become socialist in no way diminish the violence which surrounds us nor the necessity of opposing it.

Here I am then, almost where I started, but with at least this certitude: the intellectual, if he cannot keep from being one, is objectively on the side of the revolutionary forces, of historical negativity,* and he must be on that side subjectively. This is the intellectual's only chance of reality. In isolation he can do nothing (nothing save amuse himself with the masks he is given and induce those in revolt to spare themselves, thanks to literary negativity, any kind of effective action). If he ever acquires a certain power, it is only the power to catalyse the diffuse will and

---

*By which I mean everything tending toward an appropriation of the world by men and of the history which they produce in fact.

the inchoate thought which lie dormant in the facts and ask only
to be expressed in order to exist as such; the power to ask, since
he is not physically engaged in action, those questions which the
actors undergo, to all intents and purposes, without finding
either the time or the perspective to ask them.

Once everything has been said, everything still remains to be
said. My first text, in which I had wanted to say everything, fell
from my hands like a bundle of dead leaves. I thought that this
was the fault of its conception. But now the second is falling from
my hands in the same way. Everything still remains to say; everything always remains to be said.

*Hic Rhodus, hic salta.* Yes, Rhodes is here. Among other things
I have learned that I shall never be through beginning again, that
my world is this white paper, my life the activity of covering it. I
once thought life would become possible when I had said everything; and now I realize that life, for me, is to write; to start out
each time trying to say everything and to begin again immediately afterward, because everything still remains to be said.

Yet I no longer believe that to write is the nearest approach to
man's total realization. For some men in each society, it is merely
the only realization possible. For some men who cannot ignore
the fact that they bear within themselves a definitive flaw; something which has happened in their life makes it impossible for
them to recognize themselves in the reality of the image which
their acts create. Something has happened in their life, or it is
their life itself, life in general – in which we are all incomplete
individuals, incapable of accepting what we can be, ill-adapted to
our reality, devoured by needs which this civilization cannot
satisfy. We are all potential traitors; each of us *petits bourgeois*
betrays this society in his dreams, scorns his fellows, denies, in
some nocturnal portion of himself, his daylight reality. What is
offered to us? A laborious, narrowly specialized life at the heart of
an undertaking which exceeds us and is even ignorant of itself;
an ant life forever unable to recognize itself in the world it contributes to produce. We are private men – deprived men, deprived
of the human meaning of our specialized tasks, deprived of
universality as real individuals working; cogs of an inhuman

social machine which, as the mechanical resultant of our efforts, perverts our intentions and annuls us at the very moment we produce it. Our need for humanity takes refuge in the private life, in nocturnal meetings and palavers, little orgies of vain dreams and discussions during which we destroy this society and the unacceptable reality it presses upon us. Which is why this society measures an individual's success by the number and the power of the means he acquires to hold the community at a distance, to escape the common fate, to isolate himself, to differentiate himself from all others, to build himself a shell against the world: a car, comfort, house, private property – all reducing his dependence on others and his contacts with them. This society considers as the crown of life the splendid isolation of the rich and refined property owner. But to those who would prefer not to possess, to isolate and to consume at the general expense, but to give, to communicate and to construct with and for all, this society has nothing to offer.

This society distinguishes itself by the profusion of instruments of destruction, evasion and disidentification which it puts at the disposal of its members. In the first category figures alcohol; in the second, the automobile (which, incarnating the negation of Here, makes Everywhere and Nowhere gleam across its hood and affords its owner the most illusory of freedoms, the apparent liberation from the constraints and requirements of life in common;* expending on automobiles a larger part of their

---

*Constraints and requirements which the drivers, racing by thousands on the road, rediscover and re-create there statistically as the resultant (desired by no one) of thousands of efforts to escape all laws, as a law which is therefore completely alien to them and which, caught in a jam advancing slower than a train or a metro, they have the illusion of being able to avoid thanks to their dexterity and to chance. The driver's freedom is that right Marx mentions: 'to be able, in the framework of certain conditions, to take advantage of chance quite calmly.' In the image of capitalist society, the drivers – each of whom hates all the rest and desires their disappearance, for they are pure obstacles for each individual driver – are in agreement only as to the necessity of perpetuating the conditions of chance by which each individual intends to profit for himself. But the possibilities of so profiting are mutually conditioned and limiting; the efforts to profit necessarily neutralize each other according to statistical laws.

revenue than any other nation, the French drive their cars *against society* in order to escape the common fate – their localization in a country whose future is shrinking – consuming in their carburettors their savings, the houses and factories they will not build, the nation's future, or what remains of it once the efforts invested in preserving the imperial past have been deducted); in the third category, eroticism, art and literature. All of us dream of being elsewhere and Other than we are. This too contributes to our reality. We are people who cannot endure the reality we represent 'despite ourselves' except by contesting it or compensating for it by an enormous and often admirable production of the imaginary; we compensate by the profusion of our ideas for the profusion of facts which escape our grasp. We are terribly *intelligent.*

Whatever we say or do, we can never feel entirely real, there is a part of ourselves which remains unrealized, a part – of failure, of silence – which forbids us to content ourselves with whatever we live (do, say, are). An absolute distance divides us from our reality. The intellectual is the man who assumes this distance, who tries to recover the silence, the failure. The means of realization society offers men is not enough for him in this society, nor in any other; his sense of incompleteness exceeds his disagreement (or agreement) with the offered means of realization. He will never (I will never) be a great man of action; at best he will be an adventurer of action, impatient to get back to his desk to write what he has lived and thereby to recover the part of himself which action has left unrealized. I must invent the means of a complete realization which is impossible for me and whose means, for this reason, cannot be really existing means. I cannot claim that I will succeed in creating these means, nor that they will be worth more than those available to everyone else. I only know that like many others (and like every man, by right if not by fact) I must invent individual means to manifest man, and that the highest recompense I can hope for resides in this activity of creation.

It is this need for individual realization which the given means do not permit me to satisfy; it is the need of certain individuals whom an original contradiction renders sensitive to the contradictions of their time and to its share of failure (experienced, though not thought, or assumed, by everyone); it is this need which motivates the work of art. It finds no satisfaction elsewhere. The work of art is the aesthetic manifestation of negativity, the contestation of the existing human reality. It acknowledges the fact that the constituted means of realization, whatever they are, which a society, whatever it is, puts at the disposal of its members are insufficient – by the mere fact that they are constituted – to manifest man totally. The work of art contests the constituted means insofar as by their objective solidity they apparently determine the man who in fact produces *them* and conceal from him the fact that it is he who produces these means, man and nature altogether. The work of art states that a production which is not conscious of producing and does not posit man as the origin and the end of its products has no value. It is freedom taking itself for an end to the degree that it cannot be satisfied with merely being given to itself at the level of the material means of its objective realization, but demands to be at the foundation of these means, to give them to itself. The work of art manifests the fact that man is always richer than what he is, richer in virtualities than what he can be, and that he must re-create himself, constantly reinvent himself, or else fall back into the automatism and the stereotypes of a dejected solemnity, being nothing but the 'product of his product'.

Art is disidentifying; it contests the identity which society confers on the individual and which the latter assumes by the mere fact that he employs given means of realization; art is negativity and reflexive *ascesis*, because in its essence it puts freedom at the source of human reality and thus restates the revolutionary requirement that man regain possession of himself (over and against his alienations) and continually re-create himself. But because it manifests only the (subjective) requirement of re-creation, because it indicates only the possibility of new means of realization but cannot by itself produce these means, which appear during praxis, art is ineffective, or, rather, becomes effective only when mediated by an action which it cannot provoke and which belongs on another level.

Then what good is it calling men to contest if those who can respond to this appeal (who possess the culture, the time and the money) cannot give freedom the means of making itself real, and if those who work, by the logic of their situation, at creating these means, those who *are* the revolutionary contestation in action, remain absorbed by more urgent tasks? Artistic creation remains both necessary and incapable, today, of believing in itself; cut off from the real revolutionary forces, its subjective demand for freedom has no other public than those for whom art is an alibi to avoid true freedom.

This is also a reason, I think, why I have not had the patience to create a work of art. I might have been able to ten years ago. Today I regard those who put beauty above all other considerations as being on the other side, on the side of those who believe in the right to possess, to enjoy, to eat, to command and to make their escape all by themselves. This book is in many respects the negation of art, a work of art which is trying to transcend itself at the very moment it comes into being, and which refuses to be an end in itself; that is why it is not a work of art.

I am not sure that I have kept all my promises. I now believe that subjective motivations are not so important. They no longer trouble me; they are fading. The man who succeeds, even for the 'wrong reasons' (individual reasons), in committing himself to an action which transcends his contingent individuality, who regards the goal of this action as more real, more important than himself, who forgets his self-esteem and the ineffable singularity of his precious person to the point of no longer even feeling that he is making humanity a tremendous gift by declaring himself on its side – this man can say, 'It matters little enough for what subjective reasons I have come to act this way, from the moment that I know that my objective reasons are real and defensible in the world's eyes; instead of worrying about my "revolutionist fixation" or about the psychology of resentment in the proletarianized masses, why don't you come to terms with the real state of things which psychoanalysis sometimes serves you as a pretext to ignore?'

It is only natural that the situation should give me back what I have given to it, that I should find in everything I say or do at this moment that shimmer of motivations, hardly defensible in themselves, of which I was speaking earlier. But, in fact, a situation, provided one assumes it altogether, an action, provided one persists in it, always give back more than one puts into them and lead by their objective logic beyond one's original intentions. Perhaps the original choice of the bourgeois son was at the start, in its subjective intention, a revolt, a treason, a disidentification. The situation will have given him back all that. But more than that, other people and history will have conferred on his egocentric gesture an unlooked-for reality; the historical conjuncture in which he functions will have conferred upon this gesture a signification which overflows its first intention. Will he carry on this signification to the point of making it the dominant aspect of his project? It is my behaviour which will decide whether this gesture was merely a juvenile crisis or the point of departure of a commitment resolved not to let go of the thread, found by chance, of the real; to act it instead of being acted by it. It is because the world always makes us say more than we meant and continually puts us at a crossroads of possible significations that we must, in truth, continually choose ourselves.

But I cannot enact a commitment and invent a reality for myself in isolation. I can only determine the direction and the side on which I exist and, once this is done, launch in that direction an action still necessarily without real weight, dependent on my fragile and solitary will. After that, I must wait and hope that others will return this action to me weighted with the reality they will have conferred upon it. This is my present hope. I cannot go further by myself. My reality is not within my power alone, it is also what you will make of me. It will certainly exceed my intentions by a density I cannot foresee (or by the nullity in which your indifference will maintain me) and will betray them in many respects; it will compel me to new intentions, new interrogations.

We have all begun by being 'betrayed'; it is only very exceptionally that we have knowingly and deliberately engaged ourselves as we find ourselves to be. The reality of our 'innocent' intentions has led us to be what we have not wanted to be. We have never done only what we wanted to do, but always what other people and history have decided we have done. Between the intellectual who, to escape this risk, isolates himself and wills his own inaction and those who with good intentions and pious hopes decline the reality which in fact they create, but of which they declare themselves prisoners, a way must be found.

We must want action to exceed its intention, for this is the price of its reality. We must want to be engaged by others more deeply than we thought or could be by ourselves. But to be capable of really wanting this (instead of producing merely an imaginary and vacant will, masking fatalism), we must still do so knowingly; we must know the total situation in which action, once performed, will take its effect, the side and the direction on which we want to be engaged. This is what I have tried to do. It is in the limits of this intention that I have agreed to be 'betrayed' (that is, led further than I can go by myself); it is my reality in the eyes of those who are on the same side as I which is important to me. Not to bow humbly beneath their verdict, not to make myself their instrument, but to play according to the rules we have agreed on and in the determination of which a dialogue must be possible. *En attendant mieux.*

*December 1955–September 1956*

# AFTERWORD

## A discussion with André Gorz on alienation, freedom, utopia and himself*

*Translated by Hilary Pilkington (Material Word)*

Q. The titles of all of your works published in Germany (excluding *The Traitor*, which was published very late), from *Strategy For Labor: A Radical Proposal*, *Socialism And Revolution* and the preface to *Socialism and Revolution* [published separately in Germany under the title *Die Aktualität der Revolution* – Tr.] to *Farewell to the Working Class*, suggest a political or sociological content. The philosophical basis or character of your thought is not, therefore, immediately apparent. What should we see André Gorz as, first and foremost? What do you see yourself as: a sociologist, a theorist of revolution, a political strategist or a philosopher?

A.G. You are quite right to ask that question. I think of myself as a failed philosopher trying to smuggle in his original philosophical reflections by way of ostensibly political or sociological themes. What I mean by 'philosophical' is the original question

---

*This interview was given as a follow-up to a three-day seminar 'On André Gorz', organized by the Federal Youth Training Centre (*Bundesjugendschule*) of the West German Federation of Trade Unions (DGB). The interview was conducted by Martin Jander and Rainer Maischein in October 1983, and was included in a booklet summing up the seminar, published under the title *Abschied vom Proletariat? Eine Diskussion mit und über André Gorz*, by DGB Bundesvorstand Abt. Jugend, Düsseldorf.

Western philosophy has posed since the Greeks – as Bahro quite rightly, though somewhat polemically, saw. When am I really 'myself', that is, not just a product externally determined by alien forces and influences but responsible for my own actions, thoughts, feelings, values and so on?

The question immediately raised is that of the past history of the individual, for there is no other subject than the individual subject; that is clear even in Marx. We must look at the question of the history of the individual subject's relationship to the body, to the environment, to society, and whether this relationship can ever be formed in such a way that I can view it as 'my own'. Here, the question of alienation and whether it is possible to overcome it arises. For me, philosophy is not Hegel or those great creators of philosophical systems but the attempt to understand, to discover oneself and what one is, to take control of, liberate and create oneself. Life, especially human life, is self-creation, 'autopoiesis'. This is being acknowledged by system theorists again today, as it was by the young Marx; it is currently being rediscovered by biologists. Of course only a being which creates itself can, in so doing, become capable of understanding, being responsible for and emancipating itself.

But philosophical works are no longer attractive either to readers or publishers; there is no 'market' for them: they have become the exclusive preserve of professional philosophy lecturers. Unless you become a lecturer, and that was quite out of the question in my case, you can only put philosophy into practice by applying it directly to other fields. This means, unfortunately, that there is a tendency to skimp on thorough investigation and reasoning.

Q. What you are writing today is very different from the kind of books you wrote in the fifties. *The Traitor* is available in West Germany; the other two, *Fondements pour une morale* and *La morale de l'histoire*, are not. What are these books about? Do you see the subject matter of *Strategy For Labor: A Radical Proposal* and the later works as being important? What significance does it have today?

**A.G.** *Fondements pour une morale* was an exploration of the philosophical questions we have just been talking about. It was a crazy project, originally intended to run to three volumes: the first was to be about the subject in relation to itself and the world, a relation which, of course, is always also partly determined by others; the second was to be about the subject's relations to other subjects; the third about how the subject relates to society and to the collective. Of the second volume, only a rough draft exists. That was written in 1948. The third volume is partly included in the *La morale de l'histoire* and partly in *Farewell to the Working Class*, but I have not even started writing the third volume, since it took me eight years to complete the first. When it was finally finished, no publisher would touch it; a 600-page philosophical work by a nobody is not much use to a publisher – it was bound to be a financial disaster. So I decided to experiment by applying the first volume to myself: the result was *The Traitor*. Sartre wrote me a beautiful long introduction, and so I managed to get it published. Sartre had not been particularly interested in *Fondements pour une morale*, which was finally published more than twenty years later. This was because it was in a way a continuation of *Being and Nothingness*: it looked at the questions Sartre had raised – but not answered – there. What is 'authenticity'? What is the 'existential conversion', and how do we arrive at it? What does it mean to posit freedom as the highest value and at the same time the source of all values? The answers could not be derived from Sartre's ontology. It had to be inflected, sophisticated, reworked; I had to show that we always exist on several different planes with their corresponding differently structured relations to being and value. These planes are:

1. physical existence and its immediate environment, which is always culturally and socially determined, although usually blurred or repressed;

2. the immediate present of perceptual consciousness;

3. goal-orientated practice.

These three planes – past as facticity, present and future – have three corresponding types of values: the vital, the aesthetic and the ethical-practical, which can never be unified or reduced to a common denominator. Vitality, joie de vivre, creature comforts; joy in beauty and artistic creation or joy in liberating action: all may come together in the same person – this remains the ideal – but not at the same moment. This is why the differentiated organization of time – days, weeks, years and so on – has always existed. The ideal is an existence in which one can move smoothly between planes without having to sacrifice or subordinate any one of them.

This ideal remains unachievable. The empirical world is not constituted in such a way that freedom can use it creatively as a means to its own self-realization. Alienation consists in the impossibility of making the given into the means to some kind of end worth living for – in perhaps even having to abandon all other goals and values in order to maintain the bare minimum of life. Now, obviously, it would be impossible to abandon these higher values in favour of the lower ones – that is, to accept the distortion of the absolute scale of values which alienation causes – if the very valuation of the aesthetic and of values of freedom were not optional, that is, free itself, and if the spontaneous tendency to run away from freedom were not, in an ontological sense, inherent to existence just as freedom itself is. A whole host of phenomenological descriptions of various 'attitudes' was designed to demonstrate this. These attitudes included both those governed by vital values like fanaticism, resignation, the worship of force or primordiality, and those which relate to aesthetic values like the stance of the person who lives for the moment, of the poet, the mystic, the adventurer, the gambler and so on, and their existential failure. The methods of self-questioning and self-analysis demanded by the 'moral conversion' takes up a good third of this volume. *The Traitor* is its practical application.

*La morale de l'histoire*, which tackles alienation theory again, examines more closely the following question: why is it that the development of one's own freedom is rendered impossible by the actual situation, and what determines this? Furthermore, how can one class be preordained to emancipate itself and all other spheres of society, as is suggested in Marx's earlier works? For self-emancipation to be predetermined seemed to me then, and still does, to be a contradiction in terms, and I wanted to show, contrary to dialectical materialist dogmatism, that the proletariat only acts in a revolutionary and liberating way to the extent that it makes itself, in all its members, the subject of the negation and reappropriation of what material relations have made of it. There can be no material necessity behind this, otherwise there would be never any problem about revolutionary consciousness and strategy. There can be no compelling necessity to self-emancipation.

The book went on to describe the alienation of the consumer, of both the members of the masses and the entrepreneurs in the so-called 'affluent society', through the separation between work and consumption, so that liberation (that is, overcoming alienation) can never be achieved on only one of these two planes.

I wrote *La Morale de l'histoire* at the same time as Sartre was working on his *Critique of Dialectical Reason* and the mutual influence is apparent despite the fact that we were pursuing different goals. In France these reflections went quite unnoticed. *La Morale de l'histoire*, which combines the investigations of American sociologists like David Riesman and C. Wright-Mills with an existential Marxism, was to become a kind of standard Marxist textbook in Italy, Mexico and Spain, where it was copied and circulated clandestinely. In Italy and, in spite of everything, in Franco's Spain, a dialectical-critical way of thinking was much more widespread amongst intellectuals and communists, because of the influence of Croce, Labriola and Gramsci, whereas in France Hegel had remained untranslated until after the war. Nor had Stalinism penetrated either Italy or Spain, for communist parties were banned there during most of Stalin's rule.

In France, on the other hand, the Stalinist brand of Marxism was dominant from the outset. Apart from a handful of Germanists like Henri Lefèbvre, French Marxists had read only Marx's *Capital* and the shorter writings like *The Civil War in France*. Alienation was considered an anti-Marxist term and, according to orthodox Stalinism, alienation could not exist at all in a

socialist society. That was the official doctrine until recently both in
the Soviet Union and China, where two editors were dismissed
last year from the central organ of the Communist Party for
publishing an article by an old Marxist in which the argument
that alienation can continue under socialism was supported with
quotations from Marx.

Finally the few French theorists of alienation were blasted by
the heavy artillery of structuralism – mainly Althusser and
Godelier – who maintained, amongst other things, that 'People
do not make revolutions in order to achieve happiness.' Revolution has nothing to do with the human subject, because there is
no such subject.

Q. After *Farewell to the Working Class*, it was sometimes claimed
that you had also bid farewell to Sartre, but it seems to us that
this was not really the case. Sartre's political strategy and tactics
– for instance his persistent criticism of Marxism whilst continuing to argue the legitimacy of Soviet policy in a particular historical situation – was never something you indulged in in quite the
same way. So even if *Farewell to the Working Class* marks a break
with Sartre's concept of the political, does this signify a departure
from existentialist philosophy? We are more inclined to see a
continuity in your thought, retaining the fundamental principles
of existentialism right through to *Paths to Paradise*. It is a kind of
search which starts with ethics and expands outwards, going
beyond Sartre; it is a search for the transcendence of alienation
and the emancipation of the individual achieved through one's
own 'self-discovery'. What does Sartre and his existentialist
philosophy mean to you? Is there a break?

A.G. Sartre is often misjudged politically. Until 1952 he was seen
by the PCF as the chief ideological enemy and denounced both
in Moscow and Paris as the 'stinking jackal', the 'hyena at the
typewriter'. Unfortunately Lukàcs was a party to this too. In 1947
Sartre became a co-founder of the neutralist left-socialist RDR
(Rassemblement Démocratique Révolutionnaire). When it was
taken over and split by the Trotskyists, Sartre left and the RDR

disintegrated. All that remained was mutual hatred between Sartre and the Trotskyists. Sartre was a fellow traveller of the PCF and the peace movement only between 1952 and 1955. After Hungary, he openly broke with the Communists, but retained a certain sympathy for Khrushchev for a few years after that. I never consciously broke with Sartre, but when, towards the end of the fifties, he began to write off the Western proletariat, and to consider the anti-colonial uprisings – and especially the Algerian nationalist movement – to be the sole bearers of world revolution, I did not follow him; *Strategy For Labor* was my reply to his dismissal of the possibility of revolution in the industrial metropolis. From 1969, we disagreed once more – this time on the Maoists, whose religious-dogmatic attitude I could not stand. I was able to express this openly in *Les Temps Modernes*, however, without any attempt on his part to stop me. Sartre never broke with anyone on political grounds. Politics was not that important to him. Right up until the end, he saw me as one of the few who used his philosophical works creatively, in a personal way. In some respects, for instance, *Farewell to the Working Class* can be viewed as an application of his *Critique of Dialectical Reason*. I think he would have liked the book.

Q. Despite its central role in the French debate, the question of alienation has never, to my knowledge, been very significant in Germany. It is not only the central theme, alongside ethics, in your philosophy but also one of the central themes in the work of Henri Lefèbvre, where alienation and mystification are closely related. Why are the French so interested in the question of alienation, and what explains its emergence as the central theme in your own work?

A.G. For me, the concept became central when I was looking at the question of how a being can misrecognize itself, mask itself and realize itself in a way which contradicts its being. Social conditions played no role at first.

But the realization that social and material conditions mean that alienation is, from the outset, the destiny of all, became

increasingly important for me. Personally, like many others, I am
not conscious of belonging to any society, group or nation, and I
am always puzzled by these collective formations, seeing them as
something accidental that was never intended by those from
whose actions they result. This autonomization of alienated
action is excellently presented in Marx's *The German Ideology*.

As far as I am aware, the question of alienation was quite
important in Germany in the twenties and thirties, but this then
faded, even in the Frankfurt School, as there was no Communist
Party and no great Marxist debate in West Germany, while in
East Germany there was of course a Communist Party but no
debate.

In France and Italy, on the other hand, one could only be
content with Stalinist dialectical-materialist dogma if one
expected emancipation to come from the Soviet Union rather
than from the workers' movement. But if what one wanted was
the building of a hegemonic, autonomous revolutionary party, as
the PCI – but not the PCF – did, then one could not be satisfied
by the promise of an end to exploitation, for the exploited in the
West were obviously better off than the non-exploited in the
East. The end of exploitation remained unconvincing as a goal
unless it also meant the end of every form of oppression and, if
possible, of alienation. The struggle for socialism could only be
won if it was the struggle for the emancipation of all.

But to say such things was only possible if one retained a critical attitude towards the Soviet Union. The PCI was more willing
to do that, the PCF not at all. For the latter, as for dogmatic
Marxism, socialism abolishes the individual subject – regarded
as a bourgeois fantasy – by allowing everyone to experience
society as an omniscient whole in which individuals are defined,
in accordance with their true being, by the party. Individuals
have no autonomous consciousness; their consciousness is
limited to a recognition of their true being in what society thinks
about and demands of them. This religious relationship to the
party which the PCF demanded of the individual thus encountered the alienation problematic as anti-Stalinist dynamite.

**Q.** In our opinion *Farewell to the Working Class* merely represents the end of a development, a moment of decision in your relationship, which was ambivalent from the outset, to the Communist Party, the socialist states, and communist theory and practice. The ambivalence we refer to is expressed very clearly in *The Traitor.* Nevertheless there is a Marxist track in your work. What importance do Marx and Marxism still have for you? What do you retain in your theory and your orientations?

**A.G.** There has never been a better theoretical understanding of the capitalist economy than Marx's. In various places it has become dated or is contestable, but it is essential to the understanding of the development, the logic, the contradictions and the crises of the capitalist world economy. So much for the economy.

The philosophical aspects of Marx may still be regarded as fundamental in many areas: his understanding of people as 'self-producing'; his alienation theory, which is developed chiefly in *The German Ideology* – which contains a tremendous wealth of philosophical understanding and ideas – but also in the *Grundrisse* and the posthumous Chapter VI of *Capital*; in short his philosophical anthropology, which basically concerns the 'all-round development of individuality', whilst political economy and economic values are destined to wither away. For Marx this is the only possible meaning of historical development. This is not to suggest, though, that this meaning must inevitably be realized, but simply that there is no other meaning and that, if we miss it, we will sink into barbarism. Here I part with the Marxist theory of history, which, like Hegelian eschatology, takes the end of history as its starting point, in order to interpret history itself – as if this end, like the biblical prophecies of God's will, had always been written in the skies.

The economism of most Marxists has always seemed wrong to me, but we can in fact refute it using Marx himself: economic values are never fundamental and can only be seen as fundamental if the means are elevated into ends, as they are in capitalism and technocratism. Then all value-relatedness disappears;

only relative so-called exchange values remain, and the highest, absolute value is money, but this is worthless in itself. All this can be found in Marx too, who took it from the Ricardians and Owenites, and who sees in capitalism a system whose development must lead to its own negation, to the 'collapse of exchange value' and economic rationality. Unfortunately most Marxists are barely aware of this and therefore use Marx mainly as a theorist of capitalism without asking how the latter can and should be superseded.

So, as you say, there is an 'ambivalence' here too: with most Marxists one can hardly get beyond economism and capitalism, and yet outside Marxism there are no intellectual forces capable of drawing up a non-capitalist alternative and working for the abolition of capitalism itself.

Q. How important was the research for the *Fondements pour une morale* for your later work – in particular for *Paths to Paradise*? I ask this because the central theme remains the individual seeking his or her way, although this search is not developed any further. Does this mark a return to the thesis that there is no morality and the only possibility is to choose freedom? Or has the thesis changed?

A.G. The choice of freedom is the only possible morality. There can be no other. I have not changed my opinion at all on that score. This is not a thesis, though, but an insight. One ought not to see 'freedom' as something primarily political or social. The freedom referred to in existentialist philosophy is a freedom closely related to Christian theology: the individual is condemned to freedom in his being; it is given to him, or rather, the individual is given to himself as 'having-to-be-free' (*ayant-à-être-libre*). The question is only: will the individual try to escape from this condition by behaving as though he or she were the tool of something superhuman, or choose to be free by setting his or her own goals and claiming responsibility for them?

Freedom in the philosophical sense, as you see, is not something that I am entitled to, that can be given or refused me by the state or the authorities: it lies in the fact that what each of us has to do is open to question, otherwise there could be no talk at all of duty, of regulations, of 'ought to be': individuals would be biologically programmed and predetermined like bees in a hive. Freedom can only be granted to a being who *is* free, and only such a being can have this or that behaviour prescribed to him or her.

It is absurd to define morality as an acceptance of prescribed rules or codified duties. The purpose of codified behaviour, in fact, is to harmonize individual actions with the maintenance of some kind of 'order'. But what about the goals and 'morality' of this order? That is a question you are not supposed to ask. In the conduct of all 'sticklers for the rules', be they bureaucrats or technicians at a power station, the highest duty is obedience or strict adherence to the rules, which means that the goals and values of state or electricity, respectively, may not be questioned. The prescribed conduct is *heteronomous*, that is, subject to outside laws. Morality does not come into it. It is concerned only with the workings of a whole, designed to function like one huge machine.

This view, that society makes individuals function as cogs in huge machines, has existed for thousands of years in systems such as Asiatic despotism, where it was responsible for preventing the development of a culture of individual consciousness, although not, of course, of consciousness itself; what is missing is the possibility of the social expression of such a consciousness – what we would call basic or civil rights.

In Europe the conception of a person as merely 'the tool of tools', the servant of a huge machine, is relatively new. This means that the victory of technocratic despotism is not yet inevitable. Resisting it implies that individuals keep using their own wits to question the meaning, purpose, and value of mega-technology and reject a world view which takes for granted that there is an absolutely superior subject standing over each one of us, a subject knowing everything better than we do ourselves and determining for us what is right and what is wrong. It is irrelevant whether one calls this superhuman subject the State, the Führer, the Party, God, or Nature, for they are all totalitarian negations of the real subject, that is, the individual subject.

**Q.** But there are other models of freedom, for example Rosa Luxemburg's: 'Freedom is always the freedom of those who think differently.' To this extent, the concept of freedom always has something to do with others. It is not simply that I can do everything that I want to and must not be compelled to do anything that I really do not want to; only then does it become immoral, for it is not free. The problem is: how does the freedom of one person relate to that of others?

**A.G.** You must put that the other way round: it is not 'being able to do what I want' which is moral, but being able to want what I do. The 'moral cogito' practically never involves the question 'Can I do what I want?', but 'Can I want what I am doing? Can I want to be what I am making myself?' Or: 'What can I do that I can also want, for which I can take responsibility myself?' Before we decide or undertake anything, we are already active as social individuals. We come into this world, so to speak, as accomplices in and co-producers of this world, since we are immediately born into a social co-operation, a co-functioning. So, nobody asks themselves first and acts later; everyone acts first without asking themselves what they are really doing and whether they can answer for it.

The liberal conception of political freedom, as it appears in your quotation from Rosa Luxemburg too, refers exclusively to the right of the citizen to think differently from the party in power: so-called 'freedom of speech'. This posits individuals in society as individual grains in a huge pile of sand: 'each to his own', 'do your own thing' – as the Americans put it. Whereas the question 'What can I do that I can want and can want to be?' always includes the question 'How will I look to others? What will I be in their eyes? Which side am I on?' It is impossible to want one's own freedom without recognizing other people's, and wanting to be recognized by them as free, as the originator of one's actions and creations. Reciprocity is always the reciprocal recognition of the freedom of others, not merely toleration. We can only have generalized reciprocity and recognition of freedom if we are all pursuing a common goal, which each person recog-

nizes as his or her own, but which he or she can only reach with
and through the voluntary involvement of all. Then everyone will
be recognized by everyone else as a free being, and will be
addressed as such. But this is only true of course on the level of
social existence. There are other levels which can never be socialized or generalized; for instance the level of completely personal
reciprocity on which the other is recognized and loved as a
unique, incomparable subject. Love is always asocial and always
spells danger for a totalitarian order.

Q. I am still not quite clear about all this, because the concept of
freedom, as you see it, has a quite different significance
politically. You say that freedom is also always the freedom of the
other. Doesn't this individual morality, which you define as freedom, already contain all those things that have to be understood
in terms of social practice? Aren't all the problems of translating
things into political terms and the problems of social action withdrawn into this concept, so that they no longer appear in your
view of society, since for you they are already solved?

A.G. These problems are certainly not solved, since the question
'What can I do that I can want to do?' does not just remain
unanswered, but for each of us it is answered in the negative:
whatever one does in this strife-torn world and society, there will
always be reverse effects and consequences which one does not
want, which one cannot be responsible for and which prevent us
from viewing the purpose itself, as well as the action and the
means employed, as expressions of freedom that are positive
both for ourselves and for others.
   You get a clear sense of the impossibility of morality and the
alienation – in the above sense of the word – from this question.
And the next question arises immediately from this: what can I
do, in my position, in my own sphere, to change this situation?

Q. How far do you think social emancipation is really possible?
Your theory is a theory of the liberation of individuals, autonomous individuals, who, not being fully socialized, come into

conflict with the norm. How can this theory be reconciled with demands which Marx, for instance, expressed, that are social in nature, aimed at social emancipation: alienation is not only an individual thing, and its transcendence, I think, must always be a collective process.

**A.G.** I think you need to be a little more cautious in your formulations, because if you phrase it that way there is a kernel of truth in it but also a hidden danger. How can we talk about 'social emancipation', if what we mean by this is a collective process which takes place over the heads of real individuals? Liberation as a collective process which we do not all experience as our own individual liberation is precisely the 'educational dictatorship' so far practised by the Church, the omniscient Leninist party and the armed avant-garde. If in fighting for collective liberation we use methods which continue to make individuals the willing tools of something transcendental, then the means intended to bring about liberation will, in fact, continue to devour it. Collective liberation must always be individual liberation as well. I think it is important that the starting point for the struggle for collective liberation is in the individual's own desire for liberation, and that these individuals then join together, uniting in the way Marx demanded, on the basis of their common situation and goals: it can only work that way round. In order to become the subject of my actions, I must change the world, but I can only do this in co-operation with all the others. But there are dozens of forms of co-operation in which individuals are needed only as tools, as obedient soldiers. If one begins with the collective, then the individual is generally lost forever. Liberation can never be the unintended product of any given process.

The question of social emancipation is never raised by society itself, as society is not a subject which knows real desires and struggles. The question of social emancipation only arises because the real subjects, the individuals, feel social circumstances to be irreconcilable with the development of their own freedom. The social negation of each individual's experience of freedom is the experience of alienation common to us all and this can only be overcome through common action, as we change society.

Q. I still don't quite understand what seems to me to be a double-bind. On the one hand your thinking seems to contain only some kind of individual morality; if morality exists at all then it can only be freedom, the choice of freedom. On the other hand, since we live in circumstances in which freedom is impossible, in which no-one experiences freedom, nobody is able to say how we can arrive at and secure this freedom. How can this freedom develop? For you this is obviously an anonymous process beyond anyone's control.

A.G. This appears to you to be a double-bind because you see freedom as a legal state rather than what it is: the negativity of all activities and all consciousness. Only a being who *is* free can and should become free: 'Become what you are', said Goethe. The human being has to make of itself what it is. System theoreticians see this basic principle of existentialist philosophy as being applicable to all living beings, although only human beings are conscious – or capable of being conscious – of it.

Even assembly-line workers or prisoners feel they are free, that they are basically different from what society is trying to make them into: they are not and cannot be what they have been sentenced to be, and the impossibility of accepting, of getting used to this sentence constitutes their feeling of freedom, which may be frustrated or negated, but persists as negation of what negates it, even if it cannot express itself in a positive way. People will repeatedly rise up against – even rebel against – the severest repression, even when the situation appears hopeless, as for instance in the Warsaw ghetto, the concentration camps or in prison. It is precisely because the individual experiences his or her being as always free, in all circumstances, that there is no double-bind, which would require that the conditions first be created – God knows by whom – which make it possible to experience freedom.

**Q.** But isn't this just a stoicism typical of Sartre's existentialism? Can't it be summed up by saying: I may be in prison and have lost my outer freedom, but inside I feel free, happy and at home, and I can feel myself to be a free being.

**A.G.** No, that's not the way it works, and neither Sartre himself nor those behind bars were or are happy and stoical. Prisoners experience and assert their freedom by covertly building relations with fellow prisoners and constantly preparing their escape or making plans about what they will do when they are released. In this respect the testimonies of Arthur London, or the Russians who were imprisoned or in labour camps both before and after the revolution, are particularly interesting. A being can only feel oppressed if, at the same time, it can feel free, if it experiences the circumstances forced upon it as a negation of its being, its freedom.

**Q.** Yes, you see here you use the word 'feel'. I think that people who do not feel they are oppressed can, nonetheless, be oppressed. Would you agree?

**A.G.** I used to quarrel with Herbert Marcuse on this point. He maintained that alienation in neo-capitalism was so deeply rooted that people were no longer conscious of it.

**Q.** Not only in neo-capitalism, I was thinking of National Socialism or fascism too. There were a lot of people one could call 'oppressed' who nonetheless felt themselves to be elevated, recognized, accepted ('We are somebody again'). Despite this one could say they were forced – or rather drawn – into it by suggestion, propaganda and the fact that all their hopes had been destroyed by the defeat of the 1918 revolution. In any case there is a form of oppression, which is in part not experienced as such.

**A.G.** In a way, for its supporters, National Socialism was also liberation or a struggle for liberation. The *feeling* of being free and of alienation does not in itself contain the *knowledge* of the real

reasons for and circumstances in which the development of freedom is prevented, suppressed. Immediate consciousness and
experience are one thing, knowledge of the whole facts of the
matter are another and are dependent upon skills of analytical
thought which must be acquired. It is possible, therefore, to
mobilize oppressed people craving liberation from 'arch-
enemies' who are in fact nothing but cheap scapegoats being
used as easy targets for belligerent self-assertion: Jews, Bolsheviks, Slavs, Democrats, masterminds of the world-wide conspiracy against an honest people. The effect is quicker and simpler
than studying Marx. The SA did not oppress its members. It
was an organization of humiliated people, who banded together
on their own accord, and like Scheler's 'Ressentimentmenschen', set
upon all these higher values and fine people, in whose name they
were humiliated and despised. They had, at last, been
empowered by an authority ('in the name of the people') which
was elevated above all traditional values. *Formally* then, it was a
real, lived liberation, for people acted together in a concrete way
and inspired the arch-enemies with fear. In content, though, it
was an unreal, mystified liberation. You see, there are different
planes of existence and what may be valid on one, may not be so
on the others and may even be completely mistaken. The reverse
may also occur, that is, people who are equipped with the correct
knowledge of the causes of oppression fight it in a way which is
even more oppressive than the oppression being fought.

The question which arises here is: what has brought people to
this? This is where Marxist analysis becomes inadequate. Here
we need to take into account such factors as national culture,
educational methods, self-hatred, repressive disciplinary school-
ing, and so on, as Wilhelm Reich and the Frankfurt School
pointed out.

To desire freedom as the highest goal and value, is, therefore,
not a simple matter: it is the endless *labour* of liberation, through
which those who are free first *make* themselves free or at least try
to do so. This demands knowledge, method, self-discipline,
reflection and an understanding of the problems and mystifications in which the freedom of others becomes ensnared or even

turns into its opposite. This is not an anonymous process. Each person must start from the question: what have I become as a result of my cultural and educational imprints, as a result of my past, my social location and position, and to what extent can I use this so as to become the originator of my own actions? Nobody is born fully equipped with the intellectual tools to answer this question – there might not even be an answer. The absence of any way out of the situation tends then to become the subject of reflective activity in literary creation: prisoners serving life sentences, for instance, often write.

The more methodically individuals tackle this work in relation to themselves, the better they will understand others and be in a position to recognize their freedom even in its mystified guises. People who lack this ability cannot become leaders of collective struggles for liberation.

Q. In *Paths to Paradise* you suggest that making your life your own requires that, to a certain extent at least, you produce what you consume, and vice versa. You suggest that the freedom to decide what, how much, for and with whom to produce cannot prevail otherwise. You said earlier that one must differentiate between different planes of existence and therefore presumably also between different planes of liberation. In *Paths to Paradise* you suggest that the places where production and consumption coincide are important planes of existence and liberation. Why?

A.G. That is a very good question. In order to answer it, I must first of all go back to the concept of alienation, which is best presented in Marx's *The German Ideology*. Here Marx shows that 'social individuals' experience the results of their co-operation as a power alien to them, which thwarts their wishes. Why? Because the whole process of this co-operation develops according to material laws, which are neither visible nor controllable. For this process could only be controlled if everyone were co-operating voluntarily – not merely by chance – to make this control the chief goal of their labour from the outset. Ending alienation means creating conditions in which everyone recognizes the results of their social co-operation and their own labour as something created and desired by themselves and, of course, it means being able to eliminate anything which is not intended. This then means that the goals, results and development of co-operation are collectively self-determined.

In market economies, just as in authoritarian planned economies, the opposite happens: people and their co-operation are subjected to heteronomous determination by the requirements of production, profit and fixed capital; the results and the process of their co-operation are alienated from the start, it is impossible to control them. This is so deeply embedded that commodities are no longer produced in accordance with people's needs, but people's needs are geared to commodities which, functioning as the apparent subjects, require that they be purchased, and relegate the question of needs to a subordinate position. In the market economy needs for certain products are heteronomously determined in so far as it is not the use value but the symbolic value of a commodity which is extolled, lending it a certain image designed to appeal to unconscious desires. Autonomous determination of one's own needs and desires is made impossible; the whole of commodity propaganda has the ring of a perpetual warning: 'You'd better watch out, or others will have more and better things than you. How will you look then?' Everyone is always addressed as an 'other' and 'others' played off against each other. There are no autonomous individuals. Envy and fear of being disadvantaged become central to human relations. Voluntary, goal-oriented, self-determined, social co-operation is quite impossible. Scarcity and the feeling of being 'underprivileged' are reproduced on ever higher planes.

The roots of alienation, of heteronomy, are therefore in the involuntary social division of labour, which separates consumption and production. Since no one is the subject of their productive work any longer, they cannot be the subject of their consumption either. Because we do not produce what we use and do not use what we produce, in neither working nor consuming are we 'at home', as Marx put it, are we 'ourselves'.

The only possible way out is to dismantle, wherever possible,

the mega-technologies requiring the social division and fragmen-
tation of labour and replace them with voluntary co-operative
activity which is organized not for the market but according to
the needs determined by the members of the community themselves, and which guarantees autoproduction of use values, not
exchange values, that is, commodities.

Q. But, how can we reach this condition? You see possibilities of
liberation everywhere, but both the programme and the individual morality of freedom remain unclear to me.

A.G. So far as the morality of freedom is concerned, it is
basically conscious self-determination in free co-operation with
others which is itself only possible on the smaller community
level. Alienation can only be overcome on this level. Thanks to
micro-processors, local community production can play a leading role in the satisfaction of needs.

As to the programme for freedom, there are two factors
involved: its content and its realization. Both would be irrelevant
were it not for the fact that:
1. All previous programmes, which have always been modelled
on economic growth, permanent full-time employment and
increasing commodity consumption, have become unrealistic;
2. For fifteen years now, a movement has been developing whose
determining values are self-determination, production for one's
own use, conviviality and so on. More than one per cent of the
population in Denmark and Norway are actively involved in
the 'The Future In Our Hands' movement, whose members
voluntarily practice self-limitation, giving the income they save to
relief projects in countries plagued by famine.

In *Paths to Paradise*, my aim was to propose for a discussion
within such groups a clearly anti-capitalist programme involving
the whole of society. The fact that hardly anybody on the political Left is thinking about what a free, post-industrial, non-
capitalist society should look like, is a depressing indication of
the inability of the traditional Left to take on board what is new
and forward-looking and make it politically viable. I cannot do

this either of course. I can only try to interest a limited number of politically active people in new directions.

Q. In *Paths to Paradise* you offer an analysis of contemporary society which predicts its collapse. You depict an era of disintegration – of societies, values, hopes, ruling ideologies, models of crisis management and reforms, in short a disintegration of the prevailing rationality. The old order cannot go on: 'industrialism' – your term – is at an end. It seems to be an era of confusion and uncertainty about the future. What is lacking is a grand design. There is a great sense of urgency in your writing – one gets the impression that change must be our greatest priority. What we are all waiting for now, is for the grand design to be published so that we can get some idea of what form the political transformation will take. There is no shortage of critics of the existing system, there are a great number of analyses, some of which steamroller over the present, flattening everything in their way, and leave only a pure negation standing. What is really missing is the translation of this analysis and criticism into politics and into a definition of the form of politics in which this goal should and can be reached. In defining this form, though, the traditions of the liberation movements are very important. In *Paths to Paradise* you refer to the goals of the labour movement – but neither the goals nor the political forms of the labour movement seem so uniform to me. What you are really referring to is a syndicalist tradition which was never particularly significant in the German workers' movement, for example, as this was much more state-oriented. Must we not include this in thinking about a plan for a future society, ought not an intellectual, in describing the tendencies and outlines of a future society, take responsibility for connecting these to a political form?

A.G. Yes, you are quite right. My first reaction to your question is a negative one. None of the traditional parties and organizations appeals to anything outside directly material interests and concerns; none of them appeals to the desire of workers, of young people, of the unemployed and of pensioners or people

taking early retirement to have the opportunity to create something themselves, that is to produce as well as to exchange or
simply give. Only the churches are applying themselves to the
desire to give, to devote oneself, to act in a value-oriented way. In
West and East alike, more and more people are turning to the
Church, including non-believers. This seems a dangerous
development to me: the spiritual becomes separated from the
political and we end up with apolitical values and valueless
politics, until one day a new fascist party appears which, like the
NSDAP, rejects both politics and politicians and appeals to a
xenophobic need for greatness, selflessness, sacrifice, discipline,
unity and self-respect.

It would be quite appropriate, then, for socialist parties and
movements to adopt a plan for society, in both theory and practice, which foresees a victory over capitalism, over full-time wage
labour and heteronomous commodity production, in favour of
increasingly more voluntary, self-determined co-operation for
goals which are ends in themselves, since they do not create
exchange values, but aesthetic, convivial or use values.

The striving for a form of society in which non-economic
values prevail over economic values, was, from the beginning, the
driving force of the labour movement: it fought capitalism not
only because it was exploitative but also because it destroyed
autonomous production and reciprocal exchange in favour of the
infernal compulsion to engage in wage labour and commodity
relations. The desire to produce oneself, not to be totally dependent on buying and selling, to be one's own master, is still far
from extinguished amongst the working class and it is expressed
even more openly amongst higher or middle-level employees,
since they have a greater degree of cultural and existential autonomy. The theme of 'working less means work for everyone and
a better life for all' is as old as the union movement itself and is
currently being taken up again, though far too timidly.

In *Paths to Paradise* I do try to appeal to trade unionists and
socialists on this matter and it always amazes me when they do
not seem to realize this. My suggestions, on both a practical and
a tactical level, have been a standard part of normal wage

bargaining for decades: wage agreements were anticipating probable or possible increases in productivity by laying down future wage increases and/or shorter working hours or a shorter working life. At present, the most important demand will be for ever shorter working hours with no loss in wages. This has, in fact, been achieved by smaller unions in Great Britain and the United States and in certain firms in France too. It cannot be extended to the whole of the economy by striking particular agreements with each firm or industry. What is needed is a political concept and governmental action. These are also well within the socialist tradition.

Socialists must completely reject any notion of 'reducing labour costs'. If the 'wage bill' is lowered in accordance with decreasing working hours, then there will be a concomitant fall in demand. Lack of demand means that increased profits will only be reinvested in increasingly cheaper automation, leading to further cuts in the workforce. The result is a further reduction in the percentage of the population gainfully employed. It is a downward spiral on a world scale, so putting more emphasis on the export market cannot provide a solution. There is no capitalist way out of the crisis.

This means there is no alternative but to break with the law of value, with market relations, with capitalist rationality: a sufficient income for life must be made independent of the number of hours worked. The satisfaction of need must become the independent variable, labour time the dependent variable. This too is, in principle, within the tradition of the labour movement. All that is new is that the degree to which this is necessary is greater than before, so that quantity turns into quality. A life long guaranteed income linked to a reduction in the total number of hours worked over the entire course of one's life is already being suggested by both reactionary and liberal politicians as well as by economists, but in a form which will inevitably lead to the humiliation, social exclusion and cultural impoverishment of those concerned.

What must distinguish the Left from the Right today is the purpose and meaning behind this abandonment of the law of value. Right-wing politicians want to retain the so-called 'work ethic', making some meagre provision for those not employed on a full-time and productivity-linked basis, but excluding them from society. The Left must, therefore, break with the work ethic too. This should be all the easier since it is already meaningless for the majority of those gainfully employed and, as automation increases, it will inevitably gradually disappear. In education, health and administration, but also in the process industries, it is impossible to measure performance. It depends, amongst other things, on how susceptible the machinery is to breaking down.

The market economy, too, is a sacred cow, attracting worshippers long after it has been slaughtered. When I suggest financing a lifelong guaranteed income by taxing goods and services produced by automation I am merely developing a process already underway. Our price system is already largely determined by political factors rather than by questions of supply and demand. All basic essentials and socially necessary goods and services – from agricultural products to transport and health care – are subsidized, while luxury goods or those made cheap through automized production, such as cars, mineral oil products, alcohol and so on, are highly taxed. This so-called value-added or sales tax does not prevent us knowing their real production costs, nor does it hinder exports, as exported goods are not liable to such taxes.

The development of opportunities for self-activity – workshops to which everybody has access, giving everyone the opportunity to be both manually and culturally productive and to participate in maintenance work; grassroots co-operatives enabling the production, locally and on a voluntary co-operative basis, of both socially necessary and more optional goods and services – all these institutions, which would release time to be used creatively in new social relations based on reciprocity, helpfulness, a sense of community could arise – all this is thoroughly in the tradition of the socialist movement and could be immediately realized by either the unions or the left-wing parties, at least as a first step in visualizing what is possible politically.

The right to work can no longer be equated with the right to full-time employment, nor can the right to income be equated with the right to a wage. This is the crucial point. Market production via wage labour must become a secondary activity for all if we are simultaneously to escape both the crisis and capitalism.

Q. Does this mean that regaining the self-determination of individual life is a prerequisite for any kind of political freedom? Does the basis of a free society lie in the recovery of culture, of production and consumption?

A.G. Certainly, but there can be no self-determination of one's own life, if social life – intercourse with others in a broad sense – is not self-determined. The demand for self-determination, for autonomy, can today only be expressed negatively: through a withdrawal into the family and private life. Work and society remain the realm of heteronomy. The importance of strengthening the micro-social communities in which we live and work lies precisely in the fact that they provide the missing but necessary mediation between the spheres of the private individual and society as a whole. Liberated time is only meaningful if people can use it in shaping social relations and modes of co-operation.

If the political Left is not capable of putting micro-electronic technology to these uses, then this technology will be used for the compulsory internalization of heteronomy: for self-surveillance, self-normalization, self-examination with the aid of home computers – the state-financed consumption of computer programmes. Income can be made dependent upon regular self-examination. The approach of this 'autosurveillance society' has been described by Jacques Attali who bases his work on a great number of examples.

So we have a choice between increasing the micro-social shaping of one's own life and self-activity, or greater macro-social oppression and alienation.

Q. What does 'the political' mean for you? What is your conception of 'the political'?

**A.G.** In the political sphere two processes overlap: firstly, citizens shape social relations and the environment; and secondly, inter-relations within society as a whole are governed and controlled. The first of these processes occurs within what we call 'civil society'. Alienation and autonomization of social relations, though, leads to the predominance of the second process: politics becomes government, that is, it becomes a matter of who runs the state governmental apparatus and great technological collective institutions and how. Civil society withers away; it is devoured by state and government.

The political cannot continue to exist in any democratic form, that is as the activity of citizens, if one of its two roles becomes subservient to the other. The strengthening of civil society cannot entail the total withering away of the state – this would mean a return to a world of tribes and village communities. But the state and its central governing apparatus have become far too large and unsupervisable and ought to be partially dismantled, and greater scope should be given for decentralized, micro-social self-government. Micro-electronic technology can facilitate this because it simplifies both decentralization and communication, and makes time available.

**Q.** Turning to the question of the marginalization of wage labour through technological progress, you seem to see this as a very desirable process making possible the trivialization of production and eliminating the identification of the producer with his/her product, which you characterize as a conservative element in the labour process, considerably stabilizing the productive and social order. So it is not only that productive work *can* be eliminated or rather marginalized, but, in the way you outline it, it *should* be. You seem to see two sides to the matter.

**A.G.** What can and should be extensively eliminated is not productive work but heteronomous and waged work. Self-determined activities can be productive too, even if not in the capitalist sense of 'creating surplus value': they will create aesthetic and use values, rather than economic values. That's the whole point. The preeminence of the economic is only two hundred years old and is responsible for creating a kind of general schizophrenia, for, in day-to-day life, there is a general feeling that economic values are morally and aesthetically worthless and vice versa: affection, love, tenderness, children, pets, the countryside have no economic value at all and are sacrificed to the economic demands of industry. When they come home from work, though – at work they are not at home – everybody wants to have an artificial niche, where these non-economic values prevail. In themselves they would not be incompatible with work, only with wage labour directed towards maximizing profitability.

The sphere in which both the necessary and the desirable can be produced in a way which reconciles the value of work with moral and aesthetic values can only grow if disposable time is no longer scarce.

The other side to the elimination of a large part of heterono- mous wage labour is that this requires a very high level of productivity, which in turn demands the standardization of socialized labour. Everyone must be able to perform the socially required work, which does not mean that work has to become unskilled, but that a variety of skills are to become commonplace and that the final products are not personal creations. The fact that the individual becomes 'indifferent' to the result of this stan- dardized work, and would no longer identify personally with it, was seen by Marx as characteristic of an advanced socialist society. The social division and specialization of labour means that the possibility of such identification has irrevocably dis- appeared for more than ninety per cent of workers. The choice we face, then, is not between identification with the content of wage labour and its elimination, but between different ways of distributing the elimination already underway. A modern Left must make more and more disposable time available to everyone and enable everyone to engage in self-determined activities with which they can identify. This, of course, could only be achieved by superseding capitalist rationality. But it is possible to show that extensive automation will bring this to an end anyway, allowing it to survive only in appearance. So my suggestions are not unrealistic.

**Q.** Does the break with the prevailing rationality, which you describe in *Paths to Paradise* not also demand a new form of politics? If so, how do you visualize this? Which forces within the labour movement are you trying to appeal to?

**A.G.** Dany Cohn-Bendit, whose ideas I value greatly, would probably be more qualified to talk about the new form of politics than I am. He is one of the possible embodiments of these new forms, as of the morality of freedom too – and of how it can be lived with a precise awareness of the impossibilities that surround it.

These new forms will attract a lot of people if, instead of isolating them as 'alternative experiments', city neighbourhoods as well as district councils, and possibly provincial governments, take this on board by making it possible for self-help networks, associations, co-operatives and so on to put into practice and gradually expand different ways of living, producing, exchanging and communicating. For example, various self-organized forms of remote working, of job sharing, and of voluntary neighbourhood services could be experimented with, as well as different forms of consumer and service co-operatives, maintenance and production workshops and genuine control over working hours – as has, for instance, been introduced by the government in Quebec: public administration officials must put in 140 hours per month, but are free to allocate their time, with minimal restrictions, as it suits them.

There is no rational, sound reason why the SPD and the trade union movement should not test out the liberating potential of new technologies, organizational principles and ways of life. If they do not, then individual entrepreneurs will, but with a quite different intention: so-called flexi-time, for example, is an apparent concession, but the way it accommodates the demand for control over one's time is a real fraud. It is precisely because we have arrived at a turning point that we need laboratories –

districts, local authorities, medium-sized towns – where new forms of sociability and political activity are invented, tested out and consolidated. In the Netherlands, Denmark and Canada there is much less prejudice in this respect than in most other countries. What is generally missing there, though, is the theoretical dimension. In our own countries we may be better off in terms of theory, but our political parties tend to become rigidly set in unified programmes for government which they necessarily cast in universal terms.

Unified universal formulae are no longer applicable. The change in the technological and cultural climate currently underway contains the kernel of a polymorphous society in which, as in nature, lots of different sorts of projects are floating around and variety can be a source of wealth and continuous further development rather than of disintegration. This was described very well by Alvin Toffler in his latest book *Previews and Premises*.

In West Germany as well as Great Britain the position in this respect is not particularly bad. Regional government and local councils have much more scope than they do for instance in France, where everything must be approved by the head of state. The SPD, like the Labour Party, also remains ununified: different currents are still alive within it, and the party is not completely closed to any tendencies which question it politically and structurally. Whether it is capable of rejuvenation is impossible to judge from afar but it is not to be ruled out. Viewing the state, the central government, as the guarantor of the general conditions through which a reduction of working time with no loss of pay, genuine control over working hours, service co-operatives, and home-producing are made possible in various forms, and the basic necessities of life are guaranteed to all – all this is in harmony with the socialist tradition.

On the other hand there is an ever increasing demand among workers for more disposable time, more opportunities for self-activity and autonomous decision-making. The elaboration of a 'politics of time', furthering the liberation and creative and social use of the growing amount of free time, and making this possible via social institutions, would accommodate a very widespread demand. If the political Left is not willing to do this, or is not capable of doing this, we will progress further in the direction of the auto-surveillance society and dual economy along Mexican or Japanese lines.

I realize that this probably does not answer your question fully. For fifteen years we have been in a process of fermentation, from which new and unexpected things are constantly emerging. As long as the political scene is governed and monopolized by political parties concentrating solely on the exercise of state power and regarding the recasting of society as unimportant, it seems impossible to envisage what the new forms of politics might look like. I am one of the many who think that it ultimately makes little difference which party is 'in power', as we say, as long as the parties basically ask the same questions and share the same tendency to short-sightedness and the recourse to outdated recipes. It is difficult to come to any final conclusion as to whether any of the great traditional parties of the Left can rejuvenate themselves from within and open up new currents or whether they could only do so by an internal split, or alternatively be rejuvenated by having to compete with a small new political movement. In England, it took from 1789 to 1830 – fifty years – for the labour movement to be able to organize itself into an independent political force.

Q. This may be so, but it coincided with the development of industrialization and capitalism, and it was within these social and economic processes and struggles that the labour movement developed and provided itself with political and organizational forms and programmes. Your analysis and prognosis amounts rather to saying we have come to a crossroads; we have reached a moment of decision: this way leads to freedom and self-determination – that way leads to a society based on auto-surveillance, from which liberation is difficult since individuals have themselves become commodities and are bought. This is why I ask my searching questions about the urgency of the problematic you have highlighted. There is barely time for politics to develop if we take into account the speed with which the economy needs a decision to be taken – West Germany alone will have three million unemployed soon. This is also what lies behind my searching questions on the intellectual's responsibility to analyse and draw up a project for society, and whether this must not be tied into a political form, if everything is coming to a head. These kinds of analyses and projects which demand a resolution and call for urgency are familiar to us from the twenties – but it was others who resolved the matter, and others who profited.

**A.G.** You are quite right to keep pushing me on this, but I'd turn the question on its head: to what extent can intellectuals, given our present circumstances, give their analyses and ideas a political, politically viable form, without losing credibility and being drawn into the discredit that surrounds conventional politics? Without any party, movement or organization capable of translating the necessary change into political terms and carrying it through, intellectuals can only direct their efforts to those people within existing movements and organizations who are open-minded and generally looking in the same direction, but have not yet managed to achieve anything themselves. So it is essential to present the nature of the decision that is to be made as clearly as possible, and prevent these issues from being pushed to one side. Intellectuals can do no more than nurture the discussion, intervene in it. The ideas they try to communicate will only lead to political action when the pressure of events forces an immediate decision on us and brings the problem to a head. If, at this point, there are enough conscious, politically active and resolute people, then things will begin to move.

For example, although we have known about the atom bomb since 1945, the anti-nuclear campaign in Western Europe or the United States has never before had the scope it does today. It is the urgency of the decision which now faces us that has brought the problem to a head. What is remarkable is that this movement has emerged in spite of the fact that – or perhaps even because – it could offer no positive political alternative, not even an alternative conception of defence, which I find deplorable. It offers something different, something which marks a break with prevailing rationality and which is forcing at least part of the political Left to reconsider certain issues.

As far as the world economic crisis is concerned, we are still in the first stages of a lengthy process which will last for another few decades. The worst may be still to come: the financial collapse of various large banks, possibly even states. Such collapses, or the means by which they might be prevented, will deepen still further the current crisis in society and its prevailing values. The seeds sown by the alternative movement, and by proposals and theories breaking with the prevailing rationality, could then make rapid progress, or rather make possible the clarification of the two positions: on the one hand, those who advocate a society in which time is released and the growth of self-activity, independent of cash values, is encouraged; on the other hand those who favour crisis management with a dual economy and auto-surveillance. I want to make it clear that I have *no* desire to see any intensification of the crisis or any financial collapse in the wish that this will improve the chances of being able to reshape society on a new basis. In fact I see the problem the other way round: because we cannot simply continue in this way and because we are faced with terrible dilemmas, we must think seriously about radical alternatives to the status quo.

Q. We would like to return once more to the theme of the continuity of thinking and searching. Looking at the fourth part of *The Traitor*, where the traitor comes to the 'I', to him-self, one gets the feeling that this was an early formulation of the programmatic outline of *Paths to Paradise*. In *The Traitor* we are introduced to the various planes of the transcendence of alienation, the individual demand for autonomy, but also to the notion that we cannot overcome alienation completely; part of it will remain. At the end, the 'I', almost in an act of self-supplication, resolves to find, seek out, invent the means to transcend alienation, in order 'to manifest man'. In searching, this 'I' expects 'that the highest reward I can hope for resides in this activity of creation.'[1] Has André Gorz made any progress with his project?

**A.G.** Thank you for the question. I would never have thought to ask it myself. It forced me to look up the passage which you cite and I was surprised to find remarks also contained in *Paths to Paradise* and *Farewell to the Working Class*. For example:

> What is offered to us? A laborious, narrowly specialized life at the heart of an undertaking which exceeds us and is even ignorant of itself; an ant life forever unable to recognize itself in the world it contributes to produce. . . . Our need for humanity takes refuge in the private life, in nocturnal meetings and palavers, little orgies of vain dreams and discussions during which we destroy this society and the unacceptable reality it presses upon us. Which is why this society measures an individual's success by the number and the power of the means he acquires to hold the community at a distance, to escape the common fate, to isolate himself, to differentiate himself from all others, to build himself a shell against the world. . . . But to those who would prefer not to possess, to isolate and to consume at the general expense, but to give, to communicate and to construct with and for all, this society has nothing to offer.[2]

And it goes on:

> We can never feel entirely real, there is a part of ourselves which remains unrealized, a part – of failure, of silence – which forbids us to content ourselves with whatever we live (do, say, are). An absolute distance divides us from our reality. The intellectual is the man who assumes this distance, who tries to recover the silence, the failure. . . . He will never (I will never) be a great man of action. . . . I must invent the means of a complete realization, which is impossible for me and whose means, for this reason, cannot be really existing means. I cannot claim that I will succeed in creating these means. . . . I only know that like many others . . . . I must invent individual means to manifest man, and that the highest recompense I can hope for resides in this activity of creation.[3]

I had quite forgotten I had ever written anything like this. It is almost thirty years ago.

The project outlined there is obviously a literary one, for there is no other means to manifest 'the part of silence', of the ineffable and the impossible. I have made progress on this front in a quite different way from how I apparently intended. I became more modest in my aims, spent a lot of time reading newspapers and writing articles and, in so doing, lost sight of myself. Becoming involved in events somewhat journalistically – the war in Algeria, the rise of modern technocracy, the crisis in the trades unions and of dogmatic Marxism – seemed more important to me than being active in a literary way. But this was also part of a programme: for I had also written that 'the resolution of all existential problems is outside', in the real world and in keeping struggling with it until purely personal problems pale into insignificance. Newspaper articles could, at specific points in time, have a certain effect, especially in the trade union movement and among secondary school pupils and students. This taught me a lot, amongst other things to write in a way which could make even complicated things comprehensible to a wide audience. What pleased me most was when now and again a factory group reproduced some articles of mine. The 'highest reward' did not correspond exactly to the one I originally intended in *The Traitor*. In this respect I have made more progress than I had intended. What I mean is that I have made progress not 'in' the project you cite, but beyond this essentially literary intention.

The influence this had from time to time could not, of course, be a lasting one and could not express what is, in each of us at present, destined to failure or silence. This would require literary or philosophical works. *Farewell to the Working Class* was intended as both: all the 'residual values' which had been pushed onto the periphery of political theory and practice came to the fore in it. It focuses on all that is generally considered to be waste or trivia: namely that part of existence that is condemned to silence, to nonexistence. When you try to express what is silenced, every major social and philosophical system suddenly appears in all its arbitrariness, its violence. Of course *Farewell to the Working Class* could not come up with any coherent theory to replace the traditional one. Nor was that my aim: I wanted to show what happens when one brings oneself into political thought as a real complex subject. The book is designed to tempt readers to follow suit and carry out a similar experiment on themselves. In this respect it is a literary work. The theoretical insights which it contains and which have often been misunderstood are taken up again in *Paths to Paradise*, although here there is no personal involvement. I consider *Farewell to the Working Class*, which was deliberately left incomplete, to be the better, and *Paths to Paradise* the more useful book.

Of course I have made no progress in overcoming alienation: many of my hopes have come to nothing and barbarism has advanced greatly in the last twenty years. But for the author of a book, each single person able even partially to recognize or discover him/herself in it, or able to gain any insight or food for thought from it, is proof that it was not written in vain.

*Notes*

1. *The Traitor*, p. 268
2. Ibid., pp. 266–67
3. Ibid., p. 305

Printed in the United States
by Baker & Taylor Publisher Services